Networks, SMEs, and the University

Networks, SMEs, and the University

The Process of Collaboration and Open Innovation

Andrew Johnston

*Professor of Innovation and Entrepreneurship,
International Centre for Transformational Entrepreneurship
(ICTE), Coventry Business School, Coventry University, UK*

Robert Huggins

*Professor of Economic Geography and Director,
Cities Research Centre, School of Geography and Planning,
Cardiff University, Cardiff, UK*

 Edward Elgar
PUBLISHING

Cheltenham, UK • Northampton, MA, USA

Published by
Edward Elgar Publishing Limited
The Lypiatts
15 Lansdown Road
Cheltenham
Glos GL50 2JA
UK

Edward Elgar Publishing, Inc.
William Pratt House
9 Dewey Court
Northampton
Massachusetts 01060
USA

A catalogue record for this book
is available from the British Library

Library of Congress Control Number: 2020950947

This book is available electronically in the **Elgar**online
Economics subject collection
http://dx.doi.org/10.4337/9781789903386

ISBN 978 1 78990 337 9 (cased)
ISBN 978 1 78990 338 6 (eBook)

Printed and bound by CPI Group (UK) Ltd, Croydon, CR0 4YY

Contents

Figures

Tables

Foreword

Tamsin Mann

At PraxisAuril, we are concerned with a range of Knowledge Exchange (KE) policy issues, including research and development (R&D) strategy, innovation metrics and research management skills. However, SME engagement is a perennial issue for universities which are regularly urged to 'do more' in this area.

Small and Medium Sized Enterprises (SMEs) are an important group for universities, as they account for the vast majority of business types in the UK. The sheer variety of company size, structure, and business focus means that finding a common approach for knowledge exchange is challenging. There are assumptions made about 'what works' – that proximity to a university is significant, for example, or that consultancy will be preferable to longer-term research collaboration. When you start to look more closely at the dynamics of knowledge exchange with this part of the UK's business sector, many of those assumptions fall away.

Members of PraxisAuril, who in general are the intermediaries between researchers based within universities and external audiences, have deployed a wide variety of engagement models for SME audiences. Yet, according to sector data, the number and value of SME engagements increase annually but this doesn't actually tell us much about the user value, or impact, of the engagement. May be this is why 'what works' still seems elusive. As the authors put it, the data "suggests that SMEs are increasingly important to UK universities, but are universities as important to SMEs?" (p. 66).

University-SME engagement is likely to figure even more as we recover and rebuild from economic turmoil caused by the Covid-19 pandemic, whilst also trying to achieve new levels of R&D intensity (2.4% of GDP by 2027). Many SMEs were obliged to work in radically new ways during the pandemic – embracing digital innovation in particular – and some also received business support from universities to tackle acute operational challenges. Would there be a greater appetite for innovation as a result, and would relationships established in a time of crisis endure? Better understanding of why and how SMEs collaborate in 'normal' times may help us to answer those questions.

This book represents a welcome opportunity to link research to practice in a way that happens surprisingly infrequently. Through an in-depth exploration of the issues, it offers insights for university-side intermediaries who want to better understand this particular group and for policymakers trying to design incentives by putting 'flesh on the bones' of sector data. I think it will promote increased debate on SME–university collaboration and look forward to further discussions with our members and their collaborative partners about the findings and conclusions of this study and how they resonate with their own stories and experiences.

Tamsin Mann,
Director of Policy and Communication
PraxisAuril – The Professional Association for Knowledge Exchange
Practitioners
July 2020

Acknowledgements

In writing a book such as this, there are inevitably many people to thank for their support in realising this project. Firstly, we are both indebted to the interview participants who graciously provided their time and experiences regarding their university collaborations. Without these insights the book would not exist. Secondly, we would like to thank Matthew Pitman of Edward Elgar for his support for the book and his encouragement to realise this project.

Andrew Johnston would firstly like to thank Robert for being the consummate co-author and mentor, not just in the course of writing this book, but over the last 14 years of their collaboration. He is also indebted to his colleague Jeremy Head for generously stepping in and looking after his module 'Business in the European Economy' while he was absorbed in writing this book. He would also like to thank his wife Amanda, and daughters, Violet and Elsie, for providing a welcome distraction from writing for the past year. Finally, the answer to the question 'has Daddy finished his book?' is, yes, he has!

Robert Huggins would firstly like to thank Andrew for conceiving and leading the project upon which much of this book is based. Their own collaboration dates back to 2006 when they first began to ponder on and figure out the nature, prevalence, and impact of university–industry links. Alongside Andrew, thanks should also go to Hiro Izushi, Kevin Morgan, Daniel Prokop, and Piers Thompson, all of whom have helped shape an understanding of innovation and the role of universities in processes of innovation and entrepreneurship. A very special thanks also goes to Angela who provides support and love in so many ways.

1. University–industry collaboration: why it matters

1.1 INTRODUCTION

The role universities has evolved, with their 'traditional' functions of teaching and research increasingly complemented by a 'third mission'. This mission focuses on their engagement with industry and their interaction with businesses (Dasgupta and David 1994; Huggins, Prokop, and Thompson 2020; Johnston 2019; Liu, Subramanian, and Hang 2020; Thursby and Thursby 2002). This broadening of the activities of universities has seen them move away from operating as 'ivory towers' that are one step removed from society and regarded as aloof and distant. Instead, the modern university is required to behave in the opposite way.

Universities have always had a significant social impact (Hermannsson et al. 2017). For example, their so-called 'first mission', which concentrates on teaching and training via undergraduate and postgraduate courses, provides society with stocks of human capital through embedding knowledge within graduates who then apply it in the workplace. Furthermore, the university's 'second mission', centring on undertaking research and the development of new knowledge, contributes to society through building and enhancing the science base, thereby providing knowledge, and the technologies to enable societal innovation and progress. Consequently, as the impacts of universities have widened, they are no longer discussed in terms of a single 'role' but multiple 'roles'.

Universities also make a significant economic impact at both a national and regional level (Guerrero, Cunningham, and Urbano 2015; Marques et al. 2019; Valero and Van Reenen 2019; World Bank 2017). For example, university research and development (R&D) has been found to increase both gross domestic product (GDP) and productivity in an economy (Martin 1998), as well as promoting patenting activity (Jaffe 1989), therefore boosting growth and prosperity (World Bank 2017). At the sub-national level, universities have a significant impact on regional economies as higher numbers are associated with faster regional growth (Valero and Van Reenen 2019), with regional growth being positively influenced by teaching, research, and entrepreneurial activities of universities (Guerrero, Cunningham, and Urbano 2015). Therefore, universities have a broad economic impact on their host regions, be they rural or urban in character, from an economic as well as an innovation perspective (Charles 2016; Charles and Benneworth 2002; Huggins and Johnston 2009b; Salomaa 2019).

The reframing of universities as key actors in the modern economy is therefore captured in the refocusing of universities' activities away from concentrating purely on research to an accompanying emphasis on 'impact' (Doyle 2018; Soetanto and Jack 2016; Woolcott, Keast, and Pickernell 2020). Fostering this impact increasingly involves the collaboration of universities with industry in order to commercialise the 'knowledge base', that is, to ensure the work of universities is *directly* utilised by firms for competitive means (Fini et al. 2018; Jessop 2017).

The re-conceptualisation of the university also reflects a fundamental re-evaluation of the nature and characteristics of the innovation process. In the past, the competitive position of firms was typically regarded as governed by the knowledge resources they possessed (Barney 1991; Dosi 1990; Grant 1996), which in turn determined firms' ability to innovate. However, scholars increasingly recognise that these resources are not decided by the firm's ability to create knowledge alone but its ability to combine this with the procurement of knowledge from external resources. Innovation, therefore, is increasingly regarded as a socio-technical and open process of inter-organisational collaboration, facilitated by networks and alliances designed to access knowledge from externals partners (Chesbrough 2003, 2017; Enkel, Gassmann, and Chesbrough 2009; Perkmann and Walsh 2007).

University–industry collaboration refers to activities that focus on the engagement of these parties that develop and utilise knowledge, technology, or expertise for the development of new goods, services, or processes (Ankrah and Al-Tabbaa 2015; Perkmann et al. 2013). Therefore, these collaborations can be viewed as a spectrum of activities ranging from informal interactions at a personal level through to the creation of new legal entities to pursue a joint venture (Bonaccorsi and Piccaluga 1994). The focus of this book is on the formal collaboration of universities and businesses, developed in order to pursue the creation or exploitation of a new technology and the development of new products or services, new processes, or new organisational structures or forms and funded through a public grant.

The motivations for engaging in this type of collaboration are well documented. Firms benefit significantly from working with universities including increased understanding of technologies, greater levels of knowledge, the development of patents, enhanced problem-solving capabilities, recruitment of graduate employees, training opportunities, and cost reductions/efficiencies within the business (Abreu et al. 2008; Bishop, D'Este, and Neely 2011; Hagerdoorn,

Link, and Vonortas 2000; Lööf and Broström 2006). These advantages may fundamentally alter the competitiveness of a firm to enable increased sales and the broadening of the scope of their activities (Abreu et al. 2008; Hagerdoorn, Link, and Vonortas 2000; Lööf and Broström 2006). In addition, firms collaborating with a university are more likely to increase R&D expenditure and R&D employment than non-collaborators (Scandura 2016). Finally, there is evidence that firms that receive public funding to support their research experience faster subsequent growth in employment and sales than those firms that did not (Vanino, Roper, and Becker 2019).

Despite the apparent advantages, two significant points must be noted: (1) universities are typically rated lower than other actors such as customers, suppliers, and rival firms as sources of external knowledge; and (2) this lack of engagement may be explained by a number of significant barriers that may exist with respect to the facilitation of links between firms and universities (Freel 2000; Hewitt-Dundas, Gkypali, and Roper 2019; Hughes and Kitson 2012).

This book concentrates on collaborations occurring between Small and Medium Sized Enterprises (SMEs) and universities. From the perspective of an SME and the entrepreneurs running it, innovation can be a risky and costly endeavour as it consumes time and resources, both of which are limited in the context of smaller firms (Christensen 1997). The rationale for the focus on small firms is based on the fact that they possess fewer resources with which to innovate (Acs and Audretsch 1990; Huggins and Johnston 2009a), and thus stand to gain a greater benefit from engaging in U–I linkages (Motohashi 2005). Yet, firm size is typically regarded to be negatively related to the propensity to engage in collaborative linkages with universities (Laursen and Salter 2004; Mohnen and Hoareau 2003).

While existing studies suggest that SMEs may be less likely to engage in university collaboration than their larger counterparts, this finding masks several significant differences in the form and function of university collaborations for SMEs (Johnston 2020b). As a result, several important differences in the behaviour of SMEs in terms of university collaboration have been observed, including:

- SMEs are less likely to engage in formal collaborations with universities.
- SMEs are more likely to undertake a higher number of collaborations once they engage with a university.
- The outcomes of collaborations between SMEs and universities are less likely to result in a patent (and when they do, they are less likely to be cited in the development of a new patent).
- SMEs are less likely to recruit new employees through university collaboration.
- SMEs may perceive fewer barriers to U–I collaboration.
- SMEs are more likely to collaborate with local universities.

There are also studies which find that firm size is not a significant determinant of university collaboration, or that it is not SMEs that are less likely to engage in these links but only the very smallest, micro, firms (Eom and Lee 2010; Maietta 2015). Furthermore, other studies have suggested that firm size may have a negative effect on the propensity to collaborate with universities, meaning SMEs are more likely to engage in this manner (Hewitt-Dundas 2011). Finally, the influence of firm size on U–I collaboration may be context specific, with Giuliani and Arza's (2009) study of wine producing firms in Italy and Chile finding that in Chile larger firms were more likely to partner with a university, whereas in Italy smaller firms were more likely.

Given the mixed evidence as to the engagement of SMEs and universities as well as their potential benefits and drawbacks, this book aims to shed greater light on collaborations between SMEs and universities. This allows a thorough examination of the socio-technical factors underpinning the motivations, processes, and means through which SMEs develop collaborative links with universities to better inform both theory and policy. As such, this book provides a comprehensive account of collaborations between SMEs and universities. Through following Kim, Kumar, and Kumar's (2010) overview of the typical structure of a collaborative project, the following analysis documents the journey of SMEs through the process of university collaboration starting with how they develop their project and identify their needs for knowledge and expertise; assessing universities and selecting a partner; undertaking the collaboration; and evaluating the outcomes of the partnership (Kim, Kumar, and Kumar 2010).

This first chapter briefly introduces the conceptual and policy background to U–I collaboration and sets the scene for the chapters that follow. In addition, it outlines the empirical approach of the book in terms of outlining the origin of the material that underpins the empirical chapters

1.2   THE ROLE(S) OF UNIVERSITIES

There exists a long-standing academic interest in the roles and performance of universities in the economy. Theorists have long highlighted the importance of firm resources for growth and competitiveness (Penrose 1959), with explicit links made to knowledge and its crucial role in economic growth but also the need for learning-by-doing within firms in order to exploit this resource (Arrow 1962; Mokyr 2002). Consequently, while knowledge was increasingly seen as an important factor of production there were only sporadic attempts to understand the roles of knowledge creators, such as universities, in the economy.

It was Jaffe's seminal 1989 paper that started in earnest a period of intense scrutiny of the roles of universities not merely within the innovation process but also in the wider economic development process by empirically demonstrating the existence of knowledge spillovers from academic research into the wider economy (Jaffe 1989). This finding prompted an increased empirical focus on the roles of universities in the innovation process through the following decade (Feldman 1999; Henderson and Cockburn 1996; Mansfield 1995, 1998), particularly as accompanying theoretical developments around clusters and systems of innovation became popular policy tools for the purposes of economic development (Drejer, Kristensen, and Laursen 1999; Freeman 1992; Lagendijk and Charles 1999; Lundvall 1992; Nelson and Rosenberg 1993; Porter 1990, 2003).

Developments in the theories of clusters and innovation systems increasingly pointed to the importance of what Porter (1990, 2003) termed 'associated institutions', that is, non-business organisations that may play a part in the innovation process. As academics recognised the increasingly 'open' nature of the innovation process, it became ever more understood as resulting from interactions outside the boundaries of the firm, facilitated through inter-organisational networks (Chesbrough 2003; Dosi 1990). Within these debates, universities were often identified as important partners (Charles 2006; Chatterton and Goddard 2000; Goddard 1999; Goddard and Chatterton 1999), prompting greater policy interest in the phenomenon.

Consequently, a broad literature examining the phenomenon of university–industry (U–I) links now exists (Ankrah and Al-Tabbaa 2015; Geuna and Muscio 2009; Perkmann et al. 2013). However, it is not just open innovation that underpins this as the conceptual foundations of this work are broader than a single framework or theory (Cunningham and O'Reilly 2018).

At a macro level, the U–I links literature draws on the science and public policy literature that examines innovation policy in enabling U–I links (Flanagan and Uyarra 2016; Mazzucato 2016). Furthermore, the literature focuses on the role of institutions, in a broad sense, that enable entrepreneurial behaviours within universities, mould their entrepreneurial characteristics, and promote the engagement in 'third' mission activities within the organisations (Clark 1998; Guerrero and Urbano 2012; Thursby and Thursby 2002). These developments are particularly evident in the conceptualisation of the 'entrepreneurial university', which has risen to the fore in the literature explaining the associated structures that have emerged within universities in order to engage in their changing missions (Centobelli et al. 2019; Fini et al. 2018; Sharifi, Liu, and Ismail 2014).

At a meso level, the literature on U–I collaboration draws on insights from both the innovation systems and geography of innovation literatures. This focuses on the spatial dimension of U–I links, highlighting the roles of universities in the economic development process at a sub-national level, that is, the city and region (Huggins and Kitagawa 2012; Johnston and Huggins

2016; Pugh et al. 2016; Sanchez-Barrioluengo and Benneworth 2019; Uyarra 2010). As such, these insights are useful firstly for understanding the effect of a university's activities on its locale, and are formalised in the 'Triple Helix' Model of economic development, explicitly placing the university and its interaction with both industry and government at the heart of this process (Etzkowitz 2003a; Etzkowitz and Leydesdorff 2000; Ranga and Etzkowitz 2013). Secondly, this literature provides insights into the role of the physical distance between actors in the formation of U–I links (D'Este, Guy, and Iammarino 2013; D'Este and Iammarino 2010; Johnston and Huggins 2017).

While macro- and meso-level conceptual frameworks underpin the literature, it is work at the micro level that provides the greatest insights into SME–university collaboration. At this level, the focus is on the socio-technical nature of these collaborative links and draws heavily on the network and innovation alliances literature (Gulati 1999; Khanna, Gulati, and Nohria 1998). Therefore, the ability of actors to connect to one another is an important factor. Accordingly, both social capital and network capital are crucial to the formation of these links; with the former playing a role in breaking down barriers between actors from academia and industry (Al-Tabbaa and Ankrah 2016), and the latter promoting calculative network formation, ensuring that a tie will actually yield external knowledge for the firm to utilise in its innovation activities (Huggins 2010; Huggins and Johnston 2010; Huggins, Johnston, and Thompson 2012; Huggins, Prokop, and Thompson 2020).

Further insights from the innovation networks literature illuminate the importance of the similarities of collaborating actors and the social nature of these collaborative links (Gertner, Roberts, and Charles 2011; Knoben and Oerlemans 2006). These similarities are conceptualised in terms of proximities that capture the closeness of actors across several dimensions including location (spatial proximity), network membership (social proximity), cognitive understanding (technological proximity), and similarity or working culture (organisational proximity) (Aguilera, Lethiais, and Rallet 2012). Therefore, in the context of SME–university collaboration, these relational and cognitive factors are important for allowing actors to connect with and understand one another (Al-Tabbaa and Ankrah 2016, 2019).

Through a detailed examination of SME–university collaboration, the analysis presented in this book presents several new findings regarding the understanding of U–I collaboration from the perspective of SMEs. To summarise, the analysis suggests that:

- Relational and cognitive factors are important for both the formation and function of collaborative links between SMEs and universities.
- Spatial proximity plays an implicit role in the collaboration process between SMEs and universities.

- The closeness of the actors in terms of social, technological, and organisational proximity may evolve through the collaboration process.
- A broad range of outputs and outcomes underpin the success of the project.
- Successful projects are more likely to result in enduring relationships between SMEs and universities.
- Collaborative projects between SMEs and universities are path dependent in nature, with prior experience of working with universities likely to result in more successful projects.

1.3 EMPIRICAL APPROACH OF THE BOOK

Given the fact that SMEs are under-represented in terms of the study of U–I collaboration (Laursen and Salter 2004; Mohnen and Hoareau 2003), examining their interactions in greater depth may shed more light on the motivations, processes, and means by which they develop U–I links to better inform both theory and policy. In order to complete this objective, this book adopts a realist approach to present a case study focused on the socio-technical characteristics of SMEs that engaged in formal collaborative projects with universities (Bhaskar 2008; Easton 2010). Essentially this allows for an objective ontology that treats constructs as observable and independent of the observer, while concurrently allowing for a subjective interpretation of those objects. As such, the approach of this book echoes the move away from what has been termed formalist approaches to the study of economic phenomena, underpinned by utility maximisation and rational choices, towards a 'substantivist' position based around reciprocity and redistribution (Polanyi 2001). In essence, this negates the Utilitarian tradition (Granovetter 1985), whereby an idealised picture of the process is painted.

Taking a realist position in the understanding of U–I collaboration allows the empirical work to reflect the actualities of this interaction, namely, the absence of a formal market for university knowledge and the associated mechanisms through which it may be coordinated, that is, a price system. This means that the development of U–I collaboration is more akin to archaic systems based on mutual exchange and embeddedness. As such, it cannot necessarily be described as a market process.

As collaboration between universities and industry is a complex process, reducing this complexity to what Granovetter (1985) describes as 'thought experiments' may only provide an incomplete assessment of the activities of which it is comprised. Importantly, given the increasing recognition that the process of U–I collaboration is a socio-technical process (Al-Tabbaa and Ankrah 2019), this approach allows the social dimension to be explicitly considered and evaluated.

This does not suggest the primacy of a qualitative approach; it merely asserts that in seeking to explore the phenomenon of U–I collaboration in sufficient depth, this approach lends itself to uncovering the processes that underpin this interaction. Indeed, the conceptual framework draws on a wealth of quantitative studies that provide many important insights. As such, the aim is to complement the extant empirical work in the field. Therefore, in order to explore the phenomenon of university collaboration from the perspective of the SMEs involved, the book draws on material from 22 in-depth semi-structured interviews with owners/managers of SMEs, defined according to accepted conventions as those with fewer than 250 employees. The sample of firms employed between three and 120 workers, with average employment around 26, thus the book captures the experience of the small firm in this process.

The participating SMEs had mostly collaborated with universities through the Knowledge Transfer Partnership (KTP) programme. KTPs are designed to assist UK business with innovation and, by extension, also promote their growth. The aim of the programme is to promote collaboration between firms and universities, ensuring that the 'latest academic thinking' is introduced into the firm to promote innovation. These projects can last between one and three years and are part-funded by a public grant to cover the costs of the project. Consequently, an SME contributes around one-third of the costs (up to £35,000, but generally lower). In addition, the project employs a graduate with specialist knowledge of the field, referred to as the Associate, to work full time on the project at the premises of the firm.

In order to examine as broad a range of projects as possible so that a wide range of experiences of U–I interaction could be captured, no *a priori* restrictions were placed on the types of firms included; consequently, the case study features firms that operate in a diverse range of sectors such as biotechnology, engineering, finance, and digital marketing. Furthermore, the participating SMEs worked with a broad cross-section of UK universities.

To capture experiences of the respondents, the analysis utilises a narrative approach, influenced by the increasing use of these techniques in both the organisation studies (Boje 2001; Czarniawska 1998) and entrepreneurship literatures (Discua Cruz, Hamilton, and Jack 2020; Gartner 2010). This enables the key events occurring during these collaborative partnerships to be identified and allows an interpretation of the participants' perceptions of these events to be captured from their perspective. Accordingly, the semi-structured interviews, based around a loose script, enabled the use of a quasi-'life-story approach' to be used (Johansson 2004). This allows the participants to discuss events from their point of view rather than based on a pre-defined set of factors (Clandinin and Connelly 2000). Naturally, each respondent differed in their openness to the interviewer; some were happy to talk at length about the project and needed just minimal prompting. When respondents were less forthcoming, the interviewers relied more upon developing focused-interview narratives (Mishler 1986), that is, building the narratives through the probing of respondents enabling greater details of their specific projects to be captured. In line with the overall approach, this probing was accomplished while following the rules of not interrupting and letting the respondent outline the events.

Adhering to these methodological protocols ensured that the respondents were given a voice (Bauer 1996), enabling the creation of a 'multi-voiced' account from the perspective of SMEs and the process of developing an idea for a new project, the pursuit of a university collaboration to realise the projects' outcome, undertaking the project, and the projects (Ericson 2010; Fletcher 2007). Thus, while narrative approaches may be broad in scope (Larty and Hamilton 2011), the approach utilised in this book has created a set of first person descriptions of events surrounding the experiences of participating in collaborative projects with universities from those involved. The narratives are, therefore, designed to provide the story – hence the empirical chapters present quotes in order to provide the participants with a voice, and enable their words to tell the story.

Using this approach means that the analysis is concerned with connecting the individual stories into a plot in order to highlight the activities that occur within the firms (Steyaert 2007). Consequently, the analysis utilises what have been described as structuralist approaches to analysing narrative (Larty and Hamilton 2011).

1.4   STRUCTURE OF THE BOOK

The first half of the book presents a state-of-the-art literature review of university engagement among firms. Chapters 2–4 provide a comprehensive overview of the conceptual underpinnings of this literature as well as the key empirical findings. As inter-organisational collaborative partnerships have been conceptualised as a four-stage socio-technical process, this provides a structure for the empirical chapters of this book: (1) identifying needs; (2) assessing and selecting a partner; (3) implementing a partnership; and (4) reassessing the partnership (Kim et al. 2010), which further provides a guiding framework for presenting the analysis. Chapter 5 examines the policy development underpinning the promotion of U–I collaboration in the UK and examines recent patterns of engagement using publicly available data. Chapter 6 explores the process of project creation and identifying the need to procure external resources within the small firm. Chapter 7 then examines the partner selection process of SMEs when they develop the collaborative links with universities. Chapter 8 examines the dynamics of the partnership and the usefulness of the knowledge obtained from the SMEs' university partner. Chapter 9 analyses the end of the project and the relative success of the partnership. Finally, Chapter 10 summarises the findings, their contribution to the overall understanding of SME–university collaboration, and discusses their implications for SMEs, academics, knowledge exchange practitioners, and policymakers.

2. Framing collaboration: alliances, networks, and open innovation

2.1 INTRODUCTION

The competitiveness of firms was traditionally associated with the resources under their control (Barney 1991; Grant 1996; Huggins 2010; Situm 2019; Wernerfelt 1984). Accordingly, the resource-based and knowledge-based views of the firm underpin a broad body of academic work that examines the form and function of SMEs. However, implicit in these views is the point that the boundary of the firm represents the limits of its competitiveness; resources within the firm are the key. The last two decades has seen scholars develop alternative views of competitiveness, namely, focusing on inter-organisational networks and collaboration to allow firms to leverage resources from outside their boundaries.

As a result of these developments, the university has been recognised as a potential source of knowledge for firms seeking external partners, with interaction between firms and universities highlighted as a key mechanism through which firms may successfully innovate (Ankrah and Al-Tabbaa 2015; Perkmann et al. 2013). As noted in Chapter 1, a broad set of concepts underpin the study of these interactions (Cunningham and O'Reilly 2018). Given the broad conceptual underpinnings of the literature, the purpose of this chapter is to explore the concepts on which it draws. Specifically, this chapter focuses on literature on strategic alliances and open innovation, two bodies of work that are fundamental to the understanding of inter-organisational collaboration, networking, and innovation.

The Open Innovation (OI) paradigm frequently provides the conceptual underpinning of work on university–industry collaboration. This body of work posits that successful innovation is systemic in nature, resulting from combining knowledge and expertise from within the firm with that of other organisations (Chesbrough 2003; Huggins and Thompson 2017; Simard and West 2006). Yet prior to the emergence of open innovation, the literature was not silent with regard to the matter of inter-organisational innovation alliances. Indeed, there exists a well-developed literature in the fields of industrial economics, operations management, and strategy around the organisation of innovation activities into cooperative and collaborative ties.

The previous orthodoxy largely regarded the vertical integration of companies as the most efficient means by which additional resources could be appropriated for a firm (Johnston and Lawrence 1988). The evolution of the world economy and the consequent rise of post-Fordism as the dominant techno-economic paradigm of the fifth Kondratiev wave has seen a shift in emphasis away from mass production reliant upon economies of scale towards a more flexible and agile production system based around economics of scope, specialisation, and servitisation (Johnston and Lawrence 1988). This post-Fordist world focuses on flexible specialisation whereby the competitiveness of firms relies on agility and responsiveness (Piore and Sabel 1984); yet, the vertical integration of firms into large corporate behemoths does not fit with this viewpoint. Therefore, by the end of the 1980s the trend towards vertical integration had diminished, replaced by an increased focus on what have been termed relational capabilities (Lorenzoni and Lipparini 1999). These relational capabilities referred to firms' ability to interact with other actors and develop broad networks through which they may increase their knowledge and expertise.

In summary, both the strategic alliances and open innovation literatures provide important insights into the issue of collaborative innovation. The remainder of this chapter provides a critical examination of both.

2.2   ALLIANCES AND NETWORKS

While the resource-based and accompanying knowledge-based view of the firm both provide significant insights into the competitiveness of firms and the factors underpinning this, implicit in both approaches is the fact that the boundaries of the firm represent its competitive limitations. This results from viewing the resources *within* the firm as the key factors that permit the firm to innovate. As such, it is the resources that the firm controls that determine innovation. Consequently, the process of research and development (R&D) collaboration, defined by Arranz and Fdez de Arroyabe (2008) as 'the union of two or more parties, institutions or individuals, who pursue a distinct assignment together' (p. 89), allows firms to combine resources for innovation.

In general, the strategic alliance literature highlights the advantages from engaging in collaboration with external actors in order to circumvent these limitations (Arranz and Fdez de Arroyabe 2008). These strategic alliances are conceptualised as a method of sharing risks, enhancing legitimacy, and seeking new competences (Eisenhardt and Schoonhoven 1996). While still drawing heavily on the resource-based view of the firm (Barney 1991; Wernerfelt 1984), this literature views alliances as a key method for firms to augment their resource base through gaining access to additional competences, capabilities, knowledge, and expertise of external organisations (Dacin, Oliver, and Roy 2007; Van Wijk and Nadolska 2020). These alliances are typically based around a formal relationship and contractual agreement to undertake specific tasks with set objectives, although stopping short of conferring any ownership factors as a joint venture might (Walter, Lechner, and Kellermanns 2007). Accordingly, alliances are viewed as being more cost-effective than joint ventures as they are typically cheaper, while at the same time their formal nature ensures that opportunism is minimised (Mowery, Oxley, and Silverman 1998; Oxley 1997; Parkhe 1993). However, one potential drawback of these alliances may be their temporary nature, with dissolution rates of around 50% reported within the literature accompanied by failure rates as high as 70% (Sivadas and Dwyer 2000).

Advantages should outweigh the disadvantages, as inter-organisational alliances have become an expanding feature of business over the past three decades (Dacin, Oliver, and Roy 2007). In addition, strategic alliances have been observed to occur in a broad range of sectors including more traditional manufacturing sectors such as car production (Dyer 1996) and emergent knowledge-intensive manufacturing sectors such as biotechnology (Zollo, Reuer, and Singh 2002), as well as service-focused sectors such as telecommunication (Gimeno et al. 2005) and financial services (Wright and Lockett 2003).

According to Chen (1996), alliances can be characterised as either offensive or defensive in nature. A firm may enter into a strategic alliance for the purposes of advancing its competitive position and expanding its scope and operations, or it may be motivated by protecting its interests and maintaining its current market position (Chen 1996). In terms of alliance formation, the first steps typically involve the organisations assessing the nature of the potential partner's resources for complementarity and interdependence (Dyer, Singh, and Hesterly 2018). Interdependence has been identified as a key factor in the longevity of these alliances; lower levels of interdependence may promote faster returns as each partner undertakes distinct tasks with little joint working, but risks being more 'decomposable' in nature as a result (Dyer, Singh, and Hesterly 2018, p. 3148).

Conversely, higher levels of complementarity and interdependence may promote slower returns associated with less of a need to invest in relation to specific assets or knowledge sharing routines, thus ensuring the alliance runs smoothly. Based on this, Dyer and Singh (1998) posit that the value creation potential of alliances is a function of complimentary resources, relations-specific assets, knowledge sharing routines and effective governance. In addition, consideration must be given to the nature of these resources and whether they are tangible (i.e. factors such as equipment, machinery, and location) or intangible (i.e. factors such as knowledge and capabilities).

Prior work also suggests that a level of path dependency in the formation of alliances exists as firms' prior experience of engaging with other firms has been identified as a key predictor of value creation (Kale and Singh 2007). Furthermore, partner-specific experience is viewed as being of greater benefit than a firm's overall experience of partnering as this may foster trust, deter opportunism, reduce conflict, and minimise governance costs (Gulati, Lavie and Singh 2009; Kale, Singh, and Perlmutter 2000; Park and Dongcheol 1997). Dyer and Singh (1998) conceptualise this reliance upon experience as 'relational capacity'.

In general, there is mixed empirical evidence as to the importance of recurrent alliances, with Hoang and Rothermaerl (2005) presenting evidence from biotechnology firms that prior ties have a positive impact on success of joint drug development projects (Hoang and Rothaermel 2005); while Goerzen (2007) found that repeated equity-based alliances had a negative effect on the performance of Japanese multinationals (Goerzen 2007). In contrast, analysis of the performance of alliances involving Fortune 300 firms highlighted the fact that partner-specific experience is positively associated with greater performance but it was moderated by the complementarity of the two partners' assets as well as their technological and financial resources (Gulati, Lavie, and Singh 2009).

Beyond performance, partner-specific experience has also been shown to have several effects on alliances, including partner selection, governance, and the development of the alliance (Valdés-Llaneza and García-Canal 2015). In terms of partner selection, the issue of information asymmetry may be addressed and removed as the organisations will both be aware of each other's strengths and weaknesses, working practices and culture, and resources and capabilities (Valdés-Llaneza and García-Canal 2015). Therefore, projects that require a high degree of technological commitment or are focused on the development of a radical innovation may be better suited to recoupling in order to ensure partner compatibility. Prior ties allow partners to have learned and, therefore, be able to anticipate the behaviours of their partner in the course of an alliance (Lioukas and Reuer 2015) as well as providing insights into the nature of the contracts required to govern the interaction (Reuer and Devarakonda 2016). In addition, an enduring relationship appears to encourage the sharing of the firm's knowledge base as they are positively related to the probability that a firm will cite their partner's patents (Devarakonda and Reuer 2018).

The means by which partners interact with one another have also been found to have an important effect on the success of the alliance. For example, Dyer (1996) found a significant positive relationship between face-to-face contact and quality of output among car manufacturers and their suppliers, suggesting that increased interaction of partners is associated with better performing alliances. Furthermore, higher levels of contact were also associated with a quicker lead time in the production of new models (pp. 282–3). Indeed, the geographic proximity within the supply chain was associated with greater efficiencies in terms of promoting contact between partners. This evidence clearly highlights the fact that the creation and function of alliances are not solely dependent upon strategic factors but that the relational/social aspect is also important (Dyer, Singh, and Hesterly 2018; Eisenhardt and Schoonhoven 1996).

The importance of the social aspect of alliances has given rise to the 'relational view' as an important theoretical approach to understanding their function, placing inter-organisational collaboration at the heart of understanding firm strategy and performance (Dyer, Singh, and Hesterly 2018).

In terms of the development of alliances, Ring, Doz, and Olk (2005) proposed three types of collaboration 'pathways'; emerged, engineered, and embedded. Each pathway has a differing focus in the initial conditions and, following a path-dependent nature, have different implications for the activities and success of the collaboration. Underpinning the formation process are three key factors (Ring, Doz, and Olk 2005):

1.   Shared interests, which promote both a commitment and urgency to address them together.
2.   Social relationships, which permit an understanding between the parties.
3.   Interdependency, which creates the motivation to seek commonalities.

Consequently, the process of alliance formation differs according to the nature of the interests, relationships, and vision of the partners (see Table 2.1).

Embedded alliances are characterised by common shared interests, established social relationships, and a shared strategic interdependence. Emergent alliances, conversely, are based around common shared interests but weaker social relationships and a differing converging interdependency; as such, these latter factors may require work during the alliance. Finally, engineered alliances are those that are typically facilitated by actors other than the partners. Accordingly, they may share a relatively common interest, the origin of the common outside actor who facilitates the alliance but lacks direct social relationships and a similar strategic vision that drives them to seek an alliance.

While alliances have been typically viewed in terms of dyads, that is, the interaction between two organisations, interest in portfolios has recently increased (Van Wijk and Nadolska 2020). Given this, strategic alliances are viewed not just in terms of one interaction but a set of interactions an organisation may engage in. Indeed, this finding resonates with the broader networks

Table 2.1   *Characteristics of alliances*

	Emergent	Engineered	Embedded
Shared Interests	Common	Relatively common	Common
Social Relationships	Relatively weak or developing	Absent or weak	Strong
Strategic Interdependency	Converging with a growing desire to work together	Divergent – no independent desire to collaborate	Converged – actively seeking to work together

Source: Summarised from Ring, Doz and Olk (2005).

literature that highlights their diversity, being comprised of a range of actors (Huggins, Johnston, and Thompson 2012; Van Wijk and Nadolska 2020). Therefore, interaction with one partner at a time is unlikely.

The strategic alliance literature provides significant insights into the motivations, form, and function of inter-organisational collaboration. However, it is also useful to understand the differences between university–industry links and strategic alliances, and whether U–I links can be considered to be a special case of strategic alliances. In particular, the absence of equity stakes in the U–I links, which are more prevalent in strategic alliances where the relationship conveys joint ownership of the project (Gulati 1995), whose focus is on joint R&D rather than joint venture. Yet, this joint working can encompass a broad range of activities related to R&D and capability building within the firm, both formal and informal (Perkmann et al. 2013).

While U–I links may be covered by contractual agreements, they are not truly market transactions in the pure sense of the concept. In this case, the absence of a 'market' means that U–I collaboration is not based on 'purchasing' but an agreement to share resources, suggesting the pooling of resources underpins these collaborations. In contrast, strategic alliances are regarded as forming when both parties lack the means to accomplish the goals alone (Mothe and Quelin 2001), while U–I collaboration is characterised by an uneven relationship between a knowledge creator, the university, and knowledge user, the firm, designed to pursue a new project.

Therefore, while the strategic alliances literature can offer some insights into the factors underpinning the process of U–I collaboration, the fact that these types of alliances do not capture all the activities of these collaborations means that other frameworks are used to examine the phenomenon. Open innovation provides one such framework.

2.3 OPEN INNOVATION

One of the key tenets of the modern innovation literature is the fact that the process has become more systemic and open in nature (Dahlander and Gann 2010; Huizingh 2011; Roper and Hewitt-Dundas 2015). According to Chesbrough (2003), this means that 'new ideas may come from inside or outside the company' (p. 43), widening the scope for innovation within the firm as it no longer relies solely upon internal resources (Barney 1991). Instead, the OI paradigm views the process of developing new products, services, processes, and technologies as resulting from the procurement of external knowledge through interaction with outside actors by means of inter-organisational networks, rather than undertaken by firms in isolation. Thus, our understanding of the innovation process has evolved. It was formerly regarded as an individual or isolated endeavour, undertaken *within* organisations, but now more often conceptualised as an activity that crosses boundaries to take place *among* organisations. This, in turn, has led to increased efforts to identify, understand, and analyse not only the external actors who may be important to this process but also the set of relations, interactions, and behaviours that may promote their occurrence.

Indeed, within an increasingly networked world, characterised by ever higher levels of globalisation, and driven by the connectivity and low communication costs afforded by the internet, the development of and participation in inter-organisational collaboration has come to be viewed as a relatively straightforward task (Huizingh 2011; Narula 2004). Yet, increasing levels of globalisation tend to be equated with increasing competition; the result being that shorter product cycles put pressure on firms for their innovation cycles to be faster. As the ability to compete effectively is more and more linked to the ability to innovate (Schumpeter 1942 [2014]), there is even more pressure on firms to update their existing products, processes, and technologies as well as develop new ideas. It has been argued that those firms not engaging in innovative activities risk losing out to those firms that are (Koschatsky 2001).

Open innovation can be defined as 'the use of purposive inflows and outflows of knowledge to accelerate the internal innovation, and to expand the markets for external use of innovation, respectively' (Simard and West 2006, p. 221). Despite this relatively simple conceptualisation, the open innovation concept suffers from ambiguity, with many different definitions being posited in the extant literature (Dahlander and Gann 2010; Huizingh 2011). As with the strategic alliances literature, the OI paradigm clearly draws on both the resource-based and knowledge-based views of the firm, which see the competitive foundations of the firm derived from the resources at its disposal (Barney 1991; Grant 1996). As such, from this perspective, it is through the means of open innovation that these resources can be augmented. A key feature of open innovation are the knowledge-based networks which facilitate the interactions, relationships, and ties necessary to access knowledge in the form of new knowledge, expertise, technology, and skills that are leveraged into the firm in order to augment its knowledge resources (Ahuja 2000; Barney 1991; Grant 1996). Explicit in the work on open innovation is the fact that networks are greater than the sum of their parts (Randhawa, Wilden, and Hohberger 2016; Spithoven, Vanhaverbeke, and Roijakkers 2013), providing opportunities for heterogeneous organisations with heterogeneous knowledge bases to combine to produce something novel.

Open innovation can be regarded as a broad set of socio-technical processes involving the formation of inter-organisational networks between many different actors for the purposes of developing new products, processes, or technology. While the literature typically refers to a single process of open innovation, three distinct strands have been posited: (1) outside-in processes, whereby organisations seek the required knowledge and expertise from external actors; (2) inside-out processes where organisations seek to marketise their own knowledge and expertise to be used by external actors; and (3) coupled processes, where organisations seek to work jointly on projects to co-create new knowledge (Dahlander and Gann 2010; Enkel, Gassmann, and Chesbrough 2009).

Activities that are commonly referred to as open innovation typically capture the first type of interaction, where firms seek to procure knowledge and expertise from external sources, but can involve inbound or outbound flows of knowledge (Saebi and Foss 2015). However, from the perspective of U–I linkages, all three processes may potentially be utilised.

Open innovation partners are often comprised of organisations from the supply chain and their customers, suppliers, or competitors (Chesbrough 2017; Laursen and Salter 2006). Outside of the supply chain, public and commercial research institutions were cited as the most important source (Enkel, Gassmann, and Chesbrough 2009). The key to successful innovation is participation in networks which allow access to organisational partners who may possess complementary knowledge (Dittrich and Duysters 2007; Gassmann 2006; Perkmann and Walsh 2007). Underpinning this work, is the assumption that firms possess the capabilities and absorptive capacity to both obtain and successfully utilise knowledge from external partners (Cohen and Levinthal 1990; Teece 1998).

The open innovation process is not merely about general network interactions and unintentional transfer of knowledge, that is, externalities, but deliberate activities whereby actors set out to build and utilise their networks in order to obtain knowledge and expertise with which to innovate. In particular, Simard and West's (2006) interpretation of open innovation suggests that it is a calculative process, where actors are looking for specific knowledge resources to augment their current stock. This deliberate construction of networks focused on *useful* relations suggests that network capital is an important resource within the firm (Huggins and Johnston 2010; Huggins, Johnston, and Thompson 2012).

This last point highlights the fact that, in general, the OI paradigm draws heavily on concepts proposed by network scholars. Through conceptualising innovation as a complex process involving the knowledge flow between firms and other actors, the network dimension of open innovation is clearly highlighted (Meagher and Rogers 2004). Networks are typically more diverse than alliances as they cover both formal and informal interactions.

Within the network literature, two distinct forms of knowledge network have been identified; knowledge contact networks and knowledge alliance networks (Huggins, Johnston, and Thompson 2012). The former are based around formal, contracted relationships founded with the explicit aim of the joint sharing of knowledge for the purposes of innovation. Within these networks, the sharing of knowledge is a deliberate consequence of the action. In contrast, knowledge alliance networks may be characterised by less formal relationships, based around looser ties or social interaction. As a result, any sharing of knowledge may be an unintended consequence of the interaction or a pure externality (Huggins, Johnston, and Thompson 2012).

For network scholars, the focus of the network is on accessing, rather than acquiring, knowledge. Therefore, networks can be looser than a formal alliance. However, network stability is dependent upon their construction, whether in the process of their creation actors sought to form relationships within an existing network or with actors outside an existing network (Beckman, Haunschild, and Phillips 2004). As such, the structure and dynamism of these networks may vary according to their type.

As the purpose of these inter-organisational networks is clearly defined as focusing on capturing external knowledge, they can be considered to be a strategic resource developed through managerial action (Huggins, Johnston, and Thompson 2012; Huizingh 2011). The development of inter-organisational networks in this context is taken to be a strategic undertaking based on the need to access the appropriate resources into the firm, with the relationships specifically designed to access knowledge for innovation (Huggins and Johnston 2010).

Therefore, it is possible to distinguish between two main types of network resource investment as means of identifying different forms of network space (Huggins 2010). The first is social capital, in the form of social networks established across firms or other organisations through which knowledge may flow. Social capital is regarded as consisting of obligations and expectations, which are dependent on: the trustworthiness of the social environment; the information flow capabilities of social structure; and norms accompanied by sanctions (Coleman 1988). The second is network capital, in the form of more calculative and strategic networks designed specifically to facilitate knowledge flow and accrue advantage for firms (Gulati 2007; Huggins 2010). This has been identified as an important determinant of innovation performance, and therefore it is not the networking activities of firms that drive innovation but their ability to develop network resources (Huggins, Johnston, and Thompson, 2012).

Open innovation also covers a wide range of interactions designed to promote innovation, and may involve linkages that are either horizontal or vertical (Contractor and Lorange 2002; Marullo et al. 2020). However, while some scholars have focused on formal equity sharing or mergers between organisations in order to promote innovation, open innovation makes no such pre-requisites. This field therefore has a similar focus to the network literature, focusing on a broad range of alliances from informal non-permanent, cooperative relationships to formal contracted relations, the co-creation of knowledge, and joint ventures. As a result, open innovation is conceptually similar to the network paradigm being focused on a continuum of types of interaction (Dahlander and Gann 2010).

Empirical evidence suggests that those firms open to sharing knowledge tend to perform better in terms of innovation metrics (Fu 2012; Laursen and Salter 2006). Furthermore, the evidence also suggests that this relationship is in fact curvilinear, that is, there exists an optimal level of openness to promote innovative performance (Greco, Grimaldi, and Cricelli 2016). Beyond a certain level, the marginal gains from increased openness begin to decrease. As a result, it is argued that business models need to be able to accommodate open innovation (Chesbrough 2007; Saebi and Foss 2015). Furthermore, as the premise of open innovation is that external knowledge *complements* and adds to the firm's existing knowledge stock a certain level of internal innovative capabilities is required (di Benedetto 2010; Chesbrough 2003). In order for this process to be complementary, firms require the ability to be innovative themselves as well as the ability to effectively absorb and use knowledge from external sources (Cohen and Levinthal 1990; Dahlander and Gann 2010).

In addition, as the process is dynamic in nature, that is, the transfer of knowledge is undertaken as an active and deliberate activity and involves the interaction of individuals to be successfully achieved, the firm's ability to network and develop the required 'relational capital' is crucial (Sisodiya, Johnson, and Grégoire 2013).

The open innovation literature has two main drawbacks; the first is that neither the pathways of engagement nor the foundations of the relationships are examined in as much detail as is found in the strategic alliance and network literature. While there is abundant evidence regarding who collaborates with whom, it comes up short in terms of explaining how these interactions are developed and facilitated. Secondly, the open innovation literature has been criticised for a tendency to focus on larger firms at the expense of SMEs (Narula 2004; Nieto and Santamaria 2010; Spithoven, Vanhaverbeke, and Roijakkers 2013). This latter criticism arose from the results of early studies into the adoption of open innovation activities which produced evidence that larger firms were more engaged in these types of activity than SMEs (Lichtenthaler 2008; Van de Vrande et al. 2009). However, as the literature matured, scholars turned their attention to understanding open innovation among SMEs, yielding a number of key insights into the actors with which SMEs may engage (Lee et al. 2010; Marullo et al. 2020) and the positive impact for SMEs of leveraging external resources through open innovation in order to diversify (Colombo, Piva, and Rossi-Lamastra 2014).

Furthermore, SMEs are regarded as being more flexible in their use of open innovation techniques, through their ability to use different open innovation practices simultaneously in the development of new products, suggesting they are more flexible than their larger counterparts (Spithoven, Vanhaverbeke, and Roijakkers 2013). Therefore, clear differences have been identified between larger firms and SMEs in terms of their engagement in open innovation; smaller firms have been found to be less open than their larger counterparts, but tend to have a higher marginal gain from each additional linkage (Vahter, Love, and Roper 2014). For resource-constrained smaller firms, significant gains can be made from utilising external knowledge for innovation (Freel 2000; Vossen 1999). In addition, SMEs tend to focus more on inbound activities, that is, their resource constraints mean they are knowledge seekers rather than knowledge sharers (Van de Vrande et al. 2009).

Overall, the evidence suggests that open innovation is beneficial to SMEs as engagement in this process enhances innovative performance (Ebersberger et al. 2012; Hung and Chou 2013; Inauen and Schenker-Wicki 2011; Parida, Westerberg, and Frishammar 2012). However, the literature reveals that the process is more complex than simply stating that open innovation enhances performance. For example, Parida, Westerberg, and Frishammar (2012) find that different open innovation practices have different effects on innovation among SMEs, with technology sourcing positively influencing radical innovation behaviour whereas technology scouting positively influences incremental innovation. A more active strategy among SMEs is likely to be associated with greater innovation performance.

Despite the positives, open innovation is not a risk-free process and engaging in it is not a guarantee of success (di Benedetto 2010).

Several externalities have been posed that suggest there are drawbacks to this kind of endeavour:

- loss of knowledge;
- coordination costs;
- inappropriate partner choice.

Potential externalities exist with respect to participating in the open innovation process. Firstly, loss of knowledge can occur when an organisation shares its knowledge, but the partner does not reciprocate. Therefore, it is left in a position where it has shared its intellectual property for little or no return (Lichtenthaler 2005). Given this situation, there is a need for trusting relations to cement the effectiveness. Indeed, particularly in the case of SMEs, Lee et al. (2010) propose that the intervention of intermediaries to facilitate the development of alliances enables trust to develop between partners.

Secondly, the process is not costless. For example, for open innovation to be successful there is a requirement that a potential partner is identified, the relationship cemented, and then maintained; activities which, in an SME context, may consume scarce resources as they require time and effort (Sieg, Wallin, and Von Krogh 2010). In addition, the types of network the firm are engaged in may affect the level of resources required to manage. For example, networking undertaken through knowledge alliances may require greater resources to manage due to their informal nature compared with contact networks which are associated with contractually bound relations (Almeida, Dokko, and Rosenkopf 2003; Lechner and Dowling 2003; Thorpe et al. 2005). Again, in an entrepreneurial and SME context, these activities may have a disproportionate effect on resource-constrained small firms

A firm must ensure that it is working with an appropriate partner as this has been identified as a key tenet of successful collaboration (Park and Ungson 2001). While heterogeneous organisations with heterogeneous knowledge bases can contribute to each other's innovation efforts, there still needs to be a degree of complementarity between partners in order that the collaboration may be effective. Therefore, a degree of organisational proximity is required, that is, a 'closeness in the space of relations' (Knoben and Oerlemans 2006; Ponds, van Oort, and Frenken 2007) that ensures they work together and have sufficient absorptive capacity to utilise each other's knowledge. As a result, a shared language or codebook may be crucial in order that each other's knowledge may be of use (Cowan and Jonard 2003).

Finally, market failures or market absences may limit the scope of open innovation, with small firms limited by a lack of information on who may act as potential partners as well as an inability to gauge their trustworthiness (Hewitt-Dundas and Roper 2017). For those SMEs and entrepreneurs that do engage in open innovation, while there may be advantages to pursuing this type of strategy, the process is not costless or frictionless. Care must be taken to engage with the appropriate partner while minimising risks from loss of knowledge and associated search and coordination costs. Collaborations between firms and universities may address some of these issues and while open innovation is not necessarily a panacea for the promotion of innovation it is a process that may assist SMEs in their innovation activities, providing it is carefully managed.

2.4   UNIVERSITIES AND OPEN INNOVATION

The key difference between the literatures on open innovation and strategic alliances is that the latter is focused on inter-firm relations, whereas open innovation has an emphasis on U–I collaboration. For example, in introducing the concept of open innovation, Chesbrough (2003) explicitly refers to the role of universities in society as important knowledge generators and potential partners in collaborative innovation projects. He noted that:

> [U]niversities are full of professors, with deep expertise. Better yet, these professors are surrounded by graduate students, who apprentice themselves to these professors. While the science that they do is excellent, many professors and their graduate students are clearly eager to apply that science to business problems. (2003, p. 44)

The extant literature on U–I links draws heavily on the concept of open innovation, with many studies using this as a starting point as to the aims of firms engaging in this fashion (Huggins, Prokop, and Thompson 2020; Johnston 2020a; Perkmann and Walsh 2007; Striukova and Rayna 2015).

As Striukova and Rayna (2015) argue, universities have always been 'open' in nature, set up to create and disseminate knowledge into wider society. However, while the open innovation literature is clearly pertinent to the discussion of U–I links, providing a rationale for the engagement to take place, the open innovation literature itself is remarkably quiet on the potential roles of universities in the process. Instead the extant literature tends to focus on issues around the use of external partners for the development of new products, processes, and technologies. Within the open innovation literature discussions around interactions with actors external to the firm tend to focus on those within the supply chain, that is, customer and suppliers, as well as rival firms (Bigliardi and Galati 2016; Colombo, Piva, and Rossi-Lamastra 2014; Van de Vrande et al. 2009). For example, in the wider literature a willingness to share and look externally has been found to be an important facet in promoting collaborations between universities and industry (Laursen and Salter 2006) and is also important when it comes to partnering with universities specifically (Laursen and Salter 2004).

In summary, the literature on open innovation provides a clear conceptual basis for the use of universities as collaborative partners to firms. Indeed, U–I links that are governed by formal collaborative agreements and underpinned by contractual relations can be seen to be analogous to coupled open innovation (Enkel, Gassmann, and Chesbrough 2009). This is clear from the focus of the literature on formal collaborations that involve projects funded either through public grants or paid for services used by the business community (D'Este, Guy and Iammarino 2013; Guerrero, Cunningham, and Urbano 2015; Huggins, Izushi, and Prokop 2016).

Finally, the open innovation literature underpins a large proportion of empirical work that examines the phenomenon of U–I collaboration as it provides a justification for this type of interaction. Yet, this literature does not provide details as to why universities may be appropriate partners, their roles within an economy, or what characteristics collaborative universities may possess. These are examined in more detail in Chapter 3.

3. Collaboration and the 'engaged' university

Universities are frequently framed as important innovators and collaborative partners, but while the open innovation literature highlights the benefits for firms of engaging in a university collaboration, it is less forthcoming on the qualities of a university and their functions in the innovation system. In order to examine these factors, this chapter assesses the characteristics of engaged universities before assessing the role of the university in the innovation system.

3.1 THE TRANSFORMATION OF UNIVERSITIES

The recognition of universities as key actors within the Open Innovation paradigm has prompted increased interest in what has been termed their 'third mission' activities, that is, moving beyond their original two missions of teaching and research towards engaging and collaborating with business (Budyldina 2018; Plewa, Rampersad, and Ho 2019; Suckling 1980; Thursby and Thursby 2002). Accordingly, this has led to new conceptualisations of ideal types of universities according to these activities. Firstly, the concept of the 'Entrepreneurial University' (Clark 1998), characterised as institutions that have moved towards being embedded in the economic and social fabric of society, positioning themselves as leaders within the economy (Clark 1998, pp. 4–5), has gained traction within the literature. Analogous to this is Goddard, Hazelkorn, and Vallance's (2016) conceptualisation of the 'civic university', whereby the teaching, research, and business engagement activities of the institution are viewed as overlapping and complementary in nature. Business engagement (or third mission activities) are integral to the functioning of the university and not peripheral or ad hoc in nature (Goddard, Hazelkorn, and Vallance 2016). In addition, the civic university is also viewed as adaptive, and able to change and adjust to fulfil shifting objectives (Goddard and Vallance 2013; Goddard et al. 2014). Thus, the ideal type of university is one that can be described as engaged.

The genesis of the focus on 'engaged' universities is typically traced to the passing of the 1980 Bayh-Dole Act by the US government. This is viewed within the literature as a watershed moment in the expansion of universities' roles within the economy (Kenney and Patton 2009; Mowery and Sampat

2004; Nelson 2001). This piece of legislation sought to encourage the commercialisation of university research by allowing US universities to patent the discoveries made as a result of Federally funded research projects, whereas previously the intellectual property (IP) was owned by the Federal government, and also to license this IP themselves (Mowery and Sampat 2004). An important result of the introduction of the Bayh-Dole Act was the mimicking of this legislation around the world (Agrawal 2001), providing independence to universities in terms of their ownership of IP developed using their knowledge, expertise, and the human capital of their academics.

While the Bayh-Dole Act marked a turning point in the institutional framework underpinning the third mission, universities already had a long history of undertaking these activities in conjunction with business. For example, Mowery and Sampat (2004) argue that there were numerous examples of joint research and patenting activity between US universities and firms throughout the twentieth century. In addition, it is well documented how Stanford University played an important role in the post-war development of Silicon Valley and the technology firms based there (Saxenian 1994). Given this, the engagement of universities with businesses is far from a new phenomenon.

Since the passing of the Bayh-Dole Act, there has been a more concerted effort among policymakers to promote collaborative links between universities and business. Previous interaction had happened either organically where individuals moved between academia and industry, for example in the design and manufacture of components such as cathode-ray tubes or semiconductors (Roy 1972; Russell 1971; Saxenian 1994) or, alternatively, cooperation and collaboration between universities and industry was the result of specific government programmes which required the input of the academic community and industry production such as the Apollo moon landings, and the development of the nuclear bomb. In short, U–I collaboration was not necessarily the result of a general policy push to create such links but motivated by explicit need or circumstance. As such, these collaborations occurred in the absence of an explicit institutional framework designed to facilitate and support them.

In the wake of the Bayh-Dole Act, and in line with the spreading neo-liberal hegemony in economic policymaking across the globe, an institutional framework developed within industrialised economies that tended to reframe the roles of universities as central to the economic development process, with U–I links becoming an important policy instrument with respect to promoting innovation (Edler and Fagerberg 2017). Therefore, while U–I collaboration pre-dates the Bayh-Dole Act, this legislation coupled with shifts in the orthodoxy of economic policymaking enabled the reframing of the roles of universities and allowed governments worldwide to formalise the role of U–I links in innovation policy.

While this changing institutional framework has laid the foundations for an expansion of the role of the university, it has also increased pressure on universities to follow this path (Perkmann et al. 2013). Interactions between universities and business are multi-faceted, encompassing many activities, the key interest being in valorisation activities that typically have a tangible outcome (Cohen, Nelson, and Walsh 2002; Perkmann et al. 2013). This is evident from examining UK government policy over the past two decades, which stressed the need to 'reward universities for strategies and activities to enhance interaction with business', while refocusing the role of businesses towards ensuring that 'they turn into success the scientific and technical knowledge in our universities' (DTI 1998). This theme has continued through successive reviews of UK universities (Lambert 2003; Wilson 2012), and explicitly formulated as a central plank of the Industrial Strategy unveiled in November 2017 (HM Government 2017). Furthermore, organisations such as the Confederation of British Industry have also called for 'deeper' collaborations between business and universities in order to promote the continued growth of the economy (CBI 2015).

These conceptualisations of the university as 'entrepreneurial' or 'civic' in nature did not evolve in isolation. The required institutional framework to support this transformation was laid down by policymakers as they sought to implement the neo-liberal orthodoxy that characterises the post-industrial political economy (Slaughter and Leslie 1997). For example, Article 130g of the Single European Act explicitly supports the pursuit of international competitiveness through the 'implementation of research, technological development, and demonstration programmes, by promoting co-operation with undertakings, research centres and universities' (European Communities 1986, p. 10).

The move to grant universities greater levels of autonomy with the outcomes of their research and their discoveries fits with the neo-liberal orthodoxy of economic policy rule-making that has had a hegemonic control over policymakers in the industrialised world. Consequently, policy conditions were right for the rise of the engaged university across all industrialised economies; a commitment to enterprise and innovation as drivers of growth, the decentralisation of the economy, and the withdrawal of the state as an actor that leads the economic growth process to one that facilitates growth from afar.

While recent arguments suggest that the role of the state should be re-imagined as that of an innovation leader (Mazzucato 2016), it can also be argued that the positioning of universities as anchor institutions within innovation systems allows this to be achieved by certain strategic nudges without the direct intervention of the state. Therefore, as an alternative to taking a clear leadership role, the state can promote the 'entrepreneurial university' as a leading organisation in the innovation process (Clark 1998; Thorp and

Goldstein 2010), allowing governments to set the agenda through promoting direction while limiting their direct interventions.

As Clark (1998) notes, the entrepreneurial university not only engages in activities which stimulate innovation and enterprise within the economy, but it is also explicitly set up and organised to accomplish this. On the one hand, entrepreneurial universities are those that are developing novel ideas, products, services, processes, or technologies through pursuing activities where the outcome is uncertain, but are also doing so through utilising new ways of organising themselves (Abreu and Grinevich 2013; Di Gregorio and Shane 2003; Shane 2004). Therefore, the university promotes innovation both *inside and outside* of its boundaries. These engaged universities can be viewed as both an incubator and catalyst for the development of the economy by acting as a conduit for both the exploration and exploitation of knowledge (Etzkowitz 2003b; Kirby, Guerrero, and Urbano 2011; Metcalfe 2010).

The key to the successful development and implementation of entrepreneurial activities is for universities to become quicker, more flexible, and responsive, to the changing demands of society. To achieve this, the university is required to foster changes in organisational structures, promoting interaction with outside stakeholders widening its sources of income. In particular, universities must concentrate more on third stream sources, ensuring that the entire university believes in the changing mission through establishing internal cultures and practices that embrace these changes (Clark 1998). These organisational changes are typically manifest in the proliferation of Technology Transfer Offices (Siegel, Veugelers, and Wright 2007).

What types of changes are witnessed within an entrepreneurial university? Utilising a Schumpeterian framework to outline the potential transformations of engaged universities, Jessop (2017) suggests that they may engage in activities such as: (1) the introduction of new goods, such as new courses, products, or technology, and new methods; (2) new markets and supply sources, focusing on exploiting new student markets or developing closer ties to the business community; and (3) reorganisation, through the creation of new organisational forms to exploit these opportunities, for example, international campus of spin-off firms (Jessop 2017, 2018).

An increasing orientation towards, and engagement in, third mission activities is a key characteristic of engaged universities, but they cannot be considered to be as isomorphic in nature (Kitagawa, Sánchez-Barrioluengo, and Uyarra 2016). Indeed, the focus within the extant literature on equating engagement with commercialisation activities has been criticised as too narrow (Abreu and Grinevich 2013). As a result, the engaged university is treated by some scholars as dichotomous in nature, broken down into those focused on commercialisation activity and those focused more broadly on working with industry (Perkmann et al. 2013; Sánchez-Barrioluengo and Benneworth 2019).

Accordingly, commercialisation activities within universities include activities such as patenting and the creation of spin-out firms. Working with industry, on the other hand, typically focuses on the combination of commercialisation activities with broader functions such as collaborative research and technical services (Sánchez-Barrioluengo and Benneworth 2019).

This distinction mirrors definitions of technology transfer activities within the extant literature, which are typically treated as either 'soft' engagement activities, for example lectures to the business community or engaging in consultancy work or contract research that are taken to be more akin to the traditional roles of universities, or 'hard' activities, such as technology licensing and the creation of spin-off firms, which are seen as less compatible with the traditional academic pursuits of teaching and research (Caldera and Debande 2010; Philpott et al. 2011). Yet, as Philpott et al. (2011) highlight, the range of third mission activities can be seen more as a continuum than a dichotomy, and while Rasmussen, Moen, and Gulbrandsen (2006) suggest that the 'harder' activities are more likely to produce tangible outcomes, this is not exclusive to these activities alone.

According to the empirical work in this area, commercialisation of university knowledge appears to be the exception rather than the norm. For example, patenting rates among academics are low, with Lissoni et al. (2011) finding that around 4–5% of academics file a patent, while Agrawal and Henderson (2002) found that patenting accounted for only around 10% of knowledge transfers at Massachusetts Institute of Technology (MIT). In addition, it has been suggested that patenting and licensing are not always relevant to all sectors of the economy, often offering a poor proxy for effective knowledge transfer (Mowery and Sampat 2004).

This focus on commercialisation may not only ignore a broad range of activities, but may also be inappropriate for all disciplines. Indeed, commercialisation activities may be biased towards disciplines where this is more prevalent as the development of frontier knowledge is more easily commercialised through a patent or licence, such as software or biosciences (Owen-Smith and Powell 2001). It may also be that less formal means of knowledge transfer are important (Agrawal and Henderson 2002; Cohen, Nelson, and Walsh 2002).

Clearly, universities are not homogenous as they vary in terms of their stocks of knowledge and expertise, knowledge generating capacity, research outputs, grant income, and commercial linkages (Hewitt-Dundas 2012; Huggins, Johnston, and Stride 2012). Sengupta and Ray (2017) identify a level of path dependence among universities in terms of how past performance with respect to their research quality enhances their abilities with respect to knowledge and technology transfer over time.

Given these debates, what characteristics make universities central to innovation networks? Evidence suggests that the centrality of a university is determined by the activities it is involved in rather than where it is located. For example, higher levels of spin-off creation and engagement in externally funded research projects have been found to promote network centrality, whereas activities such as patenting have a negative effect (Huggins et al. 2020).

The engaged university is the cornerstone of the Triple Helix Model of economic development, which conceives the process as dependent upon the facilitation of innovation within the economy based on the interaction of university–industry–government relationships (Etzkowitz 2003a; Etzkowitz and Leydesdorff 2000; Etzkowitz and Zhou 2006; Ranga and Etzkowitz 2013; Smith and Bagchi-Sen 2010).

While innovation systems tend to be discussed as a single entity, there is evidence to suggest that they are comprised of two distinct networks, one with a focus on technology and the other on scientific development (Murray 2002). In the former, academics generally work together on projects that focus on the creation of new knowledge, or Mode 1 type activities (Gibbons et al. 1994). In the latter, academics work with businesses in order to commercialise scientific research, or Mode 2 type activities, and a key finding is that academics are more productive when they work with other academics (Murray 2002).

4. University–industry collaboration: formation and function

The previous chapters have highlighted that universities are regarded as important actors in the innovation process, encouraging policymakers to promote their anchor role with innovation systems and their interaction with firms. This chapter undertakes a critical examination of the formation of collaborative links between universities and industry, how they function, and their outcomes, providing a critical appreciation of the process through highlighting the advantages but also the drawbacks.

The fact that universities have been placed at the forefront of the open innovation process is attributed to their role as significant generators of knowledge and expertise, operating at the cutting edge of disciplines through new discoveries. Consequently, their attractiveness as partners can be explained as they offer the prospect of new knowledge but are not direct competitors to the firms (Lavie and Drori 2012). Therefore, the starting point of the chapter is the proposition that engaging with a university is a strategic decision by the firm designed to procure new knowledge and expertise, that is, it is not merely a random occurrence, but instead involves premeditation, planning, and organising.

The chapter explores the factors that underpin the formation of these collaborations, the advantages for those firms that do engage with universities, while also examining any barriers and drawbacks faced. Finally, the chapter assesses the factors that influence the success of these collaborations.

4.1 UNIVERSITY–INDUSTRY COLLABORATION

The term 'university–industry links' usually covers activities that focus on the engagement of universities with businesses to develop and utilise knowledge, technology, or expertise for the development of new goods, services, or processes (Ankrah and Al-Tabbaa 2015; Perkmann et al. 2013). The broadness of the concept has led to the term U–I links being used for all interaction between firms and universities (Perkmann and Walsh 2007). Ankrah and Al-Tabbaa (2015) proposed a set of criteria for differentiating different types of U–I link, in terms of (1) the resource involvement, (2) the length of agreement, and (3) the degree of formalisation. Collaborations with universities can clearly be viewed as a spectrum of activities. These activities range from informal interactions at a personal level with little resource commitment and a short duration through to interactions that involve larger resource commitments over a longer time-period with a high degree of formality that may eventually involve the creation of new legal entities to pursue a joint venture (Bonaccorsi and Piccaluga 1994). Formal U–I links cover a wide spectrum of activities from joint patenting, licensing, and the creation of joint ventures and spin-offs, considered to be activities associated with academic entrepreneurship, to collaborative research, contract research, and consultancy (de Wit-de Vries et al. 2019).

It is these formal collaborations which form the basis of empirical studies within the extant literature, particularly those that are approved and funded via public bodies (Bruneel, D'Este, and Salter 2010; D'Este and Patel 2007; D'Este, Guy, and Iammarino 2013; Johnston and Huggins 2016). Using Ankrah and Al-Tabbaa's (2015) criteria, these U–I collaborations focus on formal projects involving the commitment of resources from both partners, a clearly defined relationship period, and a formal contracted relationship. As such, these collaborations typically focus on the development of a new product or process.

Of course, formal interactions between universities and businesses may vary widely, even though the extant literature tends to treat them as an isomorphic construct. The drawback to this approach, however, is that empirical studies typically treat university collaboration as a binary variable; either the collaboration occurred, or it did not. As such, this 'out the door criterion', which takes the capture of public funding to initiate a project as a sign of success, does not allow a holistic understanding of the workings of U–I links (Bozeman, Rimes, and Youtie 2015). Therefore, when examining U–I links it is crucial to firstly appreciate the diversity of these links and evaluate and understand the process in terms of the form they take.

Alternative approaches to examining U–I collaboration have focused on their outcomes. Projects are examined by focusing on the results of these projects such as joint patenting (Balconi and Laboranti 2006; Crescenzi, Filippetti, and Iammarino 2017) or co-publications (Yegros-Yegros et al. 2016). These approaches have been utilised given these commercialisation activities leave a 'clear empirical trail', resulting in codified and verifiable artefacts relating to innovative outputs (Perkmann et al. 2013). Yet, the drawback to this is that these projects only comprise a small proportion of U–I collaborations (D'Este and Perkmann 2010). Furthermore, outcomes may vary, and these collaborative projects may result in a new product, an amended product, a patent, or a spin-off firm. More broadly, the project may be successful, or it may be a failure. Therefore, while a broad focus on collaborations may be 'fuzzier' conceptually, it provides an opportunity to study a broader range of U–I links, rather than those that have led to the creation of a patent or co-publication.

Understanding the nature of U–I collaboration requires an appreciation of the different types of links that exist, which may of course involve and induce divergent behaviours. For example, joint projects that involve the co-creation of knowledge will facilitate a greater level of interaction and sharing of knowledge than contract research projects. Indeed, the leitmotif of this literature is on interactions, meaning that the emphasis is on *connections* between individuals from academia with those from the world of business (Rajalo and Vadi 2017). As Perkmann and Walsh (2007) note, open innovation activities imply the existence of a relationship between actors with the entire process resulting from a strategic decision and active choice to engage with external actors in order to procure new knowledge with the end result being collaboration and co-creation activities (Chesbrough 2003; Enkel, Gassmann, and Chesbrough 2009).

Despite the focus on formal projects, informal interactions, that is, those that do not involve contracted agreements, between universities and industry are still important (Grimpe and Fier 2010; Grimpe and Hussinger 2013). These types of contact can result from meetings at events, conference presentations, talks, or belonging to shared groups (Grimpe and Hussinger 2013). Indeed, it has been suggested by both Siegel et al. (2003) and Thursby and Thursby (2004) that these projects may be motivated by the wish to circumvent formal property rights and bypass the restrictions posed by universities' rules and regulations. However, the distinction between the two may be blurred as there is evidence that the two are interlinked, with the formation of both formal and informal U–I links being influenced by similar factors (Grimpe and Fier 2010).

The prevalence of formal university links is relatively low (Freel and Harrison 2006; Hughes and Kitson 2012; Johnston and Prokop 2019), perhaps due to the low success rates for funding bids (the recent success rate in the UK is around 30%). Conversely, empirical evidence suggests that informal linkages are relatively common. For example, using data from the German Community Innovation Survey, Goel, Göktepe-Hultén, and Grimpe (2017) report that 87% of innovative German firms had an informal contact with a university, and Link, Siegel, and Bozeman (2017) found that just over half of US academics reported informal links with industry. Grimpe and Fier (2010) further find that just under half of German academics reported the same. However, while it appears that informal links may be more prevalent, empirical evidence suggests that most benefits from university collaboration result from formal collaborations (Monjon and Waelbroeck 2003).

4.2   THE FORMATION OF FORMAL UNIVERSITY–INDUSTRY LINKAGES

The operation of U–I links is regarded as having a number of stages (Barnes, Pashby, and Gibbons 2002; Plewa, Korff, Baaken et al. 2013; Plewa, Korff, Johnson et al. 2013), starting with the process of identifying and engaging potential partners, then assessing their credibility and choosing a partner, followed by engaging in the project, and finally completing the project (Johnston and Huggins 2018; Plewa, Korff, Johnson et al. 2013).

The formation of U–I links, particularly those organised on a formal basis, is a complex process influenced by many factors and involves more than simply identifying an appropriate partner and initiating collaboration. As noted in Chapter 3, universities may have been thrust into the forefront of open innovation initiatives by policymakers as a short cut to success. Indeed, while they may be regarded by firms as a 'safe' collaboration partner, given that their roles and remits are clearly understood (Powell, Koput, and Smith-Doerr 1996), the formation of a collaborative link with a university represents a strategic decision on the part of a firm with an uncertain outcome (Capaldo and Petruzzelli 2014; Mindruta 2013; Mindruta, Moeen, and Agarwal 2016).

As already indicated, strategic alliances, in the form of university collaborations, can be classified as emergent, embedded, or engineered based on the origins of the collaboration (Al-Tabbaa and Ankrah 2016, 2019). The formation of such links is often influenced by the context in which the decision is being made, as well as a myriad of biases and heuristics of the actors involved. These may be related to the characteristics of the firm, the decision makers within the firm, as well as the environment in which they are operating (Shepherd and Rudd 2014). The process may only be initiated upon the firm's recognition of a deficiency of a specific resource or competence and the realisation of the need to absorb this from elsewhere (Huggins et al. 2014; Rajalo and Vadi 2017).

In effect, the process can be conceptualised as a dual process of searching for the appropriate knowledge and expertise among potential partners as well as ensuring that the firm will also be able to absorb the knowledge. This suggests that access to the individuals with the knowledge coupled with the ability to understand it is important. Consequently, the process has both a cognitive and relational dimension. Typically, these factors are discussed in terms of spatial relations, which concern the physical closeness of the partners, and organisational relations, that is, complementarities between the partners in terms of knowledge base, methods of working, and culture (Aguilera, Lethiais, and Rallet 2012; D'Este, Guy, and Iammarino 2013; Johnston and Huggins

2016). However, before these are discussed it is pertinent to assess the potential gains from and drawbacks to university collaboration.

The extant literature highlights several key benefits to firms from engaging in a collaboration with a university. The positive effects observed from engaging in such a collaboration may include increased understanding of technologies, greater levels of knowledge, the development of patents, enhanced problem-solving capabilities, recruitment of graduate employees, training opportunities, and cost reductions/efficiencies within the business (Abreu et al. 2008; Bishop, D'Este, and Neely 2011; Hagerdoorn, Link, and Vonortas 2000; Lööf and Broström 2006). These advantages may fundamentally alter the competitiveness of a firm to enable increased sales and broadening the scope of their activities (Abreu et al. 2008; Hagerdoorn, Link, and Vonortas 2000; Lööf and Broström 2006).

The positive impact of university collaboration on research and development (R&D) activities within firms is often highlighted in the literature (Baba, Shichijo, and Sedita 2009; Maietta 2015; Soh and Subramanian 2014). The key benefit to firms from university collaboration is the boost it provides to their innovativeness, through developing patentable ideas or new competences within the firm (Belderbos et al. 2004; Faems, Van Looy, and Debackere 2005; George, Zahra, and Wood 2002; Monjon and Waelbroeck 2003). Belderbos, Carree, Diederen et al. (2004), using data on Belgian firms, found that sales resulting from innovations are higher when the firm has formally cooperated with a university. Similarly, using data on Dutch firms, Faems, Van Looy, and Debackere (2005) found that engagement with universities increased firms' turnover from product innovation. These findings indicate that university collaboration can play a positive role in developing new products within firms and, therefore, increasing the turnover of the business due to the resultant increase in sales. Indeed, the focus of university collaboration is on the provision of something new rather than the improvement of existing offerings (Faems, Van Looy, and Debackere 2005). Therefore, university collaboration makes a positive contribution to the 'newness' of the technology developed (Wirsich et al. 2016).

University collaboration may also enable organisational learning (Dada and Fogg 2016). Furthermore, this learning has been observed to influence both product and process innovation (Freel and Harrison 2006; Rouvinen 2002). However, two caveats must be noted. Firstly, those firms that are highly innovative may only benefit marginally from local university knowledge as they may already possess what has been described as 'frontier' knowledge, and instead collaborate with foreign universities in order to access new knowledge (Monjon and Waelbroeck 2003). Therefore, the benefits to firms may depend upon their own characteristics and those of their university partner. Secondly, the benefits may not be instant, with two- to three-year time-lags noted in terms of the time-period between the collaboration and the benefits being realised (Fukugawa 2013; Wirsich et al. 2016).

The evidence is not unequivocal regarding the benefits from U–I collaborations, however, and while some have observed that it may boost sales through providing the firm with new to market goods and services to sell (Belderbos, Carree, and Lokshin 2004; Hagerdoorn, Link, and Vonortas 2000), others have found there are no effects. For example, Eom and Lee (2010) suggest that university collaboration does not necessarily guarantee that a successful innovation will occur as a result, and that there is little impact on sales resulting from the collaboration. In addition, there is evidence that collaboration with universities does not have a significant effect on successful innovation within firms (Okamuro 2007). Furthermore, one factor that appears to be untouched by university collaboration is labour productivity within the firms; thus, no productivity gains are observed among collaborating firms (Belderbos, Carree, and Lokshin 2004; Eom and Lee 2010). Therefore, while firms may benefit from this type of collaboration, there is no guarantee that they will be successful.

In addition to these disputed findings, the work of Bishop et al. (2011) provides an interesting insight into the factors that may promote disparities in the benefits realised from university collaboration. Accordingly, factors such as characteristics of the partner university, the geographic proximity of the partners, firm size, and previous interactions and organisational familiarity with university collaboration all influence the benefits to firms.

Evaluating the success of university collaborations does not just focus on the changes in R&D outputs, sales, and competitiveness within the firm, nor are the effects necessarily restricted to the firm involved (Andrade, Fernandes, and Tereso 2016; Rossi and Rosli 2015). Indeed, considerable efforts have been made to assess and evaluate the success and performance of U–I collaboration within the extant literature that moves beyond performance metrics (Albats, Fiegenbaum, and Cunningham 2018; Gretsch, Salzmann, and Kock 2019; Perkmann, Neely, and Walsh 2011; Rossi and Rosli 2015; Rybnicek and Königsgruber 2019). It appears that the success of U–I collaborations is increasingly focused on understanding the extent to which they accomplish their goals, which may of course be broader than performance effects. The success of U–I collaborations can therefore be examined in terms of two factors, the outputs and the outcomes. The former relate to the project's aims and objectives such as products, services, processes, or structures and their impacts on sales, innovation, and employment, while the latter can be considered as externalities to the aims and objectives.

There are many metrics to measure the success of university collaboration in terms of outcomes (Schofield 2013; Ternouth et al. 2012). These cover a variety of factors. Firstly, kudos from an association may be an important outcome of university collaboration, whereby the reputation of the firm is enhanced through being connected with a university (Albats et al. 2018). Outputs are obviously important, but the fact that the firm can demonstrate that it is working with a university may allow them to gain credibility within their industry. Secondly, the recruitment of graduate labour has been highlighted as an important outcome – while this may not be the main objective of a project, when it occurs it can enhance the knowledge and capabilities within the firm (Al-Ashaab et al. 2011; Albats, Fiegenbaum, and Cunningham 2018). Finally, the development of an ongoing relationship may also signal success as further interaction between the parties can be viewed as evidence that the parties involved have learned to work together (Al-Ashaab et al. 2011).

Firms may also be judged as either excellent, promising, or modest collaborators based on the outcomes of their projects (Rajalo and Vadi 2017). The success element of excellent collaborators is based around the existence of 'complementary boundary crossing mechanisms' (Rajalo and Vadi 2017, p. 48) whereby membership of an existing structure or network allows the actors to transcend any organisational boundaries that may exist between the firms and the university partner. Therefore, these mechanisms allow actors to work together effectively. Conversely, those classed as promising or modest collaborators are often hampered by a lack of any previous contacts or experience of one another which impeded their communication efforts. In the case of modest collaborators there is also a mismatch in terms of trust which further negatively influenced the ability of the partners to communicate effectively (Rajalo and Vadi 2017).

In summary, university collaboration can have multiple influences on the firms involved, from direct impacts such as revenue from new products and services developed, new patents, and new capabilities to indirect impacts focused on successful outcomes such as kudos, recruitment, and an ongoing relationship.

4.3 CHARACTERISTICS OF FIRMS AND UNIVERSITY COLLABORATORS

The previous arguments highlight an interesting question; given the potential benefits of university collaboration and the low levels of actual engagements between firms and universities, what are the characteristics of the firms that do engage with them? Furthermore, given the ideal type of the 'entrepreneurial university' outlined in Chapter 3, which of these characteristics attract industry partners?

In terms of firms engaging with universities, the empirical evidence suggests that the characteristics openness, location, and sector are important determinants (Laursen and Salter 2004). Furthermore, the characteristics of the university partner may also influence the decision to collaborate in terms of prestige, reputation, and engagement, all of which have been identified as important facets of the economic development process within cities and regions (Huggins, Johnston, and Steffenson 2008; Yigitcanlar 2014). Observed patterns of engagement may be related to the characteristics of the firms and universities, the decision makers, and the environment in which they are operating (Shepherd and Rudd 2014). These are examined in more detail in the remainder of the section.

From the firm perspective, the openness of the firm is an important determinant of whether it will collaborate with a university (Fontana, Geuna, and Matt 2006; Laursen and Salter 2006), that is, the cultural make-up of the firm must be orientated towards cooperative relations with external actors. Therefore, the firm must be predisposed towards external networking as well as possessing the capital to create these networks (Huggins 2010). As well as openness, a predisposition towards R&D activities has been identified as an important characteristic of those firms that collaborate with universities, and establish a demand for knowledge within the firm (Fontana, Geuna, and Matt 2006).

The broader innovation literature highlights the fact that firm size is positively correlated with R&D collaboration (Belderbos, Carree, Diederen et al. 2004). While this pattern is also observed with respect to U–I links, with larger firms more likely to engage in formal collaboration with universities (Laursen and Salter 2004), the role of firm size is more complex than a simple dichotomy suggesting that large firms are more likely to engage with universities than SMEs.

Certainly, in light of the resource constraints faced by SMEs and entrepreneurs, the open innovation process may provide these firms with access to a broad range of knowledge and expertise outside of the firm's boundary (Chesbrough 2003; Enkel, Gassmann, and Chesbrough 2009; Madrid-Guijarro et al. 2009). Yet, the literature also suggests that SMEs and entrepreneurial firms are distinctive in their open innovation practices: (1) being less open than their larger counterparts, and tending to have a higher marginal gain from each additional linkage (Vahter, Love, and Roper 2014); (2) exhibiting more flexibility in terms of their use of different open innovation practices simultaneously in the development of new products (Spithoven, Vanhaverbeke, and Roijakkers 2013); (3) being focused more on inbound activities, that is, seeking knowledge rather than sharing it (Van de Vrande et al. 2009). In terms of open innovation, SMEs and more entrepreneurial firms are not absent from this process, but their experience of the process is different to that of larger firms.

The extant literature offers a range of insights into the form, function, and experiences of SMEs with respect to university collaboration. However, as with the literature on open innovation, empirical work on U–I linkages tends to focus on a cross-section of firms, resulting in fewer studies that focus solely on the nature of U–I links involving SMEs. However, this is not to say that the literature ignores SMEs and entrepreneurs, it does not. Indeed, this literature offers a broad examination of SMEs' U–I links across many settings, covering several countries, including the UK, USA, China, South Korea, Italy, Germany, Japan, Chile, and Sweden, as well as a range of industrial sectors including manufacturing, food and drink, knowledge-intensive business services (KIBS), and biotechnology.

The main insight from these studies is that, despite the proposed benefits of engaging with universities, non-engagement among SMEs is particularly prevalent (Hughes and Kitson 2012). Therefore, entrepreneurs and their SMEs are considered to be less likely to engage with universities than larger firms (Bodas Freitas, Geuna, and Rossi 2013; Cohen, Nelson, and Walsh 2002; Fontana, Geuna, and Matt 2006; Giuliani and Arza 2009; Laursen and Salter 2004; Laursen, Reichstein, and Salter 2011; Motohashi 2005). This mirrors the trend observed in the broader innovation literature, which highlights the fact that firm size is positively correlated with R&D collaboration (Autant-Bernard et al. 2007; Belderbos, Carree, Diederen et al. 2004). In terms of firm size, Fontana, Geuna, and Matt (2006) suggest that the observed effects are 'absolute' rather than 'relative' in nature, that is, it is the total number of employees within the firm, not just the number undertaking R&D activities. Therefore, firm size can be seen as a proxy for total resources within the firm rather than those dedicated solely to R&D activities. Given this finding, the debates around the influence of firm size focus on the absolute size of a firm in terms of its employees.

These results do not mean that entrepreneurs and SMEs do not engage with universities, only that vis-à-vis larger firms, it is the latter that are more prone to developing these links. As such, merely suggesting that SMEs are less likely to engage in collaboration with universities rather simplifies the overall relationship, hiding a more nuanced relationship between size and university collaboration. For example, while Motohashi (2005) found that firm size has a positive effect on overall probability of a firm collaborating with a university, a negative relationship is observed with the number of projects undertaken. Therefore, while larger firms may be more likely to collaborate with a university, smaller firms are more likely to engage in a higher number of projects. Additionally, Bodas Freitas, Geuna, and Rossi (2013) surveyed manufacturing firms in Italy and found that larger firms are more likely to be engaged in *formal* interaction with universities, suggesting that SMEs may be engaging in less formal activities. For SMEs, therefore, university collaboration may have different characteristics than larger firms would experience through being focused on pursuing informal interactions.

Firm size has also been found to influence the impacts of university collaboration. Firstly, Broström (2010) suggests that the focus of the collaborative project may also vary according to firm size, with larger firms more focused on short-term effects to ensure rapid organisational learning. SMEs are less focused on the quick pursuit of knowledge commercialisation and are less likely to develop patents from university collaborations, which suggests that there may be a link between resources available and this type of output (Baba, Shichijo, and Sedita 2009; Eom and Lee 2010). However, in terms of the quality of those patents, no firm size effects have been found (Soh and Subramanian 2014). Interestingly, SME patents developed in collaboration with universities tend to receive fewer forward citations, that is, cited by others in the pursuit of their own patents (Dornbusch and Neuhäusler 2015). Given this, SME patents may be viewed as less credible than those developed by larger firms.

Furthermore, the relationship between firm size and patenting from university collaboration may be non-linear, with one study suggesting an optimum firm size of 171 employees (Fukugawa 2013). Beyond this, firm size has a negative effect on the propensity to develop a patent. Consequently, firms of a medium sized nature may be the optimum organisational form for developing novel outputs from university collaboration. This is corroborated by evidence from Eom and Lee (2010) who find that while there was a significant difference in the size of those firms collaborating with universities, and those that did not, the average size of the former was 194 employees, with those that did not having 144 employees. The key point is that despite the significant difference in size, both groups show that the average firm is again medium sized, in other words an SME.

In terms of forming collaborative links with universities, smaller firms are less likely to perceive the existence of transaction-related barriers to engaging with universities than larger firms, especially those associated with the contractual aspect of the project including intellectual property (IP) and payments (Bruneel, D'Este, and Salter 2010). In contrast, no differences are observed with respect to orientation-focused barriers, such as those associated with the university partner's focus and working practices. Smaller firms may be more agile and flexible when it comes to the operation of a collaborative project, and do not concentrate on the transactional aspect of the project as closely. Importantly, in terms of the organisational aspect of the project, SMEs are no more likely to perceive barriers than larger firms, suggesting that they are no more likely to be affected by the two-worlds paradox (Hewitt-Dundas, Gkypali, and Roper 2019). In short, SMEs appear to face no greater barriers to collaborating with universities than firms in general.

The importance of the spatial proximity of the partners has also been found to vary according to firm size; Johnston and Huggins (2016) highlight the fact that for UK-based KIBS firms the distinction is not between SMEs and large firms, but micro and potentially more entrepreneurial firms (those with fewer than ten employees) and other firms. Therefore, it is the latter that are more likely to rely on geographically proximate partners. This is corroborated for the general firm population of the UK, whereby larger firms are found to be less likely to collaborate with local universities (Hewitt-Dundas 2011). More generally, SMEs may be more likely to engage in collaborations with universities that are located in closer physical proximity than their larger counterparts.

In summary, the evidence demonstrates that firm size provides a broad proxy for firms' propensity to collaborate with universities, with SMEs less likely to engage. However, it must be noted that merely focusing on this headline finding masks a myriad of variations in the collaborations and their outcomes according to firm size. Consequently, the literature identifies several key differences in the behaviour of SMEs in terms of university collaboration. These include:

- the types of activity the firms engage in, with SMEs less likely to engage in formal collaborations;
- the number of collaborations, with SMEs more likely to undertake a higher number of collaborations once they engage;
- the outcomes of collaborations between SMEs and universities are less likely to result in a patent (and when they do, they are less likely to be cited in the development of a new patent);
- SMEs are less likely to recruit new employees through university collaboration;
- SMEs may perceive fewer barriers to U–I collaboration; and
- SMEs are more likely to collaborate with local universities.

Conversely, while firm size has been shown to have an important influence on U–I collaboration, as well as its forms and outcomes, there are also studies which report the fact that firm size is not a significant determinant of U–I collaboration, or that it is only micro firms that are less likely to engage in this manner (Eom and Lee 2010; Maietta 2015), or also that firm size has a negative effect on the propensity to engage with universities (Hewitt-Dundas 2011). Furthermore, Giuliani and Arza's (2009) study of wine producing firms in Italy and Chile found that in Chile larger firms were more likely to partner with a university, whereas in Italy smaller firms were more likely, suggesting that context may be important.

In addition, the benefits from engaging with a university, such as improving understanding, gaining knowledge, problem solving, and training the workforce appear to be unrelated to firm size (Bishop, D'Este, and Neely 2011). The only area where significant differences related to firm size are observed is in the recruitment of university postgraduates, which is positively linked to firm size.

Overall, the evidence suggests that there are indeed different dynamics involved with respect to university collaboration depending on the size of the firm. Indeed, the nature of this literature, being empirical in its approach and deductive in intent, allows the observation of general trends in university collaboration and highlights differing dynamics between SMEs and larger firms. However, it would be a misunderstanding to merely assert that SMEs are of less interest, as they are less likely to collaborate with universities. As a result, the literature reveals little about the way in which SMEs may engage and their reasons for doing so, and the outcomes of this interaction.

While firm characteristics are important indicators of SMEs' propensity to engage with universities, the type of collaborations they undertake, and the outcomes, the characteristics of university partners are also important. A firm's strategic decision to enter into a formal collaboration with a university is designed to leverage resources into the business and develop new competences and ultimately products and processes (Bishop, D'Este, and Neely 2011; Mindruta 2013). Therefore, the university partner must possess the necessary knowledge to accomplish the project's aims. As these are non-market transactions, typically formal interactions that are publicly funded or substantially subsidised, the absence of a pricing mechanism means that firms require a method of assessing their potential university partners.

As already indicated, universities are not homogenous, varying in terms of their stocks of knowledge and expertise, knowledge generating capacity, commercial linkages, and the appropriateness of their knowledge and expertise to a given sector (Hewitt-Dundas 2012; Huggins, Johnston, and Stride 2012). This suggests that alternatives to market-based signals are required to highlight to firms the knowledge, expertise, and competences of universities as potential partners.

Indeed, the ethos of a university may influence the encouragement given to their academics to engage with outside actors, while their reputation and prestige may encourage or discourage external actors to engage with them (Laursen, Reichstein, and Salter 2011; Wright et al. 2008). Firstly, to firms seeking to exploit their output for commercial gain, stocks of knowledge and expertise within a university as well as the ability to generate knowledge can be important signals as to their overall performance as a knowledge creator (Acs, Anselin, and Varga 2002; Petruzzelli 2011). For example, patents possessed by a university can be interpreted as representing their unique stock of new knowledge, recorded in a codified and accessible form, as well as their ability to develop novel ideas (Azagra-Caro et al. 2017; Motoyama 2014; Petruzzelli 2011). As a result, higher knowledge stocks and a greater knowledge generation ability are associated with an increased probability of a U–I linkage forming (Hewitt-Dundas 2012).

While the quantity of knowledge produced by a university may be important, perceptions of its quality also influence the development of U–I links (Hewitt-Dundas 2011; Mansfield 1995). This suggests that quality may act as an indicator of the likely knowledge creation capability of the university, with the capacity to create more world-leading knowledge being more attractive to firms to exploit for commercial gain. Thus, institutions and departments that perform well in ranking metrics typically attract more distant partners (Hewitt-Dundas 2011; Laursen, Reichstein, and Salter 2011).

Similarly, IP has also been shown to be an important factor in the decision to choose one university over another as a partner, representing the stock of novel knowledge held by an institution (Acs, Anselin, and Varga 2002; Petruzzelli 2011). Patents can then be interpreted as a signal that the knowledge in question has a certain level of uniqueness, and is therefore only available from that institution, representing the university's stock of new knowledge in a codified and accessible form. While patent income has been shown to be considerably lower than income from collaborative links (Perkmann, King, and Pavelin 2011).

The breadth of a university's commercial links, typically covering activities such as consultancy, contract research, and collaboration, may have a bearing on the formation of U–I linkages (D'Este and Patel 2007; Huggins, Johnston, and Stride 2012). These activities represent interactions between academics and individuals *outside* of the academic world (Cohen, Nelson, and Walsh 2002). Universities with higher levels of commercial links are therefore regarded as more 'engaged' (Perkmann et al. 2013), highlighting their ability not just to create knowledge but to also exploit it, that is, Mode 2 knowledge creation (Gibbons et al. 1994). Therefore, a greater number of commercial links may merely signal the openness of a university and be indicative of an institution that is actively seeking to commercialise its knowledge (Perkmann et al. 2013).

A concept such as 'research intensity' utilises a typically academic approach to characterising universities, focusing on outputs which can be seen as resulting from Mode 1 knowledge creation, that is, 'discovery' type knowledge (Gibbons et al. 1994) and more fully understanding these signals suggests the importance played by proximities, or the closeness of the partners in terms of their location, methods of working, networking activity, and knowledge base.

4.4   UNCERTAINTIES AND THE ROLE(S) OF PROXIMITIES IN UNIVERSITY–INDUSTRY COLLABORATION

Within the alliance literature, scholars suggest that uncertainty motivates the use of strategic alliances among firms (Dyer 1996; Eisenhardt and Schoonhoven 1996). In contrast, the U–I links literature has more often discussed their formation as an uncertain process, underpinned by the organisational asymmetries between SMEs and universities rather than as a response to uncertainty (Hewitt-Dundas, Gkypali, and Roper 2019; Lavie and Drori 2012).

Despite the benefits from university collaboration, there may also be drawbacks to consider. In the absence of a pricing mechanism as a signal of the potential quality of a university as a partner, firm-level decisions are inherently uncertain. These differences may be magnified as universities and firms are viewed as operating within differing organisational contexts and institutional environments. Universities typically focus on exploration activities, while firms concentrate on exploitation activities (Lavie and Drori 2012; Petruzzelli and Rotolo 2015). Therefore, effective knowledge transfer between partners may depend upon the ability of actors to work together effectively.

These issues highlight the existence of both costs and benefits to university collaboration. Firms, therefore, face a dilemma with respect to guaranteeing that they reap the benefits of these links while also minimising the costs. However, the issue of asymmetric information is rather glossed over across most of the literature, implying that the process of developing collaborative links is costless and frictionless. In the context of U–I links, the issue of uncertainties, particularly around the compatibility of partners, ensures that costs are indeed present, and, as we will empirically illustrate later, friction exists in the process.

There is evidence that collaborating with universities can increase the probability of a 'cooperation failure', that is, the failure of the collaboration (Lhuillery and Pfister 2009). In addition, the extant literature features a number of studies where collaboration with universities has not had a significant effect on the level of R&D or innovation within firms (Miotti and Sachwald 2003; Okamuro 2007). Despite the perceived benefits of collaboration with universities there is no guarantee that they offer a short cut to success.

A number of reasons for this are posited; firstly, that actors from each organisation have different motivations, for example firms are seeking knowledge whereas academics are attempting to enhance their careers through novel research and developing a reputation in a particular field rather than attempting to commercialise an idea (D'Este and Perkmann 2010; Lam 2011), thus responding to different incentives (Garman 2011). Secondly, that actors within firms and universities work to differing timescales, with firms operating to a stricter timescale dictated by commercial demands (Walsh et al. 2007). Thirdly, it has been observed that each of the actors can use different communication styles (Wasserman and Kram 2009). Finally, other scholars question the relevance of academic research to the private sector (McGahan 2007; Rasche and Behnam 2009).

In effect, while university collaboration may be an attractive proposition for firms, at the point of initiation their outcome is largely unknown. Consequently, there are significant uncertainties involved in the formation of these links. This may be due in part to the fact that U–I linkages focus on new knowledge, ensuring that the project is focused on the beginning of the innovation process, commonly referred to as the 'fuzzy front end' whereby the process is often inexact or unfocused (Alam 2006; Montoya-Weiss and O'Driscoll 2000). At this stage of the innovation process the outcome is uncertain, a fact compounded by further uncertainties associated with collaborative partnerships, where actors must also tackle the problem of asymmetric information. This is due to both parties being unaware of the likely knowledge and capabilities possessed by their potential partner. Therefore, while participation in inter-organisational knowledge networks is viewed as addressing the uncertainties faced by the firm in terms of development and, ultimately, survival (Beckman, Haunschild, and Phillips 2004), the actual process network creation is itself an uncertain practice (Debackere and Veugelers 2005).

The broader literature on strategic alliances has highlighted a high failure rate among inter-firm collaborative linkages, with around half being unsuccessful. Accordingly, goal setting and coordinating and managing these collaborations has been cited as the most common problems encountered (Park and Ungson 2001). Indeed, collaborative partnerships based around technology development have been held up as exemplars of particularly unstable linkages and described as a 'bumpy road' to travel on for firms, typically reflecting their lack of ability to predict or anticipate the intentions and actions of their partners (Lokshin, Hagedoorn, and Letterie 2011). For these reasons, universities have been cited as 'safer' actors with which to collaborate (Powell, Koput, and Smith-Doerr 1996). Furthermore, the development of collaborative links with public institutions such as universities is perceived as less risky as they focus more on 'basic' research rather than commercial application (Miotti and Sachwald 2003).

On the flip side, the issue of differing organisational contexts and institutional environments may result in a disconnect between the motivations of the academic and industry partners involved in the project. Therefore, tensions may exist between the two groups arising from differing logics and methods of working (Bartunek and Rynes 2014; Beech, MacIntosh, and MacLean 2010).

These differences have been conceptualised as the 'two-worlds paradox' (Hewitt-Dundas, Gkypali, and Roper 2019).

Of course, these uncertainties may be addressed through contractual means, deterring opportunistic behaviour among their potential partners. However, this may merely add to the expense of a project while increasing the time taken to set it up, consuming a firm's scarce resources in addressing uncertainty through holding actors to an agreed plan of action (Williamson 1993). For smaller and entrepreneurial firms, often with fewer resources to commit to a project (Barney 1991), this may be a particular deterrent, where they prefer to devote their resources to productive activities. Furthermore, this method only allows the issues to be addressed retrospectively and does not assist the firm in its choice of an appropriate partner.

Proximities have been mooted as moderators of uncertainty as they provide the means for partners to understand one another's offer to the partnership (Fitjar and Gjelsvik 2018; Johnston and Huggins 2016). Proximity is typically discussed in terms of geography, although the concept has expanded to consider the closeness of actors along a broad spectrum of characteristics including utilising similar technology, membership of common networks or organisations, and operating in similar contexts (Boschma 2005; Devigili, Pucci, and Zanni 2019).

The spatial proximity of partners, that is, their physical closeness, is typically regarded as a positive factor in their formation (D'Este, Guy, and Iammarino 2013; Giuliani and Arza 2009; Johnston and Huggins 2016; Laursen, Reichstein, and Salter 2011). A number of reasons for this are proposed; firstly, innovation partnerships tend to perform better when the physical distance between the partners is minimised (Capaldo and Petruzzelli 2014). Secondly, spatial proximity allows the actions of potential partners to be observed, permitting an assessment of their effectiveness (Gulati 2007; Wood and Parr 2005). Thirdly, minimising the distance between partners increases the intensity of collaborative links, through promoting greater levels of face-to-face interaction (Storper and Venables 2004). Indeed, the intensity of the relationship has been found to have a positive effect on the tangible outcomes from a project leading to increased competitive advantage for a firm (Santoro 2000).

The spatial proximity of partners allows a close observation of partners, specifically their organisational routines, and offers an opportunity to assess this ability (Capaldo and Petruzzelli 2014). Where there is minimal physical distance between a firm and a university, this may allow a firm to gauge what knowledge and expertise a potential university partner possesses as well as its ability to maintain this stock.

In some cases, spatial proximity to their partner is less important, especially when the relevant knowledge and expertise is not available locally (Laursen,

Reichstein, and Salter 2011; Moodysson and Jonsson 2007). The result is that, as previously noted, universities undertaking 'world-leading' research typically attract more distant partners, suggesting that spatial proximity may be substituted for appropriate knowledge (Hewitt-Dundas 2011; Huggins, Johnston, and Stride 2012; Laursen, Reichstein, and Salter 2011; Petruzzelli 2011). Consequently, the perceived quality of the academic partner is an important determinant of both the formation of U–I linkages *and* their spatial scope (Huggins, Johnston, and Steffenson 2008; Johnston and Huggins 2017; Laursen, Reichstein, and Salter 2011).

Furthermore, recent evidence focused on the formation of collaborative links between universities and industry has suggested that the relationship between link formation and spatial proximity is curvilinear in nature, following an inverted 'U' shape, whereby beyond an optimal level the marginal influence is no longer positive (Broekel and Boschma 2012; Crescenzi, Filippetti, and Iammarino 2017; D'Este, Guy, and Iammarino 2013; Johnston and Huggins 2016). The spatial proximity of partners may, in some cases, be a limiting factor as they can be 'too close' (Ben Letaifa and Goglio-Primard 2016). While 'being there' may be an important mechanism for developing collaborative links, with spatial proximity facilitating the transferring knowledge (Asheim and Gertler 2005; Gertler 1995; Morgan 2004), merely being there is not always sufficient (Hassink and Wood 1998).

In addition, the concept of spatial proximity can be considered as less fixed and more fluid, fleeting, and flexible, whereby distances between partners can vary through the mobility of resources (Rinallo, Bathelt, and Golfetto 2017). Therefore, a lack of spatial proximity may not preclude the creation of a U–I linkage as inter-organisational networks can develop as a result of temporary spatial proximity with partners (Bathelt, 2005; Bathelt, Malmberg, and Maskell 2004; Maskell, Bathelt, and Malmberg 2006). This temporary proximity may be manifest in terms of time-limited gatherings such as conferences or exhibitions, providing actors with sufficient interaction to cement a relationship which then carries on without face-to-face contact (Maskell, Bathelt, and Malmberg 2006). Once this occurs, the ubiquity of information and communication technologies (ICT) for virtual communication means that actors can maintain these relationships at relatively little cost (Bathelt and Cohendet 2014; Herrmann, Taks, and Moors 2012).

In general, the fact that collaborative linkages can, and do, develop over significant distances, has led scholars to recognise the diversity of contextual factors (Davenport 2005) and highlight the importance of non-spatial proximities in their development (Boschma 2005; Capone and Zampi 2019; Crescenzi, Filippetti, and Iammarino 2017). Typically, non-spatial proximity is conceptualised in terms of the similarities between agents based on: shared knowledge bases or skills (technological or cognitive proximity); organisational context (organisational proximity); relationships and networks (social proximity); and shared culture (institutional proximity) (Aguilera, Lethiais, and Rallet 2012; Boschma 2005; Devigili, Pucci, and Zanni 2019; Knoben and Oerlemans 2006). The clear outcome of this is that associational factors play an important role (Cooke and Morgan 1998). However, these concepts are noted as being conceptually fuzzy (Devigili, Pucci, and Zanni 2019; Knoben and Oerlemans 2006).

One issue within the literature is that earlier studies on non-spatial proximity examined this solely in terms of organisational proximity (Oerlemans and Meeus 2005). Indeed, debates within the literature have sought to understand the trade-off between spatial and non-spatial proximity, when in fact they may both simultaneously be of influence (Healy and Morgan 2012). Therefore, while empirical evidence within the literature on the interactions between spatial and non-spatial proximities has highlighted the existence of both complementary relationships, and the fact they substitute for one another (D'Este, Guy, and Iammarino 2013; Hansen 2015; Johnston and Huggins 2016; Ponds, van Oort, and Frenken 2007), the real focus should be on connecting physical space with social space in order to capture a holistic understanding of proximities (Rutten 2017). This suggests that the interaction of actors may involve *both* a spatial and a relational dimension (Healy and Morgan 2012).

In addition, organisational proximity, that is, membership of the same firm or establishment, has been highlighted as an important factor in knowledge transfer, promoting the ease with which agents can interact through following similar routines, practices, rules, and behaviours (Torre and Rallet 2005). Organisational proximity is recognised as promoting coherence among collaborators and promotes a shared understanding between actors, and with it the ability to communicate effectively (Moodysson and Jonsson 2007). Therefore, if actors are able to understand each other and possess an equal absorptive capacity (Cohen and Levinthal 1990) to successfully transfer knowledge there is less likely to be uncertainty around whether a particular collaboration will prove effective.

A shared organisational culture signals an ability of actors to work together (Nonaka, Toyama, and Nagata 2000), with organisational proximity characterised not just by a shared understanding but also a shared experience of collaboration (D'Este, Guy, and Iammarino 2013). Prior collaboration, therefore, allows participants to build knowledge not just of each other but also the collaborative process as a whole and the relative success and/or failure of methods and approaches to working together.

It is well established within the innovation literature that membership of epistemic communities may also be an important determinant of collaborative links (Cowan, David, and Foray 2000). The fact that these communities may possess shared codebooks, that is, a shared technical language, allows them to understand one another (Henry and Pinch 2001; Pinch et al. 2003). Cognitive or technological proximity afforded by membership of epistemic communities may evolve through shared routines, behaviours, and languages of actors which develop through working in the same field and the use of a similar knowledge base (Tether, Li, and Mina 2012). Membership of these communities may be continuously evolving, allowing actors to develop ever closer ties and deeper relationships through prolonged collaboration (Balland, Boschma, and Frenken 2015). In this sense, it is not a static factor, but dynamic and evolutionary in nature.

Similarly, social proximity is based around membership of a community, focusing on ties relating to friendships, shared networks, and interactions between actors (Hansen 2015). Actors may also be from different backgrounds and industries but their interaction through events, meetings, fora, or broad-based membership organisations breeds a familiarity between them (Mattes 2012). These actors may be from different sectors, performing different roles, and work in different ways but these past interactions facilitate an understanding between them that allows effective collaboration.

Finally, institutional proximity refers to the shared environment among actors, whereby they are subject to the same rules and regulations as well as cultural norms and habits which promote a common agency (David 1998; DiMaggio 1988). Typically, this results from the actors being located in the same regional or country location (Marrocu, Paci, and Usai 2013).

Understanding how different proximities may affect different aspects of the project and that they may interact is important for assessing a potential collaboration. For example, the existence of technological proximity may not necessarily require the actors to be physically close to one another (Bathelt and Cohendet 2014; Moodysson and Jonsson 2007; Torre and Gilly 2000), but the presence of spatial proximity may promote its development (Rutten 2017). As such, there may be substitution and overlap effects between types of proximity (Hansen 2015).

These proximities are examined in terms of the formation of U–I collaboration. However, there is evidence that the function of SME–university collaboration may promote the evolution of these proximities. The relationship between the partners may evolve as the collaboration continues as they learn to work together effectively (Bjerregaard 2010; Steinmo and Rasmussen 2018). Therefore, there may be an evolutionary dimension to the cognitive and relational aspect of these. Indeed, scholars have suggested that proximities may be dynamic in nature (Balland, Boschma, and Frenken 2015), and can ebb and flow over the duration of a collaboration. This variation in the closeness of the partners is captured in Figure 4.1.

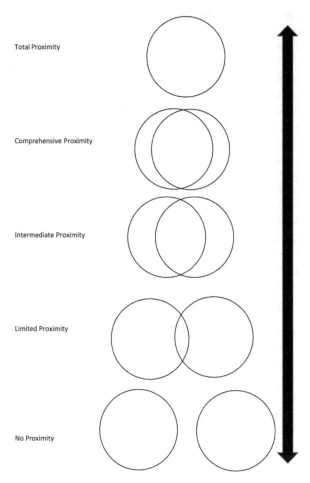

Figure 4.1   Degrees of proximity

Considering proximities as dynamic in nature (Balland, Boschma, and Frenken 2015), it also makes sense to consider them as continuous rather than binary. Therefore, proximities do not have to be treated as either present or otherwise, instead they can be assessed in terms of their degrees of completeness. Considering this, it may be more useful to examine the extent to which these factors are present. For example, spatial proximity is not necessarily absolute. Partners may be located very close together (<5 km) within the same city, or relatively close together in the same region (<50 km). In addition, working practices and knowledge bases of partners may overlap but not be perfectly matched. Therefore, in this case the proximity of partners may not be total.

Instead it can be described as comprehensive, exhibiting a high level of similarity, intermediate where the partners show some similarities, limited where there is a high level of dissimilarity, or absent, where the partners are dissimilar in character. In addition, Figure 4.1 shows that these proximities may evolve, both ebbing and flowing.

In summary, as relational and cognitive factors appear to be important in the formation and function of U–I links, they may be underpinned by a blend of proximities capturing the closeness of the partners in terms of a range of factors based on location, networks, methods of working, and knowledge base (Capone and Lazzeretti 2018; Capone and Zampi 2019; Healy and Morgan 2012; Rutten 2017; Zeller 2009). These are captured in the proximity matrix (Table 4.1).

Table 4.1   *The Proximity matrix*

	Spatial	Social	Organisational	Technological
Total Proximity	Located on same science park/ industrial estate	Members of identical networks	Identical working culture and practices	Utilise identical scientific language and knowledge base
Comprehensive Proximity	Located within same city/town	Significant overlap of actors within networks	Significant overlap of working culture, practice, and procedures	Significant overlaps in scientific language used and knowledge base
Intermediate Proximity	Located within the same region	Some overlap of actors within networks	Some similarity of working culture, practice, and procedures	Some similarity in scientific language used and knowledge base
Limited Proximity	Located within adjacent regions	Few common actors within networks	Little similarity in working culture, practice, and procedures	Little similarity in scientific language and knowledge base
No Proximity	Located in non-adjacent regions	No common actors within networks	No common working culture, practice, and procedures	No common scientific language or knowledge base

Importantly, the matrix outlines the factors that underlie the formation and function of these collaborative links between firms and universities without stressing the primacy of any single factor. Therefore, the formation and function of U–I links can be driven by many combinations of proximities, while the strength of these may also vary from link to link. Using this matrix as a framework for understanding captures the uniqueness and nuances of each.

4.5   SMES AND UNIVERSITY COLLABORATION

Within the extant literature there are a number of empirical studies focused solely on the engagement of SMEs with universities and the key issues involved. While SMEs may be under-represented in the extant literature on U–I links, there exist several studies that focus exclusively on samples of SMEs and, therefore, provide insights into the experiences and traits of these firms and their university collaborations. In addition, these studies tend to take what has been described as a 'micro-level perspective' that captures the detail of these interactions (Bjerregaard 2009).

The value of these studies are that they extend understanding of the process of university collaborations from the perspective of SMEs through examining themes such as the formation of collaborative links between SMEs and universities (Johnston and Huggins 2018; Mäkimattila, Junell, and Rantala 2015), the governance of these collaborative links and their performance (Garcia-Perez-de-Lema, Madrid-Guijarro, and Martin 2017), the role of policy initiatives to support and ferment these collaborations (Caloffi, Rossi, and Russo 2015), and the outcomes and effects of university collaborations on SMEs (Dada and Fogg 2016; Lauvås and Steinmo 2019; Rosli et al. 2018; De Zubielqui, Jones, and Lester 2016).

According to Mäkimattila, Junell, and Rantala (2015), when engaging in collaborative links with universities the emphasis for SMEs is on identifying 'the right person and the right knowledge' (p. 461). This evidence, therefore, highlights a clear socio-technical motive for engaging in U–I collaboration, that is, to create a tangible output to generate sales for the firm. Using a framework proposed by John and Martin (1984) as a means for analysing the credibility of potential external partners, Johnston and Huggins (2018) examine the influences on SMEs' perceptions of the credibility of their potential partners in terms of five factors: realism of expertise, specificity of knowledge, consistency of knowledge, comprehensiveness of research, validity of research (John and Martin 1984; Menon and Varadarajan 1992). Their analysis suggests that small firms typically utilise 'realism' in their assessment of credibility, basing their judgement on labels and affiliations of the academic partner. Importantly, this assessment tends to focus on the individual rather than the institution, highlighting the importance of the social side rather than the organisational (Johnston and Huggins 2018).

Building on this, the main theme for research on collaborations between SMEs and universities is their socio-technical nature, driven by cognitive and relational factors which influence the effectiveness of the interaction of the actors involved (Al-Tabbaa and Ankrah 2016). This is borne out by the empirical work that highlights the importance of social capital for the formation and function of these collaborations (Bjerregaard 2010; Garcia-Perez-de-Lema, Madrid-Guijarro, and Martin 2017; Mäkimattila, Junell, and Rantala 2015; Rajalo and Vadi 2017; Steinmo and Rasmussen 2018).

For example, in terms of the formation of collaborative links between SMEs and universities, Bjerregaard (2010) highlights the importance of 'short institutional distances' between the partners in that there exist a shared understanding and expectations between the parties involved. Minimising this institutional distance is often achieved through previous experience of working with universities enabling the firm to develop a sense of familiarity with their working practices. Previous collaborations between the parties have been found to be an important facilitator of these links, suggesting that the development of a link signifies a long-term commitment (Caloffi, Rossi, and Russo 2015).

Rajalo and Vadi (2017) highlight the influence of cognitive and relational factors as boundary crossing mechanisms in these collaborations. Therefore, firms rated as 'excellent collaborators' are those that were able to harness these factors, which, importantly, were not affected by whether the firm was an SME. Indeed, when examining the outcomes of university collaborations, those that were rated as excellent by Rajalo and Vadi (2017) were all SMEs. While this does not suggest the primacy of these firms in terms of performance, it does suggest that SMEs are able to successfully harness these factors in order to collaborate with universities. Similarly, Steinmo and Rasmussen's (2018) study of the cognitive and relational aspects of U–I collaborations highlighted the importance of cognitive social capital in the formation of collaborative links, enabling the development of trusting relations and a shared goal. However, this study makes no distinction in terms of firm size, and in the formation of these links SMEs were shown to utilise similar factors as their larger counterparts.

The socio-technical nature of the collaboration process is clearly highlighted within the SME-focused literature, echoing the arguments found within strategic alliances literature where complementarity and interdependence have been found to play an important part in their formation (Dyer, Singh, and Hesterly 2018). This literature also highlights the importance of prior experience of engaging with other firms, and has been identified as a key predictor of value creation (Kale and Singh 2007). The empirical evidence suggests that university collaborations for SMEs resemble the traditional strategic alliance, with the findings echoing that of alliance scholars who highlight the social and relational dimension of these interactions (Dyer and Singh 1998; Eisenhardt and Schoonhoven 1996). Consequently, university collaborations appear to have significant similarities to other R&D alliances.

Importantly, empirical studies of SME–university collaboration also emphasise the dynamic nature of these factors through highlighting their evolution over time (Bjerregaard 2010; Steinmo and Rasmussen 2018). The collaboration process for SMEs is dynamic, as the relationships between the parties can change as the project progresses. Boundaries can exist at the outset of the project, but these may blur as the collaboration continues and the proximities between the parties develop and evolve as they learn to work together effectively (Balland, Boschma, and Frenken 2015; Bjerregaard 2009). As a result, the proximities identified as important for the formation and function of collaborative links with universities may develop over the course of a project (Balland, Boschma, and Frenken 2015).

In addition to the formation and function of the project, there is evidence to suggest that the outcomes of the SMEs' projects are also influenced by cognitive and relational factors (Rosli et al. 2018). For example, a strong relationship between the parties has a positive effect on the successful development of new business opportunities for SMEs from the collaboration. The firm owner/managers' commitment to the project also has a positive effect on a successful outcome, while longer-term opportunities were positively influenced by the presence of a suitable boundary spanner in the collaboration (Rosli et al. 2018). In terms of the outcomes of SME–university collaboration, there is also evidence that the effects are indirect in nature, focused on increasing absorptive capacity of firms rather than producing outputs (De Zubielqui, Jones, and Lester 2016).

As a result of the above, the importance of cognitive and relational factors within the extant literature highlights the fact that SME–university collaborations are more embedded and emergent and less engineered in character as the relationships tend to develop in a more organic manner (Al-Tabbaa and Ankrah 2019; Ring, Doz, and Olk 2005). Therefore, the observed collaborations described in the literature all appear to develop as a result of the SMEs' own activities rather than at the direction of a third party.

Further insights suggest that the relational aspect complements the contractual. For example, a formal governance structure, based on contractual relations, has been found to have a positive effect on innovative outputs from SMEs' university collaborations (Garcia-Perez-de-Lema, Madrid-Guijarro, and Martin 2017). While relational governance structures in the form of less formal connections were not found to influence the innovative outputs directly, they had a positive influence on the formation of contractual governance. Therefore, the caveat is that relational factors may be important for the formation and function of collaborative links between SMEs and universities but are no substitute for contractual governance of the projects.

Other important insights include an examination of the factors that underpin the formation of these collaborative links. For example, using evidence from the Groningen region of the Netherlands, Delfmann and Koster (2012) find that more practice orientated colleges are perceived to be more accessible to

SMEs than traditional universities with a pure research focus. Furthermore, they find that SMEs are typically involved in more localised collaborations with a greater emphasis on face-to-face interactions.

The SME literature highlights the importance of non-spatial proximities, but it is remarkably quiet on the influence of spatial proximities. Indeed, the importance of social factors identified in the extant literature reflects that of the broader innovation literature that has questioned the importance of physical distance (Ben Letaifa and Goglio-Primard 2016). Spatial proximity to partners has been highlighted as an important factor for the open innovation activities of SMEs (Gertler 2003; Kapetaniou and Lee 2019; Lawson et al. 1998; Pickernell, Clifton, and Senyard 2009), but evidence of its influence on their collaborations with universities is surprisingly scant. Indeed, the evidence is not only limited but mixed; for example, spatial proximity has been found to be insignificant in the formation of some SME–university collaborations (Caloffi, Rossi, and Russo 2015). However, for Rosli et al. (2018) spatial proximity has been found to have a significant and positive effect on short-term business opportunities following the end of the collaboration but not longer-term opportunities. Therefore, Davenport's (2005) acknowledgement that contextual factors unique to individual firms will determine the importance of spatial or non-spatial proximities is important.

The significant contribution of the SME literature is that it highlights the role of the individual in the university collaboration process, that is, the strong theme is the role of communication between and understanding of individuals that brings together SMEs and universities in their collaborative links. This is an important insight as it brings the entrepreneur into the theorising of the U–I collaboration process. Therefore, while inter-organisational networks may be the functional form of these interactions, underpinning the observed activities are the interactions and characteristics of the individual agents involved.

In summary, the literature on firm size and university collaboration is far more nuanced than merely suggesting that SMEs are less likely to collaborate than larger firms. The evidence suggests that SMEs do collaborate with universities, yet the dynamics of these are different than for larger firms. For example, SMEs may be more likely to collaborate multiple times but less likely to patent the outcomes. Finally, through examining the workings of SME–university collaborations, the literature reveals the importance of the cognitive and relational factors in their formation and function.

5. Universities and the UK economy

5.1 INTRODUCTION

This chapter presents an overview of both the evolution of UK government policy towards universities, as well as examining the importance of universities in the context of the UK economy utilising data from publicly available sources. It provides a context for the analytical chapters that follow through discussing the current policy environment surrounding university–industry interaction, international comparisons of the importance of the higher education sector in the UK, and existing patterns of SME–university interaction.

The UK is home to a significant number of higher education institutions, with 159 established universities located within the country. In addition to these institutions, there are specialist higher education institutions that focus on specific activities such as dance, music, medicine, or teaching. In addition to these there are several new providers that have joined the higher education sector in the wake of the market reforms introduced in the 2004 Higher Education Act and the 2010 Browne Review. Therefore, given that there are over 200 organisations that purport to be a 'university' in the UK, there exists a broad choice of potential partners for SMEs looking to engage and collaborate with universities.

Despite the breadth of providers now operating in the UK's higher education sector, the university system is typically considered as a dichotomy with institutions divided between 'older' institutions, that is, those that were established prior to the 1992 Funding and Higher Education Act, and 'new' universities, those that were established as a result of the Act. In short, 'pre-1992' universities are considered to be more focused on pure academic research, while the 'post-1992' universities are typically institutions that were previously polytechnics, resulting in a focus on the application of knowledge.

5.2 UNIVERSITY–INDUSTRY COLLABORATION: POLICY BACKGROUND

As previously discussed, the passing of the Bayh-Dole Act in the USA in 1980 is seen as the initiation of interest in the interaction of universities and other organisations (Kenney and Patton 2009; Mowery and Sampat 2004).

However, within the UK, the origins of this policy push can be traced back further. Indeed, the first significant development was the establishment of the National Physical Laboratory (NPL) by the UK government in 1900 to integrate scientific knowledge with industrial activity and everyday life (Heath and Heatherington 1946; Pyatt 1983). This institution drew directly on the UK's science base providing a destination for British scientists to work after completing their doctorates. Over the following decades NPL scientists were responsible for several significant breakthroughs; for example, work on metal fatigue by Herbert Gough fed directly into the fledgling automotive and aircraft industries, while David Dye's work on waves and vibrations led to the development of extremely accurate quartz clocks and the magnetometer, which measured the Earth's magnetic field. Also, Robert Watson-Watt, whose work on antennas allowed the direction of radio waves to be determined, paved the way for the development of RADAR (Pyatt 1983).

The outbreak of World War I prompted the creation of the Department of Scientific and Industrial Research in 1916 with a remit to finance research, award fellowships and studentships, and promote the development of university research in the sciences (Heath and Heatherington 1946). Ostensibly, the Department was set up to undertake research that would promote the development of new weapons for the war effort, although following the armistice attention turned to civilian applications of this knowledge. As a result, laboratories such as the Radio Research Station were tasked with promoting research into areas such as radio waves and understanding Earth's ionosphere.

Military applications of knowledge were directed by a series of laboratories set up to pursue work relevant to all branches of the armed forces, the Admiralty Research Laboratory, the Royal Aircraft Establishment, and the Explosives Research and Development Establishment. While these were independent of universities, as with the NPL, these establishments provided homes for newly qualified scientists on leaving the university system, highlighting their reliance on university knowledge to function (Heath and Heatherington 1946; Pyatt 1983).

World War II saw these establishments play a key role in the development of new weapons and technologies. Importantly, there were significant overlaps with the UK university system as many academic scientists were seconded to these organisations. For example, Max Newman who was Professor of Mathematics at the University of Cambridge was seconded to Bletchley Park where his expertise was applied to develop ciphers and the production of the Colossus computer. Similarly, Douglas Hartree's work on differential analysers at the University of Manchester was also used in the pursuit of building the Colossus computer, with his machine made available to assist with solving equations needed to run the computer (Hendry 1989).

The end of the war saw pressure to utilise the work of these government research establishments for commercial purposes (Hendry 1989), and the beginning of the so-called 'age of techno-nationalism' promoting the use of British knowledge to ensure self-sufficiency in key areas such as food, energy, and defence (Edgerton 2019). This pressure led to the Development of Inventions Act 1948 which created the National Research Development Corporation (NRDC), a new body charged with exploiting inventions from public research and granting licences for the use of public research by other organisations (Bud and Gummett 2002). Nonetheless, the NRDC did not explicitly promote collaborations between industry and universities but existed to utilise research from military activities in the pursuit of commercial activities. For example, in the late 1950s the hovercraft developed from this process.

By the end of the 1950s the prevailing mood among some thinkers such as C.P. Snow was that the scientific advances of the industrial revolution had been wasted and that capitalist society was content to turn itself into one dominated by administrators (Snow 1959). An early proponent of highlighting the chasm between academia and industry, Snow argued that pure scientists were not interested in application of their knowledge, regarding commercialisation as a lower priority. On becoming leader of the Labour Party in 1963, Harold Wilson tapped into this current by championing a future vision of Britain as an incubator of science, occupying a central place in the development of new technology, and famously stating that 'the Britain that is going to be forged in the white heat of this revolution will be no place for restrictive practices or for outdated methods on either side of industry'.

One commitment made by Wilson in his successful 1964 election campaign was to establish a Ministry of Technology, duly set up that year. By the mid-1960s, increasing attention began to be paid to the public value of government funding for university research, with arguments stating that the scientific community must demonstrate their ability to generate important new insights within their disciplines (Abelson 1966). Implicit in these arguments was the fact that scientific research must have a direct benefit to society at large.

These moves led to an explicit focus on investigating formal links between industry and universities. In 1967 a committee was formed of industrialists and university vice-chancellors to investigate links between universities and industry in the UK (Russell 1971). Published four years later by the CBI, 'The Docksey Report' suggested that interactions were in fact widespread, particularly in the chemistry, pharmacy, and social sciences fields. However, it was a further 30 years until UK universities were brought to the forefront of innovation strategies.

Instead, the policies of this era focused on what Edgerton has termed 'defence and prestige projects' however the resulting developments such as the nuclear reactor programme or Concorde ultimately failed to secure large overseas markets (Edgerton 2019). The economic turmoil of the 1970s and early 1980s meant that science policy took a back seat to issues of macroeconomic stability. According to Agar (2019), the foundations for modern science policy emerged in 1987 with the report 'A Strategy for the Science Base', which explicitly linked science-based research to the higher education system and set out to reform the system of grant funding. This entailed focusing funding on curiosity driven research and leaving it up to market forces to ensure that it was exploited for commercial gain.

Essentially, this approach represented a shift in policy from a focus on intermediary organisations designed to link universities and industry, to a focus on supporting independent university research. The premise of this shift is evident in the subsequent policy developments; 11 years later, the 1998 White Paper 'Our Competitive Future', introduced by the Labour government, was the first to explicitly present university knowledge as an exploitable resource for the wider economy.

These developments reflect the dominance of the current economic orthodoxy within post-industrial economies such as the UK, where innovation is viewed as the key to competitiveness and growth through encouraging the continued development and refining of products, services, processes, and technologies (Porter and Ketels 2003; Slaughter and Leslie 1997). Consequently, this theme has been pursued through several subsequent policy reviews, each intended to promote the interaction of industry with the country's universities within a framework designed to marketise knowledge and the 'scientific commons' (Nelson 2004). These reviews, the Lambert Review 2003, Witty Review 2012, Wilson Review 2015, and McMillan Review 2016 each stressed the need for universities to be more commercially minded and open to working with industry, while maintaining their traditional roles of education and research. Within these reviews, repeated reference to the UK's 'world-class research and innovation system' all envisaged a key role for universities in the development of the UK economy. Indeed, the Industrial Strategy, published in 2017, unequivocally placed universities at the forefront of the policy framework and, therefore, at the centre of the innovation system (Johnston and Wells 2020). Therefore, innovation in key sectors of the future involves the exploitation of the UK's science base, ensuring that university research in these areas underpins the future prosperity of the economy.

5.3 UNIVERSITY–INDUSTRY COLLABORATION

The pursuit of realising 'value' from public research expenditure in terms of commercial exploitation has had a two-pronged effect on universities, providing both opportunities for increased income generation but also greater scrutiny of their research activities with a heightened emphasis on the impact outside of academia.

In common with other industrialised economies, university research and development (R&D) expenditure is a significant component of overall activity in the UK. According to data from the Organisation for Economic Co-operation and Development (OECD), in 2018 R&D expenditure by the higher education sector in the UK reached $11.97 billion (OECD 2019). While this is greater than that of Italy and Spain, the data from Table 5.1 shows that the UK currently lags other industrialised economies in terms of the absolute value of higher education expenditure on R&D.

Table 5.1   *Higher education expenditure on R&D for selected OECD*
                 countries, 2019

Country	Higher Education Expenditure on R&D ($000s PPP at Current Prices)
Canada	12 103
France	14 032
Germany	25 064
Italy	8 469
Japan	19 801
Spain	6 218
United Kingdom	11 976
United States	74 722

Note: PPP, purchasing power parity.
Source: OECD, *Main Science and Technology Indicators* 2019.

Figure 5.1 illustrates the relative importance of R&D expenditure by the higher education sector by displaying this expenditure as a proportion of overall R&D expenditure. Several interesting comparisons are evident vis-à-vis the UK and other countries. For example, not only is the expenditure of Germany's higher education sector on R&D in monetary terms more than twice that of the UK, it accounts for a lower proportion of total R&D (17.7% in Germany vs 22.5% in the UK). A similar pattern is observed with respect to the USA, Japan, and France, where the higher education sector is responsible for a lower proportion of total R&D. Compared to these countries the UK's total R&D expenditure is comparatively lower, but the higher education sector is relatively more important in monetary terms.

Figure 5.2 details the level of R&D expenditure by the UK higher education sector over the 30-year period 1988–2018. Overall, the pattern is one of an increasing level of R&D expenditure by this sector, highlighting the growing importance of universities to overall R&D activities within the UK over this period. However, Figure 5.2 also highlights the somewhat erratic nature of

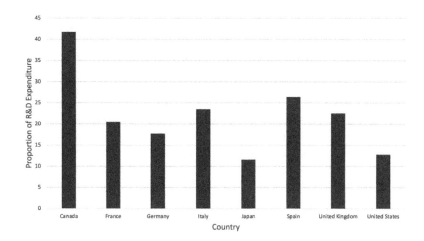

Figure 5.1   Proportion of gross domestic expenditure on R&D (GERD) accounted for by higher education

Source: OECD, *Main Science and Technology Indicators* 2019.

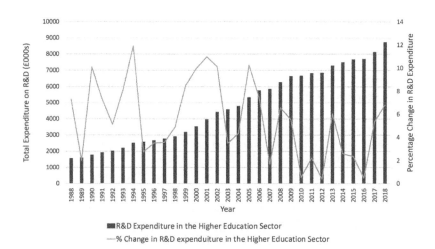

Figure 5.2   Gross expenditure on R&D by the UK higher education sector (1988–2018, £000s current prices)

Source: Office for National Statistics (ONS), Gross domestic expenditure on research and development time series (2020).

the year-on-year change during this period. Indeed, changes in R&D expenditure in the higher education sector is somewhat stop–start, recording growth rates of over 10% in several years along with growth rates of less than 2%. Furthermore, larger increases are never sustained and once the growth rate peaks it quickly recedes. Finally, the pattern of growth appears to have slowed down towards the end of the time-period, with lower growth rates recorded after 2005.

Underpinning the UK higher education sector's contribution to R&D is the funding regime supporting activities within universities. In terms of pure research funding, that is, support for projects focused on developing basic or discovery knowledge, UK universities currently receive over £3 billion per year (Vanino, Roper, and Becker 2019). This level of public funding for research has remained constant over the past decade, squeezed by the commitment to austerity. Despite the stagnation of research funding, the data shows that an increasing number of firms have been supported via public funding and the associated collaboration with universities, suggesting a move away from a model underpinned by a focus on curiosity driven research to a more commercially focused approach.

Despite the move towards a more commercially driven approach, funding for university research in the UK is still skewed towards what has been termed 'pure' research projects, that is, those that are focused on the production of new scientific knowledge. The total value of UK Research and Innovation (UKRI) funding in 2018/19 was £6.86 billion, of which around £800 million was allocated for collaborative projects, that is, those that are focused on the commercialisation of a technology or knowledge. Of the remaining £6 billion, £2.2 billion is classed as 'quality related' funding, which is allocated to universities based on their performance under the Research Evaluation Framework (REF). This is designed to guarantee a level of baseline funding for each institution, enabling them to make longer-term commitments to research and support more novel, curiosity driven projects and respond to emerging and evolving themes. The remaining £3.8 billion is allocated on a competitive basis through grant applications via discipline-specific Research Councils.

While public funding is still fundamentally geared towards pure research, substantial sums of public money are still available for commercially focused research. Indeed, the government's stated target of ensuring that 2.4% of GDP is invested in R&D by 2027 places greater significance on this funding to act as a primer for innovation in the economy. As previously noted, with universities explicitly identified within the Industrial Strategy as the key to promoting further R&D in the economy, this funding will surely grow as long as macro-economic conditions allow.

Funding to support industrial R&D is allocated through a broad range of schemes and initiatives, with the principal funding schemes being the

Collaborative R&D projects, Feasibility Studies, and Knowledge Transfer Partnerships. While these share a common aim, designed to support firms to undertake R&D activities and promote innovation, there are several differences between the schemes. The Collaborative R&D funding is designed to fund a discrete project through a partnership with another organisation. These projects may have two or more organisations, including but not restricted to universities. According to UKRI, approximately 55% of these projects utilise a university partner, highlighting their role as a facilitator of innovation.

Feasibility Studies are similar in their intent, although focused on much smaller-scale projects where the objective is to design and produce a prototype. Therefore, the focus is on proving the concept and that the technology works in a specific scenario. These projects do not necessarily produce a ready to market product or service but prove that it is indeed possible.

Knowledge Transfer Partnerships (KTPs) are designed to assist UK business with innovation and, by extension, also promote their growth. The aim of the programme is to promote collaboration between firms and universities, ensuring that the 'latest academic thinking' is introduced into the firm to promote innovation. These projects can last between one and three years and are part-funded by a public grant to cover the costs of the project. Consequently, an SME contributes around one-third of the costs (up to £35,000, but generally lower). In addition, the project employs a graduate with specialist knowledge of the field, referred to as the Associate, to work full time on the project at the premises of the firm.

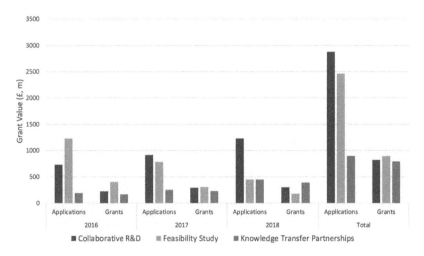

Figure 5.3   *Industry-focused research funding: total applications and grants (2016–18)*

Figure 5.3 presents data on recent applications and grants made by UKRI between 2016 and 2018 for the three main funding schemes for industry-based research, Collaborative R&D, Feasibility Studies, and KTPs. An initial examination of this data shows that applications for funding from the Collaborative R&D and KTP schemes have been increasing over the period, while those for Feasibility Studies have decreased.

Overall success rates for each scheme vary, highlighting the competitive nature of some aspects of industrial funding. For example, over this three-year period the success rates of funding through the Collaborative R&D and Feasibility Studies schemes were 29% and 36% respectively, whereas for funding through the KTP scheme 88% of projects were successful.

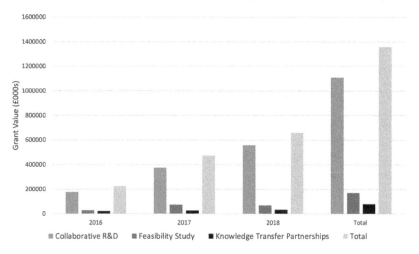

Figure 5.4   *Value of industry grants 2016–18*

Source: Authors' calculations from Gateway to Research website.

Figure 5.4 shows that the value of this grant funding has increased over the three years, with the total value of the grants from these three schemes in 2018 being over double that of 2016 (an increase from £226 million in 2016 to £659 million in 2018). It is also clear that the Collaborative R&D scheme accounts for the bulk of this funding (approximately 78%), highlighting its importance to industrial research in the UK. Therefore, publicly funded R&D makes a significant contribution to the UK economy. If the value of all grants over the three-year period under these three schemes were combined, they would total £1.35 billion. Furthermore, this would also typically be augmented by match funding or in-kind contributions from the firms involved, making the actual value of these projects higher.

Across the three schemes, the average size of the grant awarded differed considerably; for example, projects funded through the Collaborative R&D scheme were awarded £1.35 million per project on average, while those funded through Feasibility Studies averaged £190,000 per project, and those funded through KTPs averaged £100,000 per project.

Outside of public research funding, business interaction activities represent a growing stream of university income. This represents income from activities such as consultancy projects, contract research, and the use of equipment and facilities paid for directly by businesses themselves, which was worth £4.93 billion to UK universities in the 2018/19 academic year.

As shown in Table 5.2, this income has been growing steadily; UK universities generated over £2.4 billion from business interaction activities in 2003–04, since when income has grown by over 100%. Indeed, since 2003–04 income from these activities has grown every year. Furthermore, when compared to the overall turnover of the UK university sector, which totalled approximately £40.5 billion in 2018/19 (HESA 2020[1]), income from business interaction now accounts for approximately 12.2%, or around one-sixth, of income.

Table 5.2   *UK universities income from business interaction activities (2003–19)*

Year	Total Income (£, billion)	Year-on-Year Change (%)
2003–04	2.43	
2004–05	2.49	2.60
2005–06	2.62	4.95
2006–07	2.96	13.28
2007–08	3.06	3.18
2008–09	3.13	2.36
2009–10	3.19	1.80
2010–11	3.32	4.03
2011–12	3.33	0.55
2012–13	3.44	3.17
2013–14	3.72	8.07
2014–15	3.90	5.02
2015–16	4.21	7.77
2016–17	4.27	1.57
2017–18	4.58	7.26
2018–19	4.93	7.64

Source: HE-BCI Survey (HESA).

Supporting business interaction income are substantial contacts with industry. These contacts represent a range of formal interactions from consultancy to contract research, activities to support continuing professional development in businesses, licensing of intellectual property, and the provision of facilities and equipment to firms.

In 2018–19 UK universities reported over 70,000 contacts with SMEs that generated over £222 million in income. On average, these accounted for 52% of the universities' contact with industry, although only 11% of income. Furthermore, each contact is worth an average of £12,000 to a university. However, while these represent substantial numbers, non-SME contact is much more prevalent and valuable, with over 134,000 contacts reported in 2018–19 worth over £1.97 billion. In addition, the average revenue from a non-SME contact was over £19,000, or 58% higher than SME contacts.

An examination of the data at an institution level shows significant differences in the level of SME engagement. On average, a UK university reported over 500 contacts in 2018–19, and income of £1.6 million. Table 5.3 presents the top ten UK universities with respect to their income from SME interaction, number of contacts with SMEs, and average income per SME contact. In terms of income, the top ten is dominated by large research-focused universities, led by the University of Oxford which generated over £17 million from SMEs in 2018–19. Importantly, these appear to be evenly distributed across the regions, representing Scotland, North West England, Yorkshire and Humberside, London, and the South East of England. Examining contacts provides a slightly different picture as, apart from the Universities of Liverpool and Edinburgh, a different set of universities make up the top ten. Indeed, the top ten in terms of SME contacts are newer universities with a more applied focus such as the University of Hertfordshire and Coventry University. This group of institutions have at least double the average of 500 SME contacts of the typical university, with the University of Liverpool reporting over 25,000 contacts. Finally, in terms of income per SME contact the top ten universities all generated at least ten times the average of £3200.

The data examined so far suggests that SMEs are increasingly important to UK universities, but are universities as important to SMEs? To assess this, secondary data sources are used to examine patterns of university–industry interaction in the UK. We first draw on the UK Innovation Survey, which contains data from over 13,000 UK firms and is undertaken biennially. It therefore provides regular insights into innovation in the UK and the proportion of UK businesses engaging in collaborations with other organisations that chose a university as a partner. This data is presented in Table 5.4 and focuses on the reports from 2015 and 2017. The data shows that in 2017, 39% of collaborating firms reported that they were working with a university partner. This represents a significant increase in the proportion of collaborations occurring

Table 5.3   *Top ten universities for SME engagement (2019–20)*

SME Income		SME Contacts		Income per SME Contact	
University	Income (£000s)	University	Contacts	University	Income (£000s)
1. University of Oxford	17 069	University of Liverpool	25 625	Institute of Cancer Research	128.89
2. University of Liverpool	14 466	University of Hertfordshire	6 674	King's College London	110.53
3. University of Southampton	11 712	Leeds Beckett University	6 436	Nottingham Trent University	104.38
4. King's College London	10 058	Coventry University	5 226	University of Aberdeen	72.79
5. University of Nottingham	9 325	University of Northampton	2 654	University of Reading	63.62
6. University of Surrey	8 501	University of Gloucestershire	1 483	Brunel University London	63.45
7. University of Aberdeen	7 352	University of Bristol	1 252	Aberystwyth University	60.90
8. University of Edinburgh	7 258	University of Salford	1 108	University of St Andrews	53.09
9. University of Sheffield	5 969	University of Edinburgh	1 079	University of Southampton	32.72
10. University of Manchester	5 715	University of the West of England, Bristol	1 062	University of Bedfordshire	32.58

Source: HE-BCI Survey 2018/19.

with universities between 2012–14 and 2014–16, with the proportion of collaborating firms reporting that their partner was a university rising from just 21%.

Closer examination of the data shows that a lower proportion of SMEs reported collaborating with a university than larger firms for both years. In addition, the data provides insights into differences within SMEs according to the number of employees. Between 2014 and 2016, 40% of the smallest firms (those with between 10 and 49 employees) reported working with a university partner. This is higher than those with 50–99 employees, where 36.7% of collaborators reported working with a university partner, and those with 100–249 employees, where the figure was 36.2%. This is, however, lower than for larger firms (250+ employees), where 41.7% of collaborators reported working with a university.

Consequently, the data highlights some positive findings regarding the utilisation of universities by UK businesses in the course of their collaborations. However, while approximately one-third of SME collaborators report that their partner was a university, this significantly lags the proportion reporting that they collaborated with their suppliers and customers, which accounted for 81% and 74% respectively. Furthermore, universities also lagged private sector knowledge generators such as commercial R&D institutes, with 49% of collaborating firms reporting them as partners. Finally, it seems that firms are more likely to turn to their rivals to collaborate before they do a university, with over 55% of collaborators reported working with them as partners.

The UK Innovation Survey also provides insight into the relative standing of universities as sources of knowledge for UK firms. Again, this shows universities to be the least important sources of information among innovating firms, with just 3% reporting that they regard them as important. Therefore, overall, the findings from the UK Innovation Survey paint a pessimistic picture of the relative importance of universities as sources of knowledge or collaborative partners.

Table 5.4   University collaboration by firm size

Firm Size	Percentage of Collaborating Firms Working with Universities 2012–14	Percentage of Collaborating Firms Working with Universities 2014–16
10–49	20.1	40.0
50–99	24.7	36.7
100–249	22.9	36.2
250+	26.7	41.7
All	21.0	39.5

Source: UK Innovation Survey (2015, 2017).

Table 5.5   SME collaboration partners

Partner in Collaboration	Proportion of firms (%)
Suppliers of equipment, materials, services, or software	57.99
Clients or customers from the private sector	42.19
Clients or customers from the public sector	27.44
Other businesses within enterprise group	27.08
Competitors or other businesses in the same industry	21.24
Consultants, commercial labs, or private R&D institutes	19.38
Universities or other higher education institutions	13.55
Government or public research institutes	6.60

Note: N = 4406.
Source: LSBS (2015).

Further information on the attitudes of SMEs towards university collaboration can be gathered from the Longitudinal Small Business Survey (LSBS).
This annual survey contains data on over 15,000 UK SMEs, allowing for
a more detailed look at with whom innovative SMEs are partnering overall
and sectoral/spatial patterns of engagement. Again, this data perpetuates the
pessimistic view around SME–university interaction with Table 5.5 showing
that for UK SMEs, the proportion reporting that their innovation involved
collaboration with a university was 13.55%. Furthermore, the table shows
that universities again lagged other organisations as collaborative partners for
innovative SMEs, confirming the findings from the UK Innovation Survey.

The additional depth afforded by the LSBS allows an examination of the
differences between sectors in university collaboration. Table 5.6 shows variations in the proportion of innovative SMEs collaborating with universities
by sector. For example, 24.8% of innovating SMEs in the education sector
reported working with a university compared with 6.7% in the retail sector.
In addition, higher proportions of innovating SMEs collaborating with universities are found in the health/social work, arts/entertainment, information/
communication, professional/scientific, and other services sectors.

Table 5.6   SME–university collaboration by sector

Standard Industrial Classification (SIC)	Proportion of SMEs Innovating with Universities
ABDE Primary	13.1
C Manufacturing	13.6
F Construction	9.5
G Wholesale/Retail	6.7
H Transport/Storage	7.9
I Accommodation/Food	8.2
Information/Communication	14.6
Finance/Real Estate	7.7
Professional/Scientific	15.0
Administrative/Support	8.8
Education	24.8
Health/Social Work	19.2
Arts/Entertainment	19.0
Other Services	16.0

Note: N = 4406.
Source: LSBS (2015).

Finally, Table 5.7 outlines the proportion of innovative firms collaborating with universities across the regions of the UK. The data does not highlight a standout region in terms of the level of university collaboration, with the proportion ranging from 10.5% in the South East to 16.6% in Wales. Therefore, there are no major regional differences in the proportion of innovative SMEs collaborating with universities.

Table 5.7   *Regional SME–university collaboration*

Region	Proportion of SMEs Collaborating with Universities
East Midlands	15.2
East of England	11.9
London	14.1
North East	13.6
North West	14.5
South East	10.5
South West	13.2
West Midlands	11.3
Yorkshire and Humberside	12.7
Scotland	15.9
Wales	16.6
Northern Ireland	10.5

Note: N = 4406.
Source: LSBS (2015).

In summary, this chapter has provided an overview of the policy environment surrounding universities and their role in the innovation system in the UK. It outlines the current policy climate as the culmination of a set of developments stretching back to the beginning of the twentieth century. In addition, it has also illuminated the relative importance of universities to the UK business community. Indeed, SMEs account for over half of the reported industry contacts for universities, further dispelling the myth of non-engagement among these firms. In addition, while universities while may be lower down the hierarchy of potential collaborative partners for firms, a clear upward trend in the data on revenue from business interaction shows that industry engagement has been growing in the UK and that the number of contacts between SMEs and UK universities is significant, numbering in the tens of thousands.

This data provides a general picture of university–industry interaction in the UK, particularly those involving SMEs, and provides a context for the following analysis of this type of collaboration from the perspective of the firms involved. The analysis seeks to address knowledge gaps in terms of the motivations of SMEs for engaging with universities, and the activities and practices that underpin their formation and function. As noted in Chapter 4, university collaboration for SMEs follows a distinct path in terms of their outputs, some of which is evident in this data. In addition, prior studies have shown that the process of university collaboration is increasingly considered to be driven by relational and cognitive similarities between the partners. Therefore, the pertinent questions appear to be: how does the socio-technical nature of this process manifest itself to the SMEs and entrepreneurs involved? And what does it mean for the formation and function of these links?

NOTE

1. https://www.hesa.ac.uk/data-and-analysis/finances/income (accessed 14 July 2020).

6.   Ideation and motivation

6.1   INTRODUCTION

In order to explore the phenomenon of university collaboration from the perspective of the SMEs involved, the following chapters of this book draw on material from 22 in-depth semi-structured interviews with entrepreneurs within SMEs, defined according to accepted conventions as firms with fewer than 250 employees. The SMEs in this study employed between 3 and 120 workers, with average employment around 26. Except for one, the SMEs had all collaborated with universities through the Knowledge Transfer Partnership (KTP) programme.

So as to examine as broad a range of projects as possible so that a wide range of experiences of university–industry (U–I) interaction could be captured, no *a priori* restrictions were placed on the types of firms included. Consequently, the case study features firms that operate in a diverse range of sectors such as biotechnology, engineering, finance, and digital marketing (Table 6.1). Furthermore, the participating SMEs worked with a broad cross-section of UK universities and are spread across the UK geographically. Annual turnover among the SMEs ranged from £130,000 to £13 million and they had been trading for between 3 and 31 years at the time they were interviewed.

Table 6.1   Participant firms

Alias	Sector	Partner	Employees	Turnover	Age
Arc-Tech	Architectural Consultants	Coventry University	50	£3 million	5
Black-Electronics	Electronics Manufacturing	Sheffield Hallam University	27	£4 million	31
Blue Design	Design Consultancy/ 3D Printing	Manchester Metropolitan University	6	£300 000	8
Blue Finance	Accident Investigation Software and Consultancy	University of the West of Scotland	15	£4 million	22
Brown Media	Media Consultants	Salford University	31	£800 000	9

Alias	Sector	Partner	Employees	Turnover	Age
Cyan-Soft	IT Support	London Metropolitan University	17	£800 000	3
Data-Tech	Financial Data Software/ Analysis	Bournemouth University	12	£500 000	17
Edu-Tech	Education Consultant/Online Assessment	University of Wolverhampton	12	£185 000	23
Gen-Tech	Biotechnology – DNA Therapies/Technology	Birmingham University	12	£9 million	4
Green-Soft	Suppliers of Analytical Instrumentation/Equipment	Anglia Ruskin University	7	£1.2 million	6
Indigo-Consultants	Health and Social Care Consultancy	Brunel University	7	£130 000	10
Magenta-Design	Design of Play Areas	Sheffield Hallam University	40	£4 million	10
Magnolia-Support	Project Management/Support	University of Exeter	50	£13 million	5
Marine Consultants	Oil and Gas Consultancy	University of Exeter	40	£7–8 million	9
Mine-Tech	Scientific Analysis of Geological Material	Southampton University	20	£4.5 million	14
Motor-Tech	Electric Motor Simulation Software	Glyndwr University	23	£1 million	9
Patient-Tech	Medical Consultancy	University of Westminster	3	£850 000	5
Pink-Soft	Software	Aston University	27	£3.5 million	13
Purple Media	Retail/Online Marketing Consultancy	Durham University	120	£35 million	9
Red-Soft	Software	University of Plymouth	24	£230 000	10
White-Electronics	Electronic Manufacturing	University of Nottingham	80	£9–12 million	16
Yellow-Soft	Marketing Solutions/Data Management	University of the West of England	65	£5 million	20

This chapter presents the first stage of the empirical analysis of the process of developing and undertaking a collaborative project with a university from the perspective of the participating SMEs. It provides an overview of the initial development of the ideas that formed the basis of these projects and the subsequent motivation for pursuing their development with a university partner. Therefore, the chapter represents the starting point of the 'plot' that underpins the following empirical chapters, not only setting the scene for the events that followed but also providing an important contextual setting for how and why these collaborative projects were initiated.

6.2   PROJECT DEVELOPMENT

In examining the process of SME engagement with universities, the natural starting point is the beginnings of the projects themselves, establishing their origins in terms of the development of the initial ideas from which their path to fruition can be plotted.

SMEs and their entrepreneurs face competitive pressures to maintain their market position, which motivates them to develop new products and services or improve their existing offerings. Therefore, SMEs are focused on survival and longevity and see innovation as the path to ensure this. To achieve this aim, they chose to pursue their ideas though open innovation, that is, in collaboration with actors from external organisations.

The U–I collaboration process can be characterised as either a top-down or bottom-up process. In terms of the former, this involves a leading role for the university partner in suggesting a project to the firm, whereas the latter would mean the firms were developing the initial ideas themselves before seeking a university partner with which to collaborate. Therefore, establishing the first steps of SMEs in the collaboration process provides a key framing device for the following analysis.

The findings reveal that the origins of these collaborative projects lie exclusively with the SMEs themselves. The process of open innovation that forms the core of the following analysis is characterised as bottom-up in nature. It commonly begins with the SMEs identifying a new opportunity they wish to pursue. In most cases, this opportunity focuses on the firm's existing products or services and aims at extending its capabilities or adapting it for a new market. Therefore, idea development is typically designed to make improvements to the underlying competitiveness of the business through adding to its ability to deliver new products and processes. This is neatly encapsulated in the following quote:

> We needed to improve our technology. We needed to move into a field of technology that's our industry. But we don't have those skills. (Black-Electronics)

There was a recognition among these SMEs that they needed to innovate, coupled with a motivation to do so. However, this recognition realised the existence of knowledge and capabilities gaps within the firms which required addressing to undertake the planned innovation.

As Table 6.2 shows, in every case the initial idea for the project was established within the firms, highlighting the dynamism of SMEs and the prevailing sense that continuous improvement is at the heart of their strategies. The outlook of collaborating SMEs is characterised by a forward-looking mindset focused on how they can ensure their continued survival and prosperity. Despite this ability to generate new ideas, SMEs suffer from a lack of capabilities required to convert these into new products on their own. It is this realisation which drives them towards initiating a process of open innovation.

Initiating an open innovation process in SMEs then promotes an internal discussion around the means through which their projects can be realised. It was these discussions that led to a search process for resource inputs into the firm to achieve this. Importantly, while the outcome of this search process is the development of a collaborative link with a university, this was often not the explicit aim. Instead, the development of the idea is typically followed by a tentative exploration of the options available for open innovation. Accordingly, the key task for SMES is to address deficiencies or absences of skills, expertise, capabilities, or knowledge within the business to realise their projects. As they pivot towards adopting an open innovation approach, the option of a university begins to emerge as a potential solution. This reality is captured clearly by Purple Media, who stated quite simply that

> the ideation came from the business and then we went around ... looking for support. (Purple Media)

The fact that the innovation activities revealed their constraints is not necessarily regarded by SMEs as a weakness. Indeed, while the existence of these constraints may be interpreted as a barrier to the firms' pursuit of innovative ideas, SMEs see these capability gaps as inevitable. This position is summed up by the quote from Green-Soft who said that:

> we were just three people in the business and we had very limited marketing capability, mainly just from a resource perspective, but also because none of us had been sort of specifically in a role that was marketing orientated. So although we knew certain things about how it worked and so on, that wasn't especially our areas of expertise. (Green-Soft)

Therefore, the development of these new ideas represents an opportunity; their weakness is not an inability to generate ideas but their inability to dedicate sufficient resources towards their realisation.

Table 6.2   *Motivations for and sources of project ideas*

Firm	Idea Source	Motivation for Project
Arc-Tech	Firm	Firm wanted to be able to reach a higher standard with the buildings they designed in terms of CO_2 emissions. They realised that the university was interested in the same area having met through professional networks/association and pursued a collaborative project.
Black-Electronics	Firm	Firm wanted to extend their capabilities by moving into the production of different types of audio electronics
Blue Design	Firm	Had developed 3D printing technology and wanted to extend this into producing prosthetic eyes.
Blue Finance	Firm	Firm was in the process of developing a new e-learning project when contacted by the university. As they had previously engaged in the KTP programme they were aware of further opportunities in this area and believed that the new project would lend itself to a KTP.
Brown Media	Firm	Had a side-project to develop a new piece of software underway but did not have the capacity to complete it internally.
Cyan-Soft	Firm	Firm was seeking to extend the capabilities of the business through the development of a new piece of software that managed their operations more efficiently.
Data-Tech	Firm	Had recognised a need to update their application but lacked the resources to do it. Wanted to do it internally in order to create the capabilities but did not have expertise, being a small firm.
Edu-Tech	Firm	Firm had already developed a new tool and wanted to use the KTP to find the best way to get it to market.
Gen-Tech	Firm	The firm was working on developing a particular technique but struggled to master it. They consulted a university for assistance with the issue which developed into a collaborative project.
Green-Soft	Firm	Identified a capability gap within the firm and wanted to address it through bringing in additional knowledge through a collaborative project.
Indigo-Consultants	Firm	Firm realised the need to extend the capabilities of their software product in order to develop their market.
Magenta-Design	Firm	Firm wanted to increase their capabilities having realised that they required more of an understanding of their area.
Magnolia-Support	Firm	Firm was aiming to extend the capabilities of the business through increasing their expertise in project management.
Marine Consultants	Firm	Firm was aiming to expand their services into new areas.

Firm	Idea Source	Motivation for Project
Mine-Tech	Firm	Firm recognised a need for a new method of analysing core rock samples while maintaining the pressure they would be under while in situ underground. Had been working alongside the academic partner in other projects and realised there was a mutual interest which developed into a KTP.
Motor-Tech	Firm	Firm wanted to develop a new idea around a new piece of software for motor design project but didn't get far with it – realised a lack of capabilities in the area and decided to address it through a collaborative project.
Patient-Tech	Firm	Firm founded around the development of a new piece of patient management software. New project was intended to develop this product to cover new applications.
Pink-Soft	Firm	Aim was to develop new product for 'continuity of revenue', i.e. ensuring long-term survivability of the business. Identified a gap in the market and wanted to develop a new application to exploit gap as well as gather analytics from the application.
Purple Media	Firm	Follow-on from previous KTP to develop models to forecast revenue from marketing techniques.
Red-Soft	Firm	Development of new software.
White-Electronics	Firm	Application of firm's technology to develop sensors for underground workers to monitor safety.
Yellow-Soft	Firm	Development of new software for cloud computing.

The adoption of an open innovation approach thus offers the potential for SMEs to acquire the resources required to realise new ideas. Even though it may not have been their primary aim, it was a course of action seen as necessary to complete the project. Therefore, while SMEs are seeking to innovate, they may not be initially seeking to collaborate. Consequently, collaborations result from the necessity of their situation. Furthermore, while SMEs may end up pursuing an open innovation path, their intention is not necessarily to engage with a university. This poses the question as to how did these projects result in a collaboration with a university?

6.3   MOTIVATIONS FOR UNIVERSITY COLLABORATION

Deciding to pursue an open innovation approach does not mean SMEs are necessarily seeking to work with a university. Instead they begin by examining options for potential partners with the required knowledge. Indeed, initial responses to the identification of a capability gap are to first try to hire individuals with the knowledge and expertise to contribute to the business and address this gap. However, this can prove to be difficult as individuals with the required knowledge and skills are hard to find, particularly for SMEs located outside of cities and major towns in more peripheral areas. As Black-Electronics noted, for them, the process was initiated through realising:

> we needed to improve our technology. We needed to move into a field of technology that's our industry. But we don't have those skills ... hiring somebody who has these skills, proved to be virtually impossible. (Black-Electronics)

Therefore, participation in the KTP scheme provides SMEs with an opportunity to increase the expertise within and capabilities of the business through employing a graduate with the appropriate knowledge and skills in addition to accessing the wider knowledge of a university.

Once SMEs begin their search for external resources, the option of developing a collaboration with a university partner becomes clearer. The analysis established several motivations for pursuing this course of action: (1) familiarity with universities; (2) a focus on obtaining high-quality knowledge; (3) the learning experience from working with a university; (4) the funding available to work with a university; (5) the kudos of association; and (6) the timely approach from a university. These are now examined in turn.

University collaboration is generally motivated by the SMEs' familiarity with universities, or where universities are prominent members of the firms' networks. Therefore, exposure to a broad range of interactions with individual academics meant that universities were a clear option for choosing an external partner. Consequently, while SMEs may not be actively searching for a university partner in the initial stages of their project, this type of collaboration would not have been beyond the bounds of probability.

These previous interactions with universities took many forms, from engaging in previous formal collaborative links to less formal interaction such as taking placement students, giving guest lectures, assisting with designing courses in their fields, and attending conferences alongside academics (see Table 6.3 for a summary). Importantly, only a single firm (Yellow-Soft) had collaborated with their current university partner through the KTP programme. Therefore, for the other 21 SMEs, these were all new links.

From the perspective of SMEs, universities are not necessarily remote organisations with which they have no understanding or affinity. Indeed, this last point is particularly important, as this familiarity presents evidence that SMEs possess an understanding of the opportunities provided by universities, and, specifically, the knowledge and expertise they can contribute. Therefore, SMEs that had previously collaborated with universities in a formal setting would have been aware of how university collaboration functions. Indeed, even those firms that had fewer formal interactions would at least have a basic understanding of the knowledge and expertise available within a university and their potential as a collaborative partner.

Table 6.3   Prior experience of university interaction

Firm	Prior University Engagement
Arc-Tech	Had previously completed a KTP with another university.
Black-Electronics	No prior experience of working with universities.
Blue Design	Had been working with universities on formal projects as a sub-contractor.
Blue Finance	Long history of working with universities in terms of course development and guest lectures. No experience of formal collaboration though a single funded project.
Brown Media	No previous contacts or collaboration with a university.
Cyan-Soft	Had previously engaged with the incubator facilities of their university partner.
Data-Tech	No previous experience of working with a university.
Edu-Tech	Had previously been involved in four KTPs with several other universities.
Gen-Tech	No previous experience of working with universities prior to this project, but subsequently developed multiple links.
Green-Soft	Was aware of university partner as was based in a university incubator. No direct experience of working with a university.
Indigo-Consultants	History of informal collaboration with universities through hosting placement students and supporting projects. Also had substantial interaction with academics through attending conferences.
Magenta-Design	Had previously completed a KTP with another university and worked informally with universities (including partner) on projects while also delivering guest lectures.
Magnolia-Support	No experience of formal collaboration prior to the project. Individuals within the firm had experience of working with universities.
Marine Consultants	Had previously completed a KTP with another university.
Mine-Tech	Firm was established by former academics and workforce has an academic background. Consequently, firm has long history of formal collaboration with universities.
Motor-Tech	No previous experience of working with a university.
Patient-Tech	History of working informally alongside university but no previous experience of a formal funded project.
Pink-Soft	No previous experience of working with a university.
Purple Media	No previous experience of working with a university.
Red-Soft	Had worked informally with universities and offered placements to students. Had participated in academic conferences in their field.
White-Electronics	Had previously completed a small collaborative project with partner.
Yellow-Soft	Had previously completed two KTPs with same partner.

The second motivation for engaging in university collaboration is that it meant access to the high-quality knowledge and expertise they required. Indeed, SMEs' familiarity with universities means that they understand the quality of knowledge and expertise on offer. This was clearly an important consideration, as the firms were motivated to ensure that they sourced cutting-edge knowledge to develop their ideas. Therefore, it was central to the firms' strategy to seek potential partners who they regarded as being as innovative as they are.

A third motivation for undertaking a project with a university partner is that it provides the firms with a learning experience. Indeed, SMEs set out to take an open innovation approach as they recognised the gap in their capabilities to develop new goods and services to take advantage of the opportunities they saw. They also displayed the determination not just to obtain these resources from external partners but embed them permanently within the business. As a result, there was a recognition that working with a university would enable the firm to learn through the collaboration rather than just finding a party to provide a solution, such as engaging a consultant. Therefore, SMEs are motivated to engage in a university collaboration as a means of addressing their capability gap on a permanent basis. These points are illustrated in the following quote from Yellow-Soft:

> I guess it was the fact that we probably didn't have the skillset internally to build the solution ourselves. Working with a third party in the private sector would have been an option, but actually, we wanted to build the skillset in-house, to be able to work on projects like this, deliver those sorts of solutions and maintain it. So, we actually thought [a university collaboration] was a good solution. (Yellow-Soft)

There was a motivation to collaborate with universities because they provided a learning experience from the initial stages of the project. Therefore, their knowledge and expertise were useful for developing a coherent project proposal as well as a final output that corresponded with firms' vision of the potential market opportunity. As noted by Indigo-Consultants:

> I don't think we had the skills internally to specify tightly exactly what we wanted, apart from just saying, this is the end product that I want, come and do it. (Indigo-Consultants)

Another factor identified as an important motivation for engaging with a university is the associated funding. This highlights the fact that for SMEs the choice of collaborative partner is not only motivated by their need to leverage knowledge, but also investment for the potential project. In these cases, where the firm's motivation was to secure funding, the relevant knowledge and expertise was seen almost as a bonus to the firm:

> we didn't need [the university's] expertise. We needed their money, and what they were also offering was an academic input which was stuff we wanted to do anyway, and they were able to offer an academic department which would help us do what we wanted to do. (Patient-Tech)

The funding attached to university collaboration acts as a significant motivator for the SMEs to engage. While most of these collaborations were KTPs, where participating firms are required to make a financial contribution to the costs of the project, the projects still attracted funding through a public grant to cover the costs of the university partners' time. Therefore, a collaborative project via the KTP programme typically costs an SME approximately £60,000 over two years. As such, the fact that the firms found the programme to be financially attractive suggests that a publicly funded collaborative project is regarded as better value for money than alternative funding proposals would be. Therefore, as illustrated by the following quote from Data-Tech, who realised that undertaking their project with a private sector partner was unaffordable:

> I think [the project cost] was estimated at being about a two-million-pound cost to be able to ask a third party to be able to do it for us. Again, we were only a half a million-pound turnover company so, as you can see, the maths just doesn't add up. (Data-Tech)

The existence of funding to support the project – or at least in the case of the KTP programme a low cost to the firm coupled with a grant to cover the university partner's time – is clearly an important motivator for the firms to choose a university collaboration. As such, developing a collaboration with a university partner can be interpreted in some cases as a method for obtaining funding in addition to a source of knowledge and expertise.

Furthermore, the feeling among the SMEs was that the funding attached to university projects is more likely to be focused on ideas that were cutting edge in nature and less obviously commercial. SMEs consider that their ideas for a new product or process are not required to be fully developed, but to have the right potential. This is viewed as being preferable to obtaining investment from private sector sources, as these investors are perceived as less focused on the idea than its potential return on investment. For some SMEs the nature of their projects meant they considered that there would be little appetite in the private sectors to fund their ideas. For others, taking advantage of publicly available funding through a partnership with a university meant that the firms could avoid venture capitalists, as this type of investment is considered a threat to the independence of the firm.

The associated kudos of working with a university is also a key factor that motivates SMEs to choose them as a partner, acting as a signal of the stature and competitiveness of the business. SMEs are keen to stress their association with a university for marketing purposes and improving their standing within their industry. Through highlighting their university collaborations SMEs can draw attention to their prowess as an innovator and capacity to deliver new products and processes. Therefore, the existence of a formal university linkage is used to show the dynamism of the firm, as noted by the following:

> I think KTPs are good value for money, 'cause they add an awful lot of … particularly in our position as a company with the … there is a kudos and there's a sort of having a formal academic link and that's sort of spun off positively in the way that we can describe the company because it demonstrates that we're serious about what we do. (Indigo-Consultants)

In some cases, SMEs are motivated to enter university collaboration simply due to a timely approach by a university seeking to develop collaborative links. In the cases of Brown Media and Marine Consultants, they were contacted by their eventual partner in order to see if they would be interested in working with the university. This proved to be a fortuitous incident as, at the time, both firms had identified an opportunity in the market to exploit and had an idea for a project they wished to pursue. Brown Media had not considered working with a university prior to this and the contact opened a previously unconsidered avenue. Marine Consultants had previously completed a KTP so were aware of this as an option and being contacted by another university spurred them into pursuing this route and developing an idea they had been developing as a joint project. Similarly, Green-Soft became aware of the possibility of university collaboration through the marketing exercises undertaken by their eventual partner. In this case the firm approached the university, but without the university's marketing activities they would not have realised the opportunity existed and been motivated to collaborate in this way.

In addition, the case of Green-Soft highlights a case whereby previous direct experience of working in conjunction with a university was absent yet they were still motivated to develop and undertake a collaboration. For Green-Soft, this foray represented a real step into the unknown:

> I guess at the time this sort of potential collaboration was kind of all new to us. We were pretty new at running a business, never done that before, didn't have any clue as to what kind of potential linkages could be made with academic institutes. So, yeah, it was a completely new concept to us and sounded like a pretty decent idea. So we were quite keen to roll with it really. (Green-Soft)

While the potential within universities was recognised, SMEs concurrently appreciated that access may not be straightforward. Yet, in general they were still motivated to engage with universities as they considered them to be favourable partners, representing sources of knowledge that were both robust and rigorous. In short, as noted by Magnolia-Support, the motivation to engage with a university is particularly strong as it can allow a firm to

> get a very motivated, very bright person for, well, frankly, not much money, and you've essentially free access to, you know, best practice round the world, research, peer review, you know … it's a cracking deal. (Magnolia-Support)

Despite having decided to collaborate with a university, there was not a unanimous feeling among these SMEs that the option of working with a university was the optimal outcome for the firm. Instead, collaborating with a university is viewed more as an attempt to see if this method of open innovation could be the solution to completing their project. Accordingly, there was a marked view, particularly among those firms that had not previously worked with a university, that this type of engagement was an experiment. As well as this, these firms also appeared to justify this view through the realisation that these projects were not a big risk for the firm. This position is summed up by the following quote from Magnolia-Support:

> We thought it was an experiment. We allocated money and we were committed to try and make it work, but we also thought we might write the money off. I mean, it's, in a sense, almost a piece of research. You can't be sure that that investment was going to pay off and we weren't. (Magnolia-Support)

Therefore, motivation for developing university collaboration may be the lack of a penalty for failure. SMEs can merely write off the cost of the project as a loss and then move on; whereas a more formal alliance or investment with a venture capitalist would have meant that failure would have left the other party unhappy as to the outcome. In general, the analysis reflects the prevailing wisdom within the extant literature on U–I collaboration that universities are a safer partner in that firms appear to be willing to take a calculated risk in order to realise their project. This is illustrated in the quote from Pink-Soft, who stated that:

> I feel very comfortable working with the universities, and they seem to be pretty well geared up to working with commercial organisations I think. (Pink-Soft)

6.4   DISCUSSION AND CONCLUSIONS

The analysis presented in this chapter provides an overview of the ideation of SME projects, and the subsequent motivation to collaborate with a university. It highlights several key findings. Firstly, it is evident from the findings that SMEs create a collaborative project with a university after they have developed a new idea. The initial outcome of this process being that it highlights the existence of a capability gap within the firm that subsequently leads to the adoption of an open innovation approach.

The findings, therefore, reveal the process of SME–university collaboration to be 'bottom-up' in nature, beginning with the firm developing an idea and then seeking the best method for realising it. The fact that, in every case, the ideation was the result of internal activities demonstrates that SMEs can recognise both the need to innovate and possess the capability to seek and develop new opportunities. In pursuing these opportunities, SMEs aim to expand their markets or make their business more efficient and competitive. Therefore, underpinning the observed innovation activity was a desire to capture new growth, rather than merely protect their current position. Drawing on work in the strategic management literature, which posits that alliance seeking behaviour can be offensive or defensive in nature (Eisenhardt and Schoonhoven 1996), the evidence suggests that the underlying motivations for SME–university collaboration are offensive in nature.

Although the underlying strategy may have been to enhance the competitive position of the firm, the act of innovating reveals that SMEs lack sufficient resources and capabilities to achieve this alone. Therefore, the findings further indicate a resource seeking motive for engaging in open innovation among the firms, driven by the recognition of an opportunity and the accordant need to acquire the necessary knowledge resources for its effective pursuit (Hadjimanolis 2000; Lee et al. 2010). These behaviours also highlight the entrepreneurial characteristics of SMEs in terms of pursuing the discovery and creation of opportunities (Sarason, Dean, and Dillard 2006; Shane and Venkataraman 2000).

Accordingly, innovation motivates SMEs' engagement in university collaboration. The strategic intent is not necessarily to pursue a university collaboration, but a need to develop new ideas and develop new products and services. As such, SMEs may not approach the open innovation process wholly in a strategic and structured manner (Terziovski 2010). Instead, the adoption of open innovation may be more a necessity as SMEs can develop innovative ideas, but they lack the capabilities to execute these plans alone. For SMEs, an evolving process of addressing a resource gap within the firm leads to an open innovation approach. Ultimately, the subsequent search for potential partners results in working with a university.

These findings clearly suggest a role for relational and cognitive complementarities in underpinning the motivations for the firms to work with universities. For example, the importance of SMEs' familiarity with universities suggests low cognitive and relational distances between them (Bjerregaard 2009). Therefore, familiarity is a key motivation for entering into a university collaboration which is, in turn, promoted by socio-technical factors in terms of proximities between the actors.

Organisational proximity between SMEs and universities is an important motivator for engaging in this type of collaboration. To recap, organisational proximity has been defined as actors that belong to the 'same space of relations (networks), i.e. actors are in interactions of various natures' (Oerlemans and Meeus 2005, p. 94). In addition, according to Torre and Gilly (2000), organisational proximity means that actors will exhibit a 'similarity logic', in terms of being familiar with each other and, importantly, their ways of working. As such, the existence of organisational proximity is seen as facilitated by prior partnering experiences (Aguilera et al. 2012; Knoben and Oerlemans 2006). Importantly, these proximities are observed in both those firms that had previously completed a formal collaborative project with a university, as well as those who may have had more informal interactions.

As a result of prior interaction, SMEs often possess an understanding of the knowledge and expertise possessed by universities, as well as an idea of their working practices. This means they possess at least some insights into potential advantages and disadvantages of this type of collaboration. Furthermore, SMEs may also possess an understanding of the universities' technical prowess as they regarded them as possessing high-quality knowledge, which motivates them to pursue these collaborations. This suggests the existence of technological proximity which allows them to understand the nature of the universities' knowledge through a shared technical language (Cowan and Jonard 2003; Cowan, David, and Foray 2000).

While the prior experience of partnering and associated organisational proximity are important factors, the findings indicate that these serve more as a guiding factor in motivating the formation of the ties rather than a clear determinant. For example, their existence does not mean the firm would automatically choose a specific university partner with which to collaborate. Instead, it highlights which university partner may be a viable option for a collaborative partner. Had the influence of prior ties and organisational proximity been greater, these SMEs would have been formulating their project ideas with a view to collaborating with a specific university, or at least adopted a more direct path to university collaboration than was observed. Furthermore, the absence of this organisational proximity did not equate to a lack of motivation for a SME to pursue a collaborative link with a specific university. Therefore, while these proximities may be useful for motivating the formation of these links, their absence is not necessarily a barrier.

The importance of organisational proximity highlights the importance of pre-existing networks to SMEs in the formation of their collaborative link with universities. Indeed, most had a prior interaction with a university, whether formal or informal, prior to initiating their collaboration. This observation not only suggests that the participating firms were all well networked, as they were able to exploit these ties when needed, but also that they possessed a degree of network capital (Huggins 2010; Huggins, Johnston, and Thompson 2012), maintaining the relationships until such a time when the firms could exploit them for their advantage. This also suggests that membership of the same networks, or social proximity, is an important factor in the initial stages of these collaborations. This is examined in more detail in the following chapter.

The analysis further suggests that, in some cases, universities may also motivate SMEs to engage with them, and these experiences suggest that the formation of U–I links could be a two-way process of firms seeking universities and universities seeking firms. In cases whereby firms were contacted by the universities, it appears that the tactic of approaching firms did pay off for a university as it resulted in the development of collaborations. In these cases, however, it was clear that firms were receptive to the contact as they had a project idea ready to go.

In summary, the findings presented in this chapter provide an overview of the activities that initiated the formation of formal collaborations with universities. Through focusing on the genesis of the participating firms' projects and their motivations for engaging with a university a chain of events is identified that describes the process of initiating SME–university collaboration. Firstly, SMEs develop the initial project ideas, highlighting the fact that they possess the capabilities to develop new ideas and an innovative mindset within the firm. Secondly, developing new ideas reveals the existence of a capability gap within the firm, due to their relative lack of expertise, resources, and finance, which highlights the need to take an open approach to innovation. Once SMEs decide this, their search activities draw them towards universities. However, in plotting the development of SME–university collaborations, the key event appears to be the recognition that realising an idea for a new product or service requires outside input.

While there may be many factors that motivate SMEs to collaborate with universities, the closeness of the firms to universities in terms of organisational and technological proximity supports their motive to collaborate. Furthermore, these proximities are dependent upon networking activities and the presence of network capital within the firms meant that these relationships could be maintained and eventually exploited. Therefore, the socio-technical nature of SME–university collaboration is apparent from their early stages.

7. Partner selection and assessing credibility

7.1 INTRODUCTION

The second stage in the lifecycle of a collaborative project is the selection of a suitable partner. In many ways, this is the crucial stage in the process as it is through these activities that the collaboration begins to take shape, as the firm evaluates the potential of a possible university partner for delivering the knowledge and expertise required to realise their project ideas and then makes a decision as to whether to engage in a formal partnership. Therefore, for SMEs the choice of a university partner is a key milestone in the unlocking of the ivory tower, representing their ability to progress from merely highlighting their ability to innovate and a desire to achieve their goals through an open innovation process, to taking a positive step in coupling with a university to collaborate and co-create knowledge.

In order to explore this process in more depth, this chapter highlights the means through which SMEs choose a university partner. In addition, it also outlines the methods used by the participating SMEs in assessing the credibility of their potential partners when engaging in the initial stages of collaboration.

7.2 PARTNER SELECTION

Given the fact that the UK is home to a significant number of higher education institutions, with 159 established universities located within the country, SMEs have a broad choice of potential university partners. Table 7.1 provides an overview of the SMEs and their university partners, highlighting a broad range of partners. The table also presents data on the distances between the participating SMEs and their university partner. These were measured as the distance between the two with respect to the fastest road route. As evident from the table, these distances varied considerably from firm to firm. For example, Indigo-Consultants' collaboration with Brunel University involved the largest distance, with the partners separated by 340 km. In contrast, Motor-Tech and Magenta-Design were located around 1 km from their university partner.

The mean distance between the firms and their university partner was 76 km, which in the context of the UK represents approximately just over one hour's driving time. Based on this average distance, the participating firms and their partners were close enough for travel to be not be too arduous or time-consuming. Considering this evidence, for the bulk of the SMEs, face-to-face communication with their university partner would have been a straightforward exercise.

Table 7.1   Details of the SMEs' collaborative partnerships

Alias	Location	University Partner	Distance (km)[a]
Arc-Tech	Greater London	Coventry University	152.0
Blue Design	South Yorkshire	Manchester Metropolitan University	64.8
Black-Electronics	South Yorkshire	Sheffield Hallam University	3.3
Blue Finance	Perthshire	University of the West of Scotland	42.7
Brown Media	Greater Manchester	Salford University	13.0
Cyan-Soft	Inner London	London Metropolitan University	4.0
Data-Tech	Dorset	Bournemouth University	45.0
Edu-Tech	Cheshire	University of Wolverhampton	94.5
Gen-Tech	Greater London	Birmingham University	176.0
Green-Soft	Cambridgeshire	Anglia Ruskin University	16.4
Indigo-Consultants	North Yorkshire	Brunel University	340.0
Magenta-Design	South Yorkshire	Sheffield Hallam University	1.3
Magnolia-Support	Somerset	University of Exeter	57.5
Marine Consultants	Devon	University of Exeter	68.5
Mine-Tech	Warwickshire	Southampton University	170.0
Motor-Tech	Shropshire	Glyndwr University	0.8
Patient-Tech	London	University of Westminster	11.2
Pink-Soft	Warwickshire	Aston University	38.1
Purple Media	East Riding of Yorkshire	University of Durham	196.0
Red-Soft	Cornwall	University of Plymouth	96.1
White-Electronics	Derbyshire	University of Nottingham	20.6
Yellow-Soft	Gloucestershire	University of the West of England	61.2

Note: [a] Distances are measured as the fastest road route using Google Maps.

However, while this data suggests that SMEs mostly chose a university partner that was physically close there was also very little reference to the location of the university by the SMEs, in terms of the partner selection process bar an occasional reference to engaging with local partners through the firms' local networks, or an acknowledgement that the university was conveniently located for communication purposes. In terms of partner selection and an assessment of their credibility, the analysis suggests that the spatial proximity of the partner was not a significant factor.

Having established with whom SMEs collaborate, attention now turns to why they selected these partners. While the analysis reveals that a broad set of factors brought the partners together, underpinning the partner selection process was a reliance on networks and networking activity to facilitate their formation. A diverse set of networking practices are utilised by SMEs to develop these links, particularly focused on two specific activities; (1) using existing contacts to develop the collaborative link, or (2) developing links with universities through new contacts. Thus, collaborative links with university partners are established through both strong and weak ties. The following quote from Yellow-Soft illustrates the view of the process of partner selection:

> It was a kind of a networking opportunity where we were aware of several people who could help us in the business, through discussions with them, looking at what research they were doing, looking at what KTP offered us, it was a kind of natural fit that we chose to go with that university. (Yellow-Soft)

In cases whereby SMEs used existing contacts to develop a link, networking activities involved targeting university partners with which they already had a relationship. Therefore, SMEs are able to draw on contacts that had been developed through previous interactions. This was not just where they had previously worked together, but also where entrepreneurs had studied at the university (contacting ex-lecturers), had friends in academia, or exploited links with academics that they knew through trade associations, conferences, or industry events. The fact that SMEs can draw on their existing contacts with universities in order to select a partner is not necessarily surprising, as the evidence from Chapter 6 shows that many were familiar with universities through a broad range of both formal and informal interactions. Therefore, universities are not necessarily regarded as remote organisations by SMEs as several possessed the necessary contacts within universities to exploit for these purposes.

Indeed, these existing contacts sometimes represent long-standing relationships; for example, for Patient-Tech and White-Electronics, these links were relationships that had endured over a significant time-period. They noted that:

> [The academic was] an old university colleague, so it's a network, and I had ... I lost touch for a while, but he turned up and we're back in touch and the idea formed from that. (Patient-Tech)

> When I first met [the academic] he was my lecturer many, many years ago ... I've kept in touch with him all the time, yeah. Yeah, I mean over the years I've done quite a lot of projects with the University, you know, going back 25 years. (White-Electronics)

Table 7.2   *Summary of approaches to finding a university partner*

Alias	University Partner	Method of Finding University Partner
Arc-Tech	Coventry University	Networking – existing contact
Black-Electronics	Sheffield Hallam University	Recommendation
Blue Design	Manchester Metropolitan University	Networking – new contact
Blue Finance	University of the West of Scotland	Networking – existing contact
Brown Media	Salford University	Contacted by university
Cyan-Soft	London Metropolitan University	Networking – new contact
Data-Tech	Bournemouth University	Google search
Edu-Tech	University of Wolverhampton	Recommendation
Gen-Tech	Birmingham University	Networking – existing contact
Green-Soft	Anglia Ruskin University	Contacted by university
Indigo-Consultants	Brunel University	Networking – existing contact
Magenta-Design	Sheffield Hallam University	Networking – new contact
Magnolia-Support	University of Exeter	Networking – new contact
Marine Consultants	University of Exeter	Contacted by university
Mine-Tech	Southampton University	Networking – existing contact
Motor-Tech	Glyndwr University	Recommendation
Patient-Tech	University of Westminster	Networking – existing contact
Pink-Soft	Aston University	Networking – new contact
Purple Media	University of Durham	Networking – new contact
Red-Soft	University of Plymouth	Recommendation
White-Electronics	University of Nottingham	Networking – existing contact
Yellow-Soft	University of the West of England	Networking – new contact

For other SMEs, the process of partner selection is based around building new contacts. In these cases, SMEs use their networking capabilities to initiate a search for a partner that typically utilises existing ties to generate potential leads or uses them as a sounding board to uncover potential partners. This process is illustrated in the following quote from Purple Media:

> So I mean we looked around at where the best universities were for Statistics and Maths … by asking around [my network]. Nothing scientific. No modelling involved, I'm afraid. Just by asking around where the good universities were. (Purple Media)

Therefore, if contacts with universities did not exist, the first point of contact for the participating SMEs was their existing network ties in order to seek potential partners.

Existing network ties are also important where the SMEs' choice of a university partner was prompted by a recommendation. These recommendations originated from a variety of sources, such as the spouse of the managing director. Furthermore, where recommendations came from outside their network, for example through the funding bodies responsible for the overall programme (the former Technology Strategy Board, or local Knowledge Transfer Partnership (KTP) advisors), the firms sought to identify if any actors within their existing networks were working with the university. When they are able to identify mutual connections, SMEs then tend to feel more confident that a university is an appropriate partner. In addition, this process is also utilised where SMEs are contacted by the university partner directly. In these cases, firms then sought to identify a mutual contact from their own networks to assist them in selecting a partner. This led to them collaborating with a university with whom they had an indirect relationship.

While the location of a partner is not explicitly highlighted as an important factor in the partner selection process, local collaborations appear to be the preferred course of action among SMEs as several mentioned that the distance between them and their partners was relatively small. This position is, however, nuanced by the fact that minimising the distance between the partners is not the main attraction of pursuing a local collaborative link with a university. Instead, it is more likely to be a result of the existing spatial scope of the networking efforts of the firms and the fact that they focus on their immediate geographic area. The evidence then suggests that spatial proximity with their university partner has an indirect influence on the partner selection process. The following quote from Yellow-Soft illustrates this argument:

> So we had a relationship through a couple of people at the University, based on our marketing background locality, Bristol is probably forty minutes away from us. (Yellow-Soft)

Conversely, there were several instances of SMEs developing collaborative links with non-local universities. In these cases, there is no suggestion that the distance involved acted as a barrier to the tie forming. In these cases, the SMEs' prior networking activity had a greater spatial scope. For example, the tie that formed over the greatest distance – that of Indigo-Consultants – was based on an existing relationship. In this case, it was purely coincidence that the academic partner had family ties near to the location of the firm, so travelling to the area was not a problem. Furthermore, for Mine-Tech, which also engaged in a long-distance collaboration, the relationship was the result of an existing link. In this case, the fact that it was based on an enduring relationship was considered to negate any issues of distance.

Indeed, the average distance of 76 km between partners highlights the fact that these collaborative relationships were not hyper-local in character, meaning they would all have involved some travel when face-to-face interaction was necessary. Even with the local bias within the firms' networks, collaboration mostly involved a degree of travel. Given this, the absence of high degrees of spatial proximity between partners during the project cannot be considered to be a constraint on these firms. In fact, the firms often expressed the opinion that meetings could be held when necessary, it depended on the needs of the project rather than the physical distance between the partners. For example, Arc-Tech typified this attitude with their comment that:

> If we want to call a meeting, people are prepared to travel. We've been over there a few times, they come over here, so it's not ... you know, it's obviously easier if you were a bit closer but it's a do-able kind of distance. (Arc-Tech)

This quote suggests a desire to minimise distance between the firm and its partner but a willingness to work around this distance to realise the project's objectives.

Based on this evidence, for SMEs, unlocking the ivory tower appears, at least initially, to be a relatively straightforward process as all were able to find a partner given the existence of a broad range of networking opportunities. In identifying a university partner, the SMEs either exploited existing ties, strong and weak, or sought to develop new ties, reflecting the importance of all types of ties regardless of strength.

Yet, despite the reliance upon networks and networking to develop these collaborative links, uncertainties did indeed exist among the SMEs at the outset of the collaboration. Firstly, these uncertainties focused on the nature of the collaboration process and the associated bureaucracy. For some of the participating firms, the uncertainties stemmed from not knowing the way the projects were supposed to function. Indeed, despite a general familiarity with universities, there was still room for doubt regarding the systems and protocols of the project. This was illustrated by the following quote from Mine-Tech:

> we didn't really know how the KTP system worked in the first instance. 'Cause it was new to us. Completely new to us. (Mine-Tech)

The bureaucracy associated with university collaboration may also cause some uncertainty for SMEs. This is because SMEs were used to working quickly, responding to changes, and working to tight deadlines. As a result, the lead times for securing the project funding, coupled with the form filling, and waiting for responses and feedback, proved frustrating. Having found a partner for their project, firms subsequently faced a wait to see if it would be funded when they wished to immediately pursue the project.

The second area of uncertainty among the respondents focused on how the relationship would work and whether the partners were indeed compatible. The firms saw one of their key strengths as agility and were concerned around the capacity of their university partner to work in a similar fashion.

In summary, the partner selection process was underpinned by a general networking approach, with several different processes at work in terms of how this networking was undertaken. In addition, while uncertainties were still present for several of the firms, the process of partner selection was relatively straightforward in that the participating SMEs were all able to find a partner. However, despite the relative simplicity of the partner selection process, *ex post*, there was a recognition that, for some firms, the search process was rather myopic in nature. For example, Green-Soft reflected on their search process:

> they were the only ones that we had any meaningful discussions with and I guess in reality it really should have happened the other way round. We should have decided that we wanted a KTP and then gone out and selected the right partner to work with on that KTP, whereas that wasn't how it happened at all. You know, it's easy to look back in hindsight and say actually that was probably in part our fault. But on the other hand we didn't know any better at that stage in our development as a company. So we just sort of went with what was in front of us because it seemed reasonably good and positive. (Green-Soft)

Therefore, a lack of prior contacts with universities results in a rather narrow search process. This, in turn, can lead to the risk of becoming locked-in with an unsuitable partner. This introduces the second question that is dealt with in this chapter, how did the SMEs assess the suitability of the university partner?

7.3   ASSESSING CREDIBILITY

The findings have established that the process of partner selection is based on networking activity, but this has only explained the identification of a potential partner rather than their choice. Therefore, in order to select the partner, SMEs are required to assess their credibility. Credibility in this sense regards the promise of a partner and the extent to which the firm considers they will deliver the required knowledge and expertise in the course of collaboration.

From Chapter 4, recall that John and Martin's (1984) framework for analysing the credibility of potential external partners has previously been used to examine the means through which SMEs assess the credibility of potential partners (see Johnston and Huggins 2018). This framework operationalises credibility through five factors: realism of expertise, specificity of knowledge, consistency of knowledge, comprehensiveness of research, and validity of research (John and Martin 1984; Menon and Varadarajan 1992) and is again used below to analyse the factors that highlighted the credibility of the university as a collaborative partner.

With respect to understanding and assessing credibility in the context of U–I links, the first factor, *realism,* is based around the firm's perceptions of the extent to which an academic partner's knowledge fits the prospective project. Here, credibility comes from the ability of the partner to highlight the fact that they possess knowledge that may be relevant to the project. Secondly, *specificity* refers to the academic partner's ability to stipulate a focus for the firm's project, thereby confirming their ability to take the idea and develop it. Thirdly, *consistency* highlights the existence of a clear logic in the academic partner's plan and whether it clearly applies to the firm's project. Fourthly, *comprehensiveness* refers to a lack of apparent gaps in the academic partner's knowledge from the firms' point of view. Finally, *validity* refers to the fact that the academic partner has made valid assumptions with respect to the firm's project (John and Martin 1984). Furthermore, credibility is typically conceptualised as having two dimensions, source credibility and information credibility (Gupta and Wilemon 1988), that is, the importance of *who* is communicating a particular message, as well as *what* is being communicated.

The findings so far highlight the fact that SMEs are driven by an awareness of the need to find the right expertise to address the capability gap they faced. This means they need to be confident that the academic partner is able to solve their problem for them, so that they would then feel comfortable that they were working with the right people. Consequently, there is a clear objective among SMEs to select a partner that was appropriate to their needs. This is highlighted in the following quotation from Black-Electronics, who noted that

> the business has to be sure that the university has exceptional academic standard, be best in class in that sector. And ensure that everybody around it has been fed by that exceptional academic standard ... you have to learn that. (Black-Electronics)

In terms of assessing the credibility of their potential partners, the analysis suggests that this is a process most SMEs go through when forming a link with a university. Therefore, nearly all the firms made at least some assessment of the potential of their collaborative partner to deliver on their promised contribution. Interestingly, when exploring the assessment of credibility, the analysis reveals that the firms did not necessarily see themselves as collaborating with a *university* but with an individual *academic.* Assessments of the credibility of a potential partner most commonly focus on the individual academic they would be working alongside and not the university as an organisation. In terms of assessing credibility, the SMEs clearly focus on the individual as its source.

This individual agent approach is perhaps unsurprising given the importance of inter-personal links highlighted in the findings so far. Section 7.2 highlighted the importance of networks and networking in the process of partner selection, which in turn are based around factors such as previous contacts and interactions. Therefore, assessing credibility took a highly personalised approach with SMEs usually focusing on individuals. In addition, when contacts did not exist, the reliance on the firms' existing network contacts also meant that a personal recommendation was likely.

The foremost indicator of credibility was the completeness and realism of an individual academic's knowledge. This is manifested in the extent to which the firms believed that the proposed academic supervisor of the project possessed a broad knowledge of the relevant field and that it was also closely related to the firms' projects. Therefore, SMEs judge the ability of their potential academic partner on whether or not they considered that the level of knowledge and expertise is simultaneously broad enough to have an overview of the field in question but also specific enough so that it fits the projects the firms are pursuing. In this respect, SMEs are clearly thorough in terms of ensuring their partners would fit their project.

SMEs typically interpret the completeness and realism of a potential academic partner's knowledge through observing labels associated with them, typically their titles and experience. While this information is freely available through university websites or other public portals, this method of judging credibility could be viewed as more naive than strategic in intent as the SMEs were simply observing their job title or the department in which the academic worked. As a result, credibility is generally assumed from noting that the potential partner is a professor in a relevant discipline or works in a department reflecting the area of expertise they were seeking.

Using this method means that SMES primarily take the completeness and realism of the knowledge of the academic at face value from their credentials. That is not to say that, for example, a professor of Mathematics may not be an appropriate partner for a firm seeking knowledge in this area. Yet Mathematics is a broad field, therefore access to specific knowledge may not be guaranteed. However, these characteristics are at least observable and understandable to the SMEs, highlighting to them that they are looking in the right areas for a partner or developing a link with individuals in broadly the right area.

SMEs tend to follow up opening contacts with a face-to-face meeting to 'sense-check' their initial judgements. For example, the following quote from Green-Soft describes how their initial scepticism vanished on meeting their potential partner and learning about his career and ensuing knowledge and expertise:

> One of the things that actually convinced me very early on was, and again I believe this was a very smart sales guy from [the university] that basically did this, he introduced us to the [academic] that would be, if we proceeded with the project, who was going to be the academic supervisor of the KTP ... And I guess I changed more or less instantly from being very, very sceptical about the relationship to meeting [the academic] and realising well, wow, this guy has actually been out in the big wide world; he's done a lot of quite heavy-hitting jobs in industry for some pretty major organisations; he's worked in places all around the world, this is somebody who could be extremely helpful and useful to the business. (Green-Soft)

Again, the inter-personal nature of these links is highlighted through the importance of the characteristics of the academic partner. To the firms, it was the characteristics of the individual that signalled the fact that the academic partner had the right knowledge and skills for the project. The precedence of inter-personal relationships over inter-organisational relationships was also highlighted through evidence that long-standing relationships with academics provided the respondents with an insight into the field in which they operated and, accordingly, their expertise. While SMEs focus on factors such as titles as a signal of an academic's ability to the firms, when this is accompanied by the existence of a shared history between the parties, it allows the respondent to *understand* the partner's work in the field and confirm to them that it fitted their need.

> I'd just known [the academic] for a long time there. I just knew he knew a lot about [our area of business]. He'd written a lot of papers. He'd speak at conferences. (Magenta-Design)

It is noteworthy that the importance of the individual again comes to the fore here. The respondents are not talking about the characteristics and capabilities of a university but the person with whom they would be working in the future. Hence, for SMEs, credibility typically refers to the individual rather than the institution, the person and not the university.

Furthermore, experience and familiarity of an academic's work allows SMEs to interpret the realism of their potential partner's knowledge in terms of how it relates to their proposed project. This means that SMEs possess an understanding of how the potential partner's work relates to the field in which the firm was operating. The following quotes illustrate this process:

> Well [the academic partner's] background was in the field ... that we were looking at, and we've got some experience here in that field as well so, you know, from talking to people and from the papers that are produced and the types of things they talk about, you can get a good feel for their expertise. (Mine-Tech)

[T]he [academic] concerned had published papers, which we read and thought were appropriate and, you know, evidenced the fact that she had a good knowledge of the kind of area that we were interested in really, in terms of carrying out a kind of a study. [T]hrough discussion and meeting with her and also [her head of department], who's got a good reputation in the area, we felt that there was a kind of matching of interests ... she's actually carrying out studies that feed into studying government standards. (Arc-Tech)

Accordingly, in these examples, a shared background provides SMEs with the ability to judge credibility through assessing the realism of a potential partner's knowledge because they were able to understand it. For example, the following quote from Mine-Tech illustrates how the firm's background was useful:

[Mine-Tech has] come out of academia really. So ... the guys who started ... [the business] worked at the Institute of Oceanographic Sciences in Surrey a long time ago now. So we all come, initially, from an academic background. (Mine-Tech)

Despite the general reliance on credentials and titles as signals of realism, and therefore credibility, there were those who do not value these. For example, some were not convinced of the value of academic research in their area,

I think actually, in our field, the research isn't particularly cutting edge and our interest is in the applied end, of which there isn't a huge amount. There's some, but it tends to be repeated. So, the benefit is more the sort of, the kudos by association. (Indigo-Consultants)

Assessing credibility through a person's credentials may not always be enough and what may appear to some entrepreneurs as legitimate qualifications are seen by others as unsatisfactory. Therefore, there may be limits to the importance of realism as a means of judging credibility. While it may provide a relatively trustworthy signal of credibility, it is not a guarantee that the partner will be appropriate to the firm's needs. Indeed, some entrepreneurs considered that it was only possible to accurately assess the compatibility of their university partner and evaluate their appropriateness through actually working together. Blue Finance typified this stance when they observed that their proposed partner

was a professor, he was a technology professor, and he had the required skills and he headed a department doing that, but clearly it seemed it was just about getting the money for his Department, because, I'm being absolutely honest in this, I did not see him once after the contract was signed ... unless you're actually doing a project jointly with them, you just don't know and maybe universities need to know more about business and businesses need to know more about universities. It may be more of a two-way process. (Blue Finance)

In addition to assessing credibility through completeness and realism, SMEs also assess their potential partners in terms of specificity of their knowledge, that is, the extent to which they are able to stipulate a specific focus for their project based on their expertise. When an academic is able to do this, SMEs interpret it as a positive signal of the individual's credibility. This process is highlighted in the following quote from Edu-Tech, who noted that prior to their initial meetings with the prospective partner the individual concerned

> had done his homework, so he came along and he knew something about the business, he'd quickly grasped what we were trying to do, was asking the right sort of questions. Even in the first meeting he was talking about the kind of things he might do with the associate. So that just builds confidence. So that's what made us comfortable, I guess. (Edu-Tech)

As this indicates, the firm was positively influenced in their assessment of the partner's credibility through their ability to engage in the project, clearly highlighting an understanding of what they were trying to achieve. In these cases, SMEs utilise *both* source credibility and information credibility, through focusing on who was conveying the message but also what they were saying.

However, there were also examples where SMEs' lack of knowledge (which was the primary reason for taking an open innovation approach in the first place) also meant that they were open to relying on the interpretations of the academic in order to explain potential solutions or directions. The following quote from Purple Media highlights this naivety, as the firm's lack of knowledge and expertise in the field of statistics is highlighted:

> Well we aren't mathematicians but when we first started talking to him, his first question was, 'What type of statistical modelling do you want to use?' And we had no idea there were different types of statistical modelling. So actually it was just about having a general conversation with him and his engagement in the project and his willingness and openness to give us advice from the start about how we might approach the project I think was really helpful. (Purple Media)

Therefore, SMEs may find the input from the academic to be helpful, but their response in turn highlights their own ignorance of the area. This then pours doubt on the ability of the firm to accurately assess specificity. Indeed, as specificity was not as prevalent as realism for highlighting the credibility of a potential partner it suggests there may be more barriers to using this approach, particularly as it is not as immediately 'obvious' to the firms and requires interpretation.

There were also drawbacks to relying on specificity as a means of evaluating credibility. For example, potential partners may be able to stipulate a focus for the project and engage with the firm's idea, but it did not necessarily mean that they could or would deliver on these promises. This was the case for Gen-Tech, where the academic was judged as credible through suggesting ways to tackle the firm's project, but in reality, could not deliver.

> They [the academic partner] said oh, you've got to try this, you've got to do this, you've got to do this, you've got to do this; we've got this equipment that's going to help that. Do you know what, that's science. You have to … some people will say, we can do it, and then they can't. Others will say they can't do it, and they can do it. Others say you've got to do some kind of empirical development of it and we'll either get lucky or we won't. What happened with us is that we embarked on this KTP in good faith and whilst we very, very much liked the KTP student, who was excellent, we didn't get anything from the University. There was no knowledge transfer. (Gen-Tech)

The situation faced by Gen-Tech highlights the need for experience to judge credibility through specificity. SMEs are required to understand what is being said by a potential partner, interpret this in relation to their proposed project, and, subsequently, make an informed decision on whether this course of action is feasible and desirable.

Further examination of the means by which SMEs examine the credibility of their partner highlights the fact that those judging credibility through specificity typically had greater levels of previous experience of working with a university in a formal capacity (Table 7.3). Therefore, there appears to be a link between this type of experience and an ability to judge whether or not an academic is able to suggest an appropriate direction for the project.

Beyond the completeness, realism, and specificity of a potential partner's knowledge, the analysis reveals that SMEs also assess the credibility of potential partners through association. This again focuses on source credibility but is nuanced in terms of seeking shared network connections with the potential partners. This process highlights the importance of networks at this stage of the process; allowing the firms to indirectly observe the credibility of the potential partner but relying on information from other sources. For example, in the case of Brown Media, where two universities approached the firm through cold calling, they chose to partner with the university that was working with shared connections.

Similarly, Arc-Tech and Magnolia-Support relied upon association to assess the credibility of their potential partners. In these cases, it was not about seeking common network ties, but observing whom the university had previously worked with and then assessing their stature as a means of judging their likely effectiveness. The credibility of a potential academic partner is not always judged from within the networks but also through observing the fact that they are working with well-known and respected firms. For example, Rolls Royce is often cited as an example of a top company to work with, and

Table 7.3   *Methods of searching and assessing partners and prior university interaction*

Alias	Search Method	Method of Assessing Credibility of Partner	Previous Contact with Universities
Arc-Tech	Networking – existing contact	Realism/completeness/ specificity	Formal
Black-Electronics	Recommendation	Other	None
Blue Design	Networking – new contact	Other	Formal
Blue Finance	Networking – existing contact	Realism	Formal/informal
Brown Media	Contacted by university	Other	None
Cyan-Soft	Networking – new contact	Realism	Market based
Data-Tech	Search engine	Other	None
Edu-Tech	Recommendation	Specificity	Formal
Gen-Tech	Networking – existing contact	Realism/specificity	None
Green-Soft	Contacted by university	Realism	Formal
Indigo-Consultants	Networking – existing contact	Realism	Informal
Magenta-Design	Networking – new contact	Realism	Formal/informal
Magnolia-Support	Networking – new contact	Other	None
Marine Consultants	Contacted by university	Realism/completeness	Formal
Mine-Tech	Networking – existing contact	Realism/completeness	Formal
Motor-Tech	Recommendation	Realism	None
Patient-Tech	Networking – existing contact	Realism	Informal
Pink-Soft	Networking – new contact	Realism	None
Purple Media	Networking – new contact	Specificity	Formal
Red-Soft	Recommendation	Other	Informal
White-Electronics	Networking – existing contact	Realism/completeness	Formal
Yellow-Soft	Networking – new contact	Realism/specificity	Formal

therefore there is credibility by association where a university is working with them. Consequently, there are cases where SMEs assess credibility through indirect means rather than through focusing on the partner alone.

In the case of Black-Electronics, credibility was judged through the fact that the university partner was recommended by the funding body. Based on this, they were content to rely on the recommendation in order to find a partner and therefore took it as a sign that the partner was appropriate to their needs. Therefore, the words or actions of other trusted actors can be important indirect signals of credibility to firms.

Finally, while the analysis suggests that the participating firms make use of a wide range of factors to assess the credibility of the universities, highlighting its importance to the partner selection process, there was one case where the firm made no assessment of the credibility of their potential university partner. For Data-Tech the process of partner selection appears to have been more of a shot in the dark in that the firm relied on what they stated as 'blind faith' that the partnership would work. The firm identified a partner and then formed the collaboration, all the while merely hoping it would work successfully.

7.4   DISCUSSION AND CONCLUSIONS

The selection of a university partner and the concurrent assessment of their credibility has been identified as an important part of the formation of collaborative linkages between SMEs and universities (Johnston and Huggins 2018). The findings presented in this chapter provide clear insights into these processes, underscoring their key features as well as their complexities and nuances. In terms of partner selection, networks and networking again emerge as significant drivers in the formation of these U–I links. Consequently, significant inter-personal perspective is evident in this process, particularly as the assessment of credibility is judged at an individual, not organisational, level, examining the person rather than the university. The findings presented in this chapter provide further evidence that the formation of university links is a socio-technical process (Al-Tabbaa and Ankrah 2016, 2019), underpinned by a reliance on both relational and cognitive factors to facilitate their development.

The prominence of networking activities indicates that these SMEs were well connected, possessing useful linkages that enabled them to identify and connect with a university partner. Therefore, it appears that the firms possessed the required network capital to allow them to develop, curate, and maintain calculative links with individuals for exploitation when required. This evidence corroborates the arguments of Eisenhardt and Schoonhoven (1996), who suggested that firms in 'strong social positions' are best placed to develop strategic alliances. Indeed, within the U–I links literature network embeddedness has been found to simplify the process of developing these collaborations (Thune and Gulbrandsen 2014). The findings also echo the logic that the formation of alliances are driven by both 'strategic needs and social opportunities' (Eisenhardt and Schoonhoven 1996). Combining the findings from both this and the preceding chapter establishes the need for knowledge among the firms, coupled with the opportunities to connect through networking, and the use of inter-personal connections to establish the alliance with a university.

The social characterisation of the process of forming SME–university links is predominantly derived directly and indirectly from a reliance upon networks and networking, or inter-personal relationships, to identify and select a university partner. Therefore, it is very much relational in character, concentrated around the ability of SMEs to connect to an external actor in order to collaborate (Steinmo 2015; Steinmo and Rasmussen 2018). Secondly, the technical characterisation is derived from the need for SMEs to be able to identify a partner who possesses the appropriate knowledge and expertise through identifying and understanding their characteristics and assessing the credibility, or perceived ability, to deliver.

This highlights the importance of network capital (Huggins 2010), as within these inter-personal networks there exists an element of calculation as the participating firms maintained a broad set of ties that proved useful in pursuing an existing university contact through to a formal collaboration or developing a new university contact with whom to collaborate. Therefore, these results suggest that Eisenhardt and Schoonhoven's (1996) arguments are best augmented to propose that a strong social position coupled with strong networking capabilities is the key to the development of alliances with universities.

Importantly, this socio-technical characterisation suggests that U–I links cannot be considered as a pure market transaction. Indeed, the findings show that while SMEs clearly intend to work with the most suitable partner, a university or academic with the appropriate knowledge and expertise, the process does not resemble a market transaction as the firms were not buying knowledge from the universities. Indeed, the SMEs' motivations were focused on resources, specifically the need to address the lack of knowledge and expertise within the firms required to accomplish the goals of their projects (Yasuda 2005).

The lack of a 'market' for university knowledge means that traditional signals of quality, such as price, are not available to SMEs as a tool to assess potential partners. Indeed, as Eisenhardt and Schoonhoven (1996) argue, an efficient market for knowledge will therefore provide a mechanism for firms to judge its quality and value. In a typical market this may assist with judging the quality of potential partners or their potential to address their project. However, with no market-based indicators to judge the potential quality of a partner's knowledge or expertise, and no concrete means to assess their credibility, the firms have had to rely upon a different set of mechanisms.

During the process of partner selection, SMEs seek to assess the credibility of the universities through several means. The findings highlight the predominance of source credibility, that is, the SMEs focused on those delivering the message rather than the message itself. This assessment is made at the inter-personal rather than inter-organisational level, with SMEs assessing the individual academic and not the university. Credibility is typically evaluated through assessing the realism and completeness of an individual's knowledge, achieved through observing the credentials of the potential partner. Based on this evidence, it appears that from the perspective of SMEs, unlocking the ivory tower does not require an understanding of the whole organisation but can be achieved through focusing on the people with whom they wish to work.

From an SME perspective, large organisations such as universities may be difficult to understand and assess holistically. The firms' search process may not necessarily be focused on a university's knowledge and expertise but a means of accessing knowledge through an individual they can interact with. Hence, the formation of a university link is very much reliant upon social factors (Lauvås and Steinmo 2019; Steinmo 2015).

The findings also reveal that a smaller group of SMEs were assessing credibility through utilising a combination of source and information credibility. Generally, these firms were those that had greater experience of previously working with a university, indicating that they have developed or possess the relational and cognitive capacity to engage with both the academic and their knowledge, that is, the source and their message. Those SMEs with greater social, technical, and organisational proximity were able to use a broader set of factors for assessing their potential partner (Knoben and Oerlemans 2006).

This greater experience of interacting with universities allows a more active process of credibility assessment. Therefore, the relational aspect of the formation of SME–university collaborative links is complemented by the cognitive aspect in the partner selection process. For example, organisational proximity, through shared working practices (Knoben and Oerlemans 2006), was developed where SMEs had worked with a university previously, allowing a degree of familiarity to develop. The ability to assess credibility using the specificity of knowledge may rely on the existence of organisational proximity as it is SMEs with prior collaboration with a university that typically utilise this method. In addition, greater levels of technological proximity, that is, expertise in a similar field and a shared scientific language (Cowan and Jonard 2003; Cowan, David, and Foray 2000), mean SMEs can gain a more nuanced understanding of their partner's potential.

This understanding allows firms to broaden the focus of their assessment from the basis of the potential partner's knowledge to how they would apply that knowledge. This allows a different assessment of credibility from realism and completeness to the partners' engagement in the SMEs' projects. In these cases, the SME can judge whether the potential partner was engaging with their project through specifying a direction to take, thereby highlighting the usefulness of the knowledge and expertise.

The extent to which proximities exist between partners may vary. For example, working with a university in an informal manner may lead to the development of less organisational proximity than engaging in several successful formal collaborations. In addition, technological proximity also varies according to the prowess of SMEs in terms of their understanding of a field, as it is clear that some SMEs have a better understanding of the field than others. These results, therefore, highlight variations in proximities between the SMEs and the universities, suggesting that they can be considered to be more of a continuum than a dichotomous construct. This is illustrated in Figure 7.1.

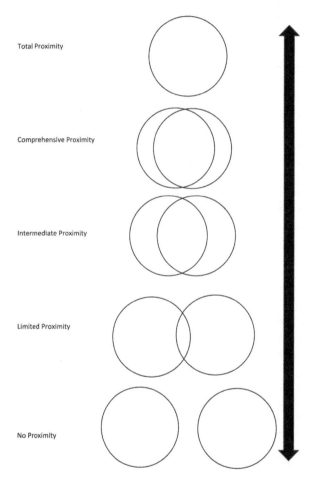

Figure 7.1   Degrees of proximity – revisited

Using organisational proximity as an example, Figure 7.1 illustrates that in the context of U–I collaboration, organisational proximity can vary substantially. Using a Venn diagram to highlight commonalities between the actors, there may be cases where two actors have no experience of working together, no common methods or working culture, resulting in a significant distance between the two and no proximity, illustrated by the separation of the circles. However, where a firm has some experience of interacting with universities, the proximity may be described as intermediate, illustrated by the partial overlap of the circles. Significant experience of collaboration may ensure proximity is comprehensive in nature, highlighting a near merger of organisational cultures and practices. Finally, total organisational proximity would entail actors working within a single firm or university department, represented by a single circle as the overlap is perfect.

There are also examples whereby relational and cognitive factors play a less prominent role in the partner selection process for SMEs. For example, networking ability was not required where the SME received a direct approach from a university, or they were just 'clutching at straws' in seeking any partner. However, in these cases the relational aspect can still be regarded as important since while direct networking was not a factor in these cases, their network ties still played a prominent role in the process by allowing an assessment of credibility to be performed. Again, this shows that there are multiple ways a firm may engage with a university. Indeed, as with variations in the proximities, the narrative also highlighted the strength of the SMEs' network ties varied too (Granovetter 1973). Importantly, the evidence also highlighted the strength of weak ties, whereby the SMEs are able to use their broader network to generate links to universities where none existed.

In these cases, SMEs make indirect assessments of credibility. Firstly, the opinions of those recommending the university are taken as a sign of credibility. In addition, their broader network of ties allows them to assess the credibility of potential partners. For example, there were examples of SMEs observing with whom the universities worked in order to judge their credibility. This outcome highlights the importance of an alliance portfolio, whereby SMEs are engaged in broad networks that offer a wide range of relationships (Van Wijk and Nadolska 2020). The broadness of the network then appears to allow SMEs to assess and understand university partners' characteristics either directly or by association.

The findings highlight the importance of context in understanding the formation of these SME–university links. The evidence suggests that variations in relational and cognitive factors may require SMEs to use varying means of building network ties and assessing the credibility of the potential partner. Indeed, this is highlighted by the fact that the participating SMEs were all able to unlock the ivory tower and successfully find a university partner.

Despite the importance of geographic proximity to the formation of U–I links noted in the extant literature (Crescenzi, Filippetti, and Iammarino 2017; D'Este, Guy, and Iammarino 2013; Johnston and Huggins 2016; Muscio 2013), there is little explicit reference to distances in the findings. Indeed, the evidence presented in Table 7.1 shows that while these collaborations occurred over a range of distances, the average distance between partners of 76 km suggests that they are relatively local collaborations. Therefore, the prima facie characteristics of these collaborative partnerships suggest that physical closeness may be a factor in the formation of these links. In general, while a slight preference for local universities was revealed in the analysis, this did not appear to be a deliberate strategy.

SMEs appear to base their search strategy on local networks not because of the perceived benefits of local connections or a feeling that they were part of any kind of broader ecosystem such as a cluster. It does not appear as if these collaborations were the result of tapping into a local milieu, and, in Marshallian terms, there was no feeling among firms that knowledge was 'in the air', or resulting from a spillover process (Jaffe 1989; Marshall 1970). Instead SMEs are more likely to rely on existing networks which are typically local in character as the starting point of their search process. The ability to network locally may, in some cases, provide an opportunity to assess a potential partner, and the findings suggest that it plays a limited role as there was only one case where local interactions were mentioned as a means for developing a collaborative link with a university.

As a result, the local focus of the networking efforts of the participating SMEs may be due to the resource constraints they faced, resulting in a limited spatial horizon over which to conduct their search activities. Furthermore, where the university partner made the first contact with the firm, the distance between the two partners was less than the average, suggesting that in these cases the observed closeness may be due to the university partner's local search activities and their focus on working with local firms. This is perhaps unsurprising as many universities state that part of their remit is to boost innovation within their locality.

In summary, this chapter has examined the partner selection process and associated assessments of their credibility for SMEs and found that this process varies widely. The findings outlined the fact that the formation of these collaborative links with universities relies heavily on relational and cognitive factors, supported by networking activities and proximities between the partners. However, there is not a single route to selecting a university partner as several variations were identified and the findings highlight the importance of context. For example, there is no single way to assess credibility as this appears to depend upon the level of previous interaction with universities. Furthermore, some SMEs were happy to rely on others. Importantly, this assessment of credibility appears to apply to the individual rather than the university. Therefore, while the narrative highlights the fact that the assessment of credibility does take place in the partner selection process, there are a multitude of methods for its undertaking.

This process illustrates the existence of bounded rationality in the assessment of credibility. This is because the firms cannot have perfect knowledge or foresight in terms of partner selection and the mechanisms for assessing credibility are not scientifically rigorous but more rules of thumb. Of course it cannot be expected that firms will make an accurate judgement every time, only that they make the best possible judgement they can at a particular time given the information they possess and the capacity to assess it. Therefore, this can be considered to be a process of effectuation (Sarasvathy 2001).

Given the non-market nature of these activities this partner selection process reflects the social foundations that exists in place of a pricing mechanism. Indeed, the suggestion that the partner selection process is focused on the individual rather than the university has important consequences for a market-based system for university knowledge. Therefore, any pricing mechanism for university knowledge may not be entirely useful alone since the system would be at the organisational level. Furthermore, given the bounded decision-making process of SMEs, it appears pertinent to question whether there exists information that is sufficient in terms of depth and accessibility that would smooth the process of partner selection. The findings suggest that SMEs ignore 'traditional' academic rankings metrics and, therefore, available information on universities is either not useful or inaccessible to them. Furthermore, if the process of U–I collaboration were to be realigned so that it was more of a market-based system, would pricing reflect individuals or the university?

8. Absorbing and utilising knowledge

8.1 INTRODUCTION

The findings so far have highlighted the processes that underpin the initial stages of the projects, that is, the generation of ideas and the selection of a university partner. To develop an in-depth insight into the entire process of U–I collaboration, this chapter moves on from the formation to the function of these projects over the course of the collaboration. In doing so, the chapter sheds light on the use and absorption of university knowledge by SMEs. As this is relatively overlooked within the extant literature, the chapter seeks to add some novel insights into the processes that drive U–I collaboration.

In order to present a clear understanding of these factors, the chapter first tackles the utilisation of knowledge by SMEs, examining who uses the knowledge within the firms. Following this, the chapter then focuses on the absorption of the knowledge into the firm and the overall learning process.

8.2 UTILISING UNIVERSITY KNOWLEDGE IN SMES

This section presents an analysis that explores who uses the knowledge generated in the course of the collaborations within SMEs, enabling greater light to be shone on the workings of U–I collaborations. In addition, the section explores the value of the knowledge to the firm in terms of when it was used. That is, is it a process of developing knowledge and expertise that can be utilised straightaway or is it a process that takes time to develop knowledge and then disseminate it through the business? The first consideration is who within the firm was working on the project, that is, the individuals that make up the project team.

Importantly, there was little evidence of significant R&D departments within the firms, with R&D activities therefore not formally organised. Given these conditions, SMEs organise collaborative projects around a small team who are responsible for creating and delivering the outputs. Therefore, in the first instance, the primary focus of the knowledge transfer was the individuals within these teams.

The make-up of these teams is fluid in nature and somewhat ad hoc in their construction, with individuals co-opted to the project as and when they were required. The core member of the team is the Knowledge Transfer Partnership (KTP) Associate, a graduate employed specifically to work full time on the project and carry out the day-to-day tasks associated with developing it. While the Associate is technically employed by the university partner and paid through the project grant, they are physically based within the SME and can be regarded as a full-time employee.

As well as the Associate, the project teams were generally comprised of employees of the SMEs who were working directly within fields relevant to the project. The entrepreneur running the business was also an active participant. In addition, membership of the project team varies according to its stage and the knowledge and expertise required at the time. While the core team is relatively small at any given time, SMEs are keen to make all their resources available to the project to ensure its success. Therefore, while the core team may have been relatively small, they are usually able to access the firm's entire resource base to function to ensure that the team was embedded into the firm.

It was generally recognised within the SMEs that the project should benefit the entirety of the firm, not just the project team. Given this, the project team was regarded as the initial conduit for the transfer and absorption of the knowledge developed in the course of undertaking the various tasks associated with it. So, while a small team was assigned to the project it was not the intention that these would be the sole recipients of the knowledge but that it is eventually transferred to all aspects of the firm.

While collaborative projects are important to SMEs, there is also the concurrent pressure to keep the business going while the project is undertaken. Collaborative projects are not necessarily the sole priority of SMEs but one of several activities occurring within the firms at any one time. Consequently, at times a degree of separation exists between the project team and the rest of the business. This is illustrated in the case of Data-Tech who recalled that during the period their project was running:

> we [also] had to keep the company going and support the KTP whilst it was doing that, so it was quite segregated. In fact, it was challenging at times. (Date-Tech)

However, for the very smallest SMEs, their size meant that the collaborative project tended to dominate all other activities. This is because the project often involved the whole firm and there may be situations when other activities within the firm are compromised when the project is prioritised and vice versa. Indeed, in the dynamic and fast-moving context of business, the focus of the firm could ebb and flow between focusing on 'everyday' activities and the collaborative project.

The presence of the KTP Associate means that there is always at least one member of the project team completely focused on its objectives. Therefore, the influence of the Associate may be higher when SMEs possess fewer resources as they represent a larger proportion of the resources available to the project. In general, the pivotal role of the Associate in the functioning of these projects is clear as they are an exclusive resource and key conduit for knowledge creation within the team and its transfer between the team and through the rest of the business. SMEs regard proactiveness as an important attribute of their Associates, as this is a key trait for enabling knowledge transfer to occur. This is illustrated by Magenta-Design, who praised the Associate on their project.

> The [Associate] that we recruited was an exceptional candidate. She made it her business to engage with everyone … She tend[ed] to work alone but people were saying 'well when she does something but we don't know what it is'. But she made it her business to go out there and say 'right, okay, this is me. This is what I'm doing and how can it impact you'. (Magenta-Design)

This quote illustrates the importance of the KTP Associate as a 'bridging role' between the university and the firm. Thus, the analysis reveals that knowledge transfer is not exclusively dependent on the academic partners per se but also the KTP Associate as they had direct contact with both the university and the firm.

Another key to the effective transfer of knowledge is the ability of the KTP Associate to combine and communicate effectively with their colleagues. As such, where the Associate lacks this ability, the project could be seriously disrupted. For example, for Brown Media, the lack of interaction and embeddedness of their KTP Associate was highlighted as one of the reasons as to why there was minimal knowledge transfer from this project. Where a KTP Associate does not engage effectively, a bottleneck is created whereby the knowledge created by the project does not get transferred into the rest of the firm.

The main entry mode for the university knowledge into SMEs is through the project team, of which the KTP Associate is a key member. Therefore, the process of knowledge transfer into an SME is based around a two-step flow. Firstly, knowledge is transferred and developed among the members of the teams working directly on the project. Secondly, the knowledge is then distributed across the rest of the business. This second step occurs either through temporary extensions of the team as other members of the firm join the team, or through deliberate sharing activities designed to spread the knowledge among the rest of the workforce in order to cement the learning into the firm.

However, the smaller the firm, the less significant the 'second step' will be as the project team tends to cover a greater proportion of the workforce.

When examining the time frames for knowledge creation and transfer, the analysis reveals that this is not always an instantaneous process as time-lags exist between the generation of the knowledge and when it became usable. However, while knowledge transfer may not be instant, SMEs are generally able to begin using the knowledge from the project prior to its conclusion and SMEs are able to reap the benefits of their investments relatively quickly. This outcome is illustrated by the following quote from Purple Media:

> I think probably after the first four to six months we started seeing some benefits of how we might do things differently. So it's been an evolution over the course of the project rather than not gaining any benefit until after the two years. So it's been useful from almost day one. (Purple Media)

This quote is also illustrative of the time frames involved, highlighting there may be a period of several months before SMEs are able to start using the knowledge from the project. Therefore, the projects do not appear to promote instant changes within SMEs. Instead, the processes adopted appear to have promoted steady progress on the outputs so that after the initial development phase has been successfully traversed useful results are developed and utilised by the firms. As Yellow-Soft noted:

> there was a continual transfer of knowledge throughout the project. So, it was quite well staged, and we were able to take that on board and use it in other areas. (Yellow-Soft)

Approximately half of the SMEs reported the fact that they were able to utilise the knowledge created prior to the end of the project, and it appears that these were, in the main, well-designed projects. Although some reported that it took longer to utilise the knowledge due to the nature of the project. For example, it was around 15 months (of a 24-month project) until Magenta-Design was able to use the knowledge from their project.

## 8.3	ABSORBING/MAKING SENSE OF UNIVERSITY KNOWLEDGE

Having examined the use of knowledge from the projects and the time frames over which this occurred, this section examines the nature of the absorption process within the participating firms, specifically the extent to which SMEs are able to understand and absorb the knowledge from their university partners.

To absorb knowledge, it must be communicated clearly so that it can first be understood. Here the focus is on the academic partner and whether they were able to impart their knowledge to SMEs. Therefore, it is important to understand how they were perceived by the firm during the project and the extent to which SMEs learn from them.

Overall, the findings reveal that SMEs are able to effectively understand their academic partners as they reported few issues in terms of being able to understand and make sense of their academic partners' words and actions. Furthermore, understanding the university partner is possible because SMEs and their entrepreneurs possess knowledge and expertise in the project areas. As SMEs work in the same area as the academic partners and deal with the same technologies, there was a sufficient overlap in the knowledge bases of the collaborators. The following quote from Yellow-Soft illustrates this point, with the respondent commenting that

> the academic supervisor, their skillset was very closely related to what we were doing, in terms of software development, cloud-based software development, and the technologies around that. (Yellow-Soft)

While SMEs tend to possess the relevant knowledge to engage successfully with their academic partners, they also recognise that the academics are the experts in the field. This means that SMEs accept that there may be occasions where they are not able to understand the academic partner as they simply did not possess as much knowledge. This is illustrated by the following quote from Magenta-Design,

> the whole point was obviously that they've got a knowledge base that you haven't.

Therefore, a lack of understanding of the partner's knowledge was recognised as a learning experience rather than a barrier to the ongoing project.

The key to understanding their partner's knowledge is not necessarily based on the SME's expertise, but the similarities of the methods of working between the two partners. Here it was important that the SME perceived their academic partner to be 'business focused', as they consider it important that academics are commercially savvy focusing on the application of knowledge and technology rather than the science underpinning it. This suggests that communication between the parties may be aided by commonalities in both their motivations and methods of working. These commercially savvy academics are described as 'not academic academics' or 'not true academics', which, to the respondents, meant that they felt able to focus on the commercial rather than scientific aspects of the project. In the course of these collaborations SMEs are also learning how to work effectively with their academic partner as the project progressed, suggesting that this was not fixed but evolutionary in nature.

Inter-personal interaction is a key factor in facilitating an effective working relationship between the actors. Therefore, SMEs need to build relationships with individuals during the project to absorb knowledge. To work effectively, the teams are required to first familiarise themselves with each other, their knowledge and role, and their methods of working in order to be able to communicate effectively. The following quote from White-Electronics illustrates this:

> you know, it probably took the first three months to realise who people were, what they did, what the benefits were. Were they there just 'cause they wanted their name on the piece of paper ... So, I think, you know, probably after three months we knew what everybody did and what the good bits were and the bad bits were and you work round that. (White-Electronics)

The existence of this learning phase provides evidence as to why U–I collaboration does not necessarily involve an instantaneous process of knowledge transfer. Instead, the parties must first work out how the other wishes to operate and then begin to work accordingly. Even though many of the ties originated from the SMEs' networking activities, the project teams still had to develop. In other words, the teams were required to first coalesce around the project and its objectives and then organise themselves into a pattern of work.

SMEs also perceive that collaborative projects must balance research and commercialisation objectives with respect to the rigour and usefulness of the knowledge from the project. For example, Purple Media commented on the fact that from their point of view the statistical model underpinning their project did not need to be 100% right, merely good enough to 'do the job' to generate revenue. Therefore, from the SMEs' perspective, the application of a technology may be more focused on making it work rather than scientific discovery.

In some cases, SMEs are also able to engage in academic-focused outputs, contributing to the publication of academic papers that drew on the results of their collaboration. In these cases, it was clear that the academic team had developed knowledge which was novel enough to publish. In the case of Edu-Tech, there was clear evidence that they had picked up on academic traits as they were discussing journal rankings and publication metrics, which are key performance indicators of the higher education sector. Indeed, this firm's website draws attention to academic outputs produced during the collaboration. Other SMEs spoke of less formal learning activities for the academics resulting from these projects, including the development of case studies for teaching purposes, as well as cementing a relationship with the firm so that individuals from there could act as external speakers for the university.

Therefore, the learning opportunities for the academic partners may be broader than learning about the commercial side of the business and how it operates.

From the point of view of the academic partners, they may have been able to learn about the application of knowledge through observing the difference between developing a technology and its commercialisation. From the SME perspective, the application of a technology may be more focused on making it work rather than scientific discovery. These experiences suggest that there are some potential learning points for the academics through industrial collaboration and that the direction of knowledge flow can be two-way.

8.4   BARRIERS ENCOUNTERED

Despite the relative success of some firms in working with their university partner, and the clear examples of the smooth transfer of knowledge and learning experiences, there were also barriers encountered during these projects and this section examines these barriers.

Importantly, while all respondents highlighted the existence of barriers during their projects, the majority appear to have been solved in the course of the project. References to different working methods and timescales are therefore common, as well as technical issues with the development of the technologies underpinning the projects. In the main, these appear to have been anticipated and factored into the firms' expectations, allowing the project participants to circumvent them successfully. The fact that there were barriers is unsurprising, given the complexity of the projects and the organisational asymmetries outlined in Chapter 4.

The findings reveal that the barriers faced by SMEs include a lack of relevant knowledge among the academic partners, communication issues between the two parties, differing methods of working, variations in the commitment to the time frames in which the projects needed to be completed, the associated bureaucracy, and recruitment of the KTP Associate.

A key barrier facing SMEs is a lack of effective knowledge transfer from the university partner. In these cases, it was felt that their academic partner simply did not possess the required knowledge and expertise. Three firms, Black-Electronics, Blue Finance, and Cyan-Soft, reported a failure of the project due to the failure of their partner to deliver the knowledge and expertise necessary. Where SMEs encounter a lack of knowledge transfer, they were able to source the required knowledge from another source. For example, in the case of Black-Electronics, they were able to complete their project with another partner. However, Blue Finance and Cyan-Soft did not follow this course, stating that they had benefitted from some aspects of the project, namely horizon scanning and some cataloguing of activities. Therefore, where there is little useful knowledge transfer SMEs are happy to salvage what they can from the project.

The second barrier encountered by SMEs concerned issues of miscommunication between actors that prevent the effective transfer of knowledge. The experience of Patient-Tech in their collaboration illustrates the issue faced. Here, the firm considered that the university did not deliver the knowledge and expertise the firm required, instead providing what they viewed to be generic training opportunities for the KTP Associate without listening to the needs of the business. In addition, Cyan-Soft were not able to arrange a face-to-face meeting with their partner despite the two partners being located within close spatial proximity (both are located in London around 15 km apart). This is illustrated by the following quote:

> I guess that would be difficult if it had been a distance away, that would have been difficult. I'm a great believer in any kind of interaction like that. Your communications are much more effective if you're stood in front of somebody just like they are in a sales situation. And whilst we have marvellous electronic tools these days with email and Skype and so on, which are definitely very, very valuable tools, you still can't beat being stood in front of somebody to get your point across, whether you're selling them something or whether you're teaching them something or whether you're learning something from them, I think. So, yes, I agree, the local nature of that probably was quite beneficial. (Cyan-Soft)

In order to avoid this type of barrier, SMEs need to focus on communication, establishing an appropriate method of working, understanding the needs and requirements of the partner, and recognising the differences that may exist in order to address them. Arc-Tech summed up this approach when they stated that:

> you have to recognise that there are different interests at work, but then negotiate the sort of middle ground that makes it kind of effective for both parties, understanding what both parties' interests are. But then in practice, making sure that there is kind of an integrity and the negotiation around that middle ground and then an acceptable methodology that isn't going to impact negatively on you as a business. (Arc-Tech)

This indicates that projects must involve continuous communication and clearly state the progress of these projects across the relevant participant actors.

Similar communication issues were encountered by Brown Media, which found that a lack of communication created a lack of clarity as to the knowledge being transferred into the firm. This subsequently left them unsure as to whether the project was progressing as planned. In some respects, this reflected the previous example of Patient-Tech in terms of a lack of clear communication between the partners, as the respondents from Brown Media referred to a lack of a 'road map' for the project or an awareness of the stages that have been passed in the course of the project. Therefore, they were not able to understand the project's progression, putting this down to differences in working cultures between the two parties:

> Academics are academics and, you know, having a commercial head on, although they are, through the KTP, you know, interacting with businesses, the day-to-day running of a business and what, you know, the value of this thing, whatever it's going to be, really kind of don't really get. They don't understand external pressures. So for them it's a project. (Brown Media)

These barriers highlight two possible issues during SME–university collaborative projects; namely a lack of effective communication, and also a lack of absorptive capacity for both partners to understand the activities or requirements of the other partner. As such, these findings highlight the need for SMEs to not only be able to communicate clearly but also possess the capacity to understand their partner.

Differences in methods of working can be a barrier for SMEs, particularly in terms of the priority given to the project. This was best illustrated by Data-Tech who highlighted incompatibilities in the way they and their partners viewed the progression of the project as a significant barrier. Their position is illustrated in the following quote:

> the real world is not about starting at the beginning of a project, carrying on and then completing it. The real world is starting at the beginning of the project and having everybody fire just about every piece of ammunition at you to put you off course, and you still have to deliver on the original date. So that's the real world. (Data-Tech)

The observed barriers suggest that SMEs are indeed subject to the 'two-worlds paradox', whereby the two sets of partners had a different way of working and running a project. In addition, this paradox was also observed in terms of time management with the observed differences centring on the deadlines for completing work. In the case of Cyan-Soft the firm was pressing for hard deadlines, whereas the academic partner was more sanguine:

> My business partner at the time was managing it from our point of view and he basically gave the academic a deadline and said that we need a deadline for when we will have a deadline for when we will see some kind of output from the project. And the academic delayed on that and so my business partner went back and said okay, well we need a deadline for a deadline for a deadline of when we're going to have an output for the project. And he responded saying that IT projects take as long as IT projects take. (Cyan-Soft)

However, SMEs do accept that the academic partners may work in dissimilar ways, as illustrated by the following quote from Gen-Tech:

> Often with academia, they would do things to suit their own academic interests and not necessarily the commercial benefit. (Gen-Tech)

Therefore, for SMEs, collaborative partnerships with universities require careful management and if they are properly managed and communication issues are addressed the barriers should not be insurmountable.

For Edu-Tech, their main barrier was the pressure they felt to deliver the results within the two-year time frame as mandated by the funding body responsible for KTPs (at the time this was the Technology Strategy Board, then Innovate UK, and now UK Research and Innovation). For this firm, the time frame they were working to was approximately five to ten years as they do not regard their sector as fast moving. Instead their requirement is for sufficient time for new developments to be recognised by their market and, consequently, their collaborative project was the first part of a plan for delivering successful outputs over the medium term.

There were also examples of barriers caused by the bureaucracy associated with the projects. In particular, the university partners' methods of employing Associates and accounting for expenditure were highlighted as particular obstacles. SMEs may struggle to recruit Associates or may find the candidates proposed by their partners unsuitable. The same frustrations were also present in terms of the legal and financial aspects of the collaborations, particularly the slow progress in negotiating over rights to intellectual property and expense claims.

SMEs also face obstacles once the KTP Associates are in post. In particular, their retention can be hampered by the fact that the duration of these projects is mandated at two years, meaning that those employed through the project inevitably found themselves on fixed-term contracts. As a result, there were several cases where the KTP Associate, with the end of their contract looming large in their sights, left prior to the project's completion in order to take up another job. There were also several cases where KTP Associates found direct employment within the business after the completion of the project.

In addition, SMEs find the design of the KTP itself presented a barrier, placing too much responsibility on the Associate for delivering the project's aims. This means the academic supervisor then takes a back seat. Magnolia-Support drew attention to this issue with respect to inducing change within the firms:

> So that was certainly a tough ask for the post-grad. He needed quite a bit of support really, 'cause you couldn't ask him to be at the forefront of changing the company.

You could ask him to be at the forefront of articulating what he was focused on, but not in actually making changes. (Magnolia-Support)

Therefore, SMEs encounter a broad range of barriers, which all have varying effects. Some of the more serious barriers encountered were those that ultimately prevented the effective functioning of the project and were typically terminal. The most serious barriers in terms of effects were those concerning a lack of engagement or the provision of relevant knowledge and expertise.

8.5   DISCUSSION AND CONCLUSIONS

The findings presented in this chapter highlight the processes through which the knowledge developed during these collaborative projects was utilised and absorbed into SMEs. They also indicate the barriers faced by SMEs during their collaboration, highlighting the fact that addressing and overcoming barriers is an integral part of the collaborative process. The analysis showcases several important findings: (1) the focused nature of the project teams; (2) participation in collaborative both projects creates and consumes resources within the SME; (3) the role of the KTP Associates as boundary spanners; (4) usable knowledge was generated and used during the project; (5) the continued importance and evolution of technological and organisational proximities during the project; and (6) those within the participating SMEs considered that learning was mutual..

Collaboration processes typically generated knowledge through the creation of a small, focused team within SMEs. In most cases, this minimised interruptions and allowed the team to focus on the project, while enabling the rest of the business to keep functioning. Considering this evidence, it is clear that participation in a collaborative link with a university does consume the resources of the SMEs as they progress. This resource consumption was compounded by the existence of a short time-lag prior to the knowledge generated by the project being 'usable'. In addition, where SMEs commit personnel to the project teams during their development an issue arises in terms of their ability to undertake their usual roles.

This aspect is a somewhat overlooked aspect of U–I collaboration, and within a resource-constrained environment such as SMEs, engaging in a collaboration will necessarily consume scarce resources. The evidence shows that within each case, the participating SMEs all commit personnel to the project teams during their development, the opportunity cost of which was their ability to undertake their usual roles. There was also an unambiguous admission by firms that committing resources to the projects diverted them away from everyday operations. This outcome could be particularly important in micro firms (those with fewer than ten employees), where the findings suggested that a large proportion of the workforce could be dedicated to the project.

SMEs may be able to utilise knowledge from collaborative projects while they are still in progress. Projects do not necessarily need to be completed before the firm can exploit the knowledge generated. However, even in the case of early utilisation there were still time-lags. Therefore, the absorption and subsequent use of knowledge requires time. These results highlight an important point, that is, collaborative links between SMEs and universities may take time to develop internally. This means that examining these collaborations in terms of the 'out the door' criterion (Bozeman, Rimes, and Youti 2015) misses the crucial development of the relationship after its initiation.

The findings highlight the key role of the KTP Associate in underpinning the functioning of SME–university collaboration through the KTP programme. These individuals usually operate as a boundary spanner, echoing the findings of Rosli, Rossi and Yip (2018) who attribute this ability to their neutral stance, being focused on the project only and therefore independent of the firm and university. These individuals were clearly, and rightly, identified as at the centre of all project-related activities within SMEs. Therefore, individuals who can strengthen the relationship between the partner organisations play a key role in these collaborations, which corroborates existing evidence that these are the key to successful collaborations (Bansal et al. 2012; Gulati 2007).

The boundary spanning activities of the KTP Associates involved them being the 'go-between' not only within the SME but also between the SME and the university. While Rosli, Rossi and Yip (2018) suggest that their independence is an important factor, the evidence above indicates that effective communication and proactivity were the key to performing this role successfully. If these factors were absent, there could be a tendency for the knowledge and expertise developed during the project to remain embedded within the Associate and not be transferred to the firm.

The SME literature typically cites entrepreneurs as drivers of collaboration within these firms (Siegel et al. 2008), and this evidence of the key role of the Associates suggests that other actors are also important in this process. Indeed, previous work has argued that boundary spanning activities are undertaken by technology transfer offices, actors from the partner firm, or the academics (Bartunek and Rynes 2014; Jain and George 2007; Wasserman and Kram 2009). Therefore, one of the advantages of the KTP programme is that it has a built-in agent who is tasked with this activity. However, given the socio-technical nature of the U–I collaboration process, these Associates require relational and cognitive similarities with both parties to act as an effective boundary spanner. Given the apparent disconnects between academia and industry, and the 'two-worlds' paradox (Bartunek and Rynes 2014;

Hewitt-Dundas, Gkypali, and Roper 2019; Lavie and Drori 2012), this may be asking a lot of a recent graduate.

With respect to the operation of the project, it must be noted that there is also a subtle difference between the operation of the project and the absorption of knowledge into SMEs. While the Associates had a central role as the pivot around which the project functioned, they were not solely responsible for absorption of knowledge. In one respect they were fundamental to the day-to-day running of the project as it was their full-time focus in a team that could be transitory as members joined and left depending on the task in hand. Therefore, the churn in the project team membership promoted the transfer of knowledge.

The existing literature often examines U–I links as a bilateral collaboration, that is, a single firm and university work together. In reality, they are typically operationalised by a team of many individuals. Therefore, the observed absorptive capacity of SMEs was contingent upon those within the firm being able to understand their academic partners. This appears to have been achieved through the existence of technological proximity between the two partners and allows SMEs to understand their partners and results from the fact that the firms were working in the same technological field as the universities.

In general, SMEs are able to understand the knowledge developed and transferred into the firm during the project, indicating the existence of a significant absorptive capacity. This was not unexpected, given the capacity of the firms to develop project ideas, and they clearly have a level of capability in this area. Yet within the extant literature there is often a supposition that university knowledge is a substitute for a lack of knowledge within the firm (Gruber, Harhoff, and Hoisl 2013). However, these cases suggest that university knowledge can be considered as a complement to SMEs' existing knowledge. So while the existing literature has highlighted the importance of complementary knowledge among partners (Brouthers, Brouthers, and Wilkinson 1995), SMEs are not necessarily seeking knowledge that was similar to their own, but knowledge that would fit their project. This is an important distinction.

The fact that SMEs are able to work effectively with their partners during the collaboration process suggests sufficient organisational and technological proximity between the two may have assisted in the communication of knowledge between the actors (Aguilera, Lethiais, and Rallet 2012; Knoben and Oerlemans 2006). During the course of the projects, proximities may evolve as partners learn together. While prior work has highlighted the evolution of relationships through the course of U–I collaboration (Thune and Gulbrandsen 2014), less consideration has been given to the dynamics of proximities (Balland, Boschma, and Frenken 2015).

Indeed, proximities are typically conceptualised as a static resource, either they exist between parties or they do not. Furthermore, when considering the 'two-worlds' paradox and the differences between firms and universities that may prevent effective collaboration, this is again treated as a constant (Bansal et al. 2012). However, these results suggest that these proximities can evolve during the course of a project, narrowing the gap between SMEs and their university partners and tackling the paradox. Furthermore, in many cases these proximities were in evidence prior to the collaboration, and the degree of evolution may be linked to their original strength.

The fact that SMEs experienced obstacles in the course of the projects suggests that the organisational and technological proximity between the actors did not evolve to become complete. Indeed, the barriers the SMEs encountered concerning a lack of commercial focus of the university partner suggest the existence of two worlds (Bartunek and Rynes 2014; Hewitt-Dundas, Gkypali, and Roper 2019). Therefore, a certain relational and cognitive distance between the partners may always be in evidence and the impetus is to minimise its influence rather than try to eradicate it. Indeed, the importance of communication between parties is typically held as an important element in ensuring that the projects run smoothly. Understandably, communication is key to SMEs and universities learning to work together and therefore promoting the evolution of their proximities.

In summary, this chapter presents details of the implementation of the projects and the details of their operationalisation. In doing so, the chapter has highlighted several key findings. Firstly, the collaboration process is focused on a small team of individuals within the SME which pivots around the KTP Associate. Within these collaborations the Associate plays a crucial role, firstly as a permanent member of the team tasked with working full time on the project in the team, and, secondly, as a boundary spanner between the university and the firm.

Secondly, the chapter highlights how usable knowledge can be generated in the course of the projects and that it is not necessary to wait for the conclusion of the project in order to exploit this knowledge. It is relatively commonplace for SMEs to be able to use the knowledge generated in the course of a collaborative project prior to its completion. Therefore, for some firms participation in collaborative links with universities yields new knowledge relatively quickly. In addition, this is also a signal that a project would be successful in achieving its objectives (discussed in more detail in Chapter 9). However, the early use of knowledge is not an instantaneous occurrence, with the project and project team typically requiring a period to embed themselves initially in the collaboration.

In common with the preceding chapters, the importance of relational and cognitive factors was again to the fore, with the role of technological and organisational proximity found to be important to the operation of these projects. This closeness not only assisted SMEs in understanding and absorbing the knowledge generated during the projects but may evolve during the lifetime of the project. Previously, proximities have been discussed within the extant literature in static terms, that is, they are either present or absent. In terms of the two-worlds paradox, which suggests that there are fundamental barriers to the effective collaboration of firms and universities, it appears that these barriers may diminish through the course of projects.

Through exploring the barriers encountered during these projects, the analysis suggests that they are a typical part of the collaboration process. As no two organisations will be totally homogenous in terms of working practices and culture, it may not be possible to eradicate these barriers completely. However, the evidence presented in this chapter illustrates that communication is the key to maintaining these relationships throughout the duration of the project. Finally, the chapter shows that undertaking collaborative projects with universities does involve the consumption of resources within the firm. It is not a costless process in terms of the opportunity costs involved whereby a trade-off may exist between the pursuit of 'everyday' activities and pursuing the project's objectives.

9. Understanding the results of collaboration

9.1 INTRODUCTION

This chapter tackles the final part of the collaboration process, assessing SMEs' perceptions of the success of the final outputs and outcomes of their projects. The objectives of U–I collaboration are typically the exploitation of cutting-edge knowledge for the purposes of innovation, resulting in the development of new products, processes, technologies, or organisational forms. The chapter provides an overview of the outcomes of these projects in order to consider the extent to which they were considered to be successful by the firms and the reasons behind this assessment.

As noted in Chapter 4, the success of U–I collaboration can be viewed more broadly than simply focusing on outputs, that is, a new product or process created from the collaboration. Instead, the outcomes of these projects can be wider in scope. Several factors can be examined in terms of 'success' and this chapter considers both the extent to which the projects achieved the objectives they were designed for *and* the other outcomes from the projects. The analysis of success is discussed in terms of outputs, relating to factors associated with the main product or service developed in the course of the project, and 'outcomes', which relate to a broader set of factors not directly linked to what was produced by the collaboration.

9.2 ASSESSING 'SUCCESS'

While there are several methods for SMEs to assess their satisfaction with the project in terms of fulfilling their aims, they primarily gauged the success of the project in terms of emphasising the completion of the project's main output (see summary in Table 9.1). The main finding is that collaborative projects between SMEs and universities typically fulfilled their objectives, with SMEs taking the development of a tangible product or service from the collaboration as a sign of its success. This manifested itself not only in terms of the creation of a product, but also whether it worked effectively.

Table 9.1   *Perceived success in terms of projects fulfilling their objectives*

Firm	Extent to which project objectives were met
Arc-Tech	Very successful; has provided firm with a lot of useful data to incorporate into their work
Black-Electronics	Unsuccessful; outside assistance was required to finish the project
Blue-Design	Successful; the project achieved its objectives
Blue Finance	Complete failure; nothing emerged
Brown Media	Unsuccessful; Associate left business and project was sidelined and left unfinished due to lack of resources
Cyan-Soft	Unsuccessful
Data-Tech	Successful; firm has doubled its client roster as a result
Edu-Tech	Very successful; product launched on time and generated sales quickly
Gen-Tech	Unsuccessful; partner did not have the knowledge it thought they had
Green-Soft	Project failed due to university administrators – achieved goals outside of project with same academic
Indigo-Consultants	Successful; product works as it envisaged
Magenta-Design	Successful; firm feels outcomes have changed the way the industry works
Magnolia-Support	Successful; project worked as intended
Marine Consultants	Unsuccessful; project ended early due to lack of progress
Mine-Tech	Commercially and scientifically successful
Motor-Tech	Project not successful due to lack of market – secondary aim of recruitment successful though
Patient-Tech	Some success but much less than expected
Pink-Soft	Not an unqualified success, outcome short of what was hoped
Purple Media	Successful; the output was delivered successfully and led to a 20% increase in performance
Red-Soft	Successful; met the aims of the project
White-Electronics	Successful; project met its aims and firm and university formed a joint venture to exploit the new product
Yellow-Soft	Successful; delivered all the objectives

In addition to the possession of a tangible output, SMEs also evaluate the market performance of an output as a sign of the project's success. This is interpreted in terms of direct impacts on the competitive position of the firm with respect to sales or customers. Analytical approaches to assessing this are typical among SMEs, who sought to explicitly quantify the changes to produce clear evidence. The success of the project is also examined in terms of its impact on the target market using metrics such as changes in revenues, range of product/services offered, or the total numbers of clients. Therefore, the development of a new product or service through collaboration provides SMEs with an opportunity for market expansion, creating new possibilities to be fulfilled. This approach is illustrated by the following quotes from Purple Media and Pink-Soft who discussed the success of their projects in quantitative terms:

> So we've measured [success] on a very, surprisingly, mathematical basis. So we've looked at uplifting delivery to our clients. So we've seen a 20% uplift in performance on average across the board to our clients. So actually it's been a really, really significant improvement to our clients and therefore to us in terms of what we can offer our clients. (Purple Media)

> Our target for year one was 14,000, we achieved that in two months. We've got a project coming through where they're likely to buy in a similar project about 25,000 tests. So we're pretty confident we're going to be way, way ahead of our plans for the next five years. (Pink-Soft)

SMEs may also use broader metrics to assess the success of their collaborative project. For example, Magenta-Design's assessment focused on changes within the firm's market. The aim of their project was to develop children's play areas with landscaping in mind and, since the completion of their project, they noticed other firms in the sector were following this trend. Therefore, undertaking their project enabled them to pursue this trend ahead of their competitors, boosting their sales. The following quote illustrates their position:

> I wouldn't be so bold or arrogant to say that we've changed the market, but we were kind of part of a movement that sort of helped to move the market along. So we were nudging it in the same direction as a few other people. And it was incredibly successful for us, and we went through some ridiculous amount of growth during that time. (Magenta-Design)

For this firm, the success of the project was viewed in terms of a contribution to the broader sector, rather than just within the firm itself. Therefore, there may be broader spillover effects from the outputs and outcomes of U–I collaboration as other firms respond to the knowledge/technology developed and the markets change accordingly.

Conversely, the failure of a project is assessed in similar terms. Indeed, understanding the lack of success in some ways is more useful than the reasons a project was regarded as successful. The main reasons for failure are again couched in terms of the outputs, specifically a failure of the collaboration to deliver something that worked. The reasons for lack of success stemmed from the failure of the partner university to provide the required knowledge, a failure to embed the knowledge developed in the course of the project into the business, and a lack of market for the finished output. In addition, there was some evidence that the role of the Knowledge Transfer Partnership (KTP) Associate is related to an unsuccessful outcome.

Where a project fails due to a lack of input from the university partner, there was considerable frustration among the SMEs. For Gen-Tech, the project was regarded as unsuccessful as it did not add anything to the business. Their frustration concerned the fact that the university partner did not possess the knowledge they initially thought. This meant that another partner was sought, who eventually successfully solved the problems encountered and completed the project accordingly.

> We employed somebody else out of another group and they cracked it almost instantly. So it was a bit of a waste of time. (Gen-Tech)

For Black-Electronics, a similar experience was described, with the firm setting out to improve their technology through engaging in a KTP, but the project was not successful as the academic partner did not possess the required knowledge. Ultimately, they had to search for and recruit a different partner to complete the project. This experience reveals a hidden cost of the failure of the project, namely the time it takes to complete an unsuccessful project is wasted for an SME, which, in a resource-constrained environment, is invaluable.

While unsuccessful collaboration may deplete resources without providing any benefits, it can provide a learning experience for SMEs. This leaves them in a stronger position to reassess the project and undertake a successful search for an appropriate partner with the required knowledge to complete the project. This was the strategy utilised by Indigo-Consultants, who ultimately regarded their project as a success rather than failure.

The failure of the output to meet the firms' expectations did not always equate to the failure of the project, as these examples indicate that the idea could be resurrected and rescued. It is also important to note that a failed collaboration does not necessarily mean an unviable project, as there were cases where the objectives were met successfully through collaborating with an alternative partner. Therefore, in these cases the SMEs' ideas were ultimately proved to be feasible; the failure to realise their potential lay in the collaboration process triggered by ineffective partner selection.

The failure of the collaboration process was also an issue for Blue Finance, resulting from a mismatch between their demands and the knowledge their university partner could offer. For example, where they required technical support in creating their output, the university offered them support to build content for it, but the required collaboration was not forthcoming. This was compounded by the fact that the original academic partner did not engage in the project and, once he was replaced, the second academic partner did not possess the required expertise. This was a source of enormous frustration for the firm, particularly as they regarded themselves as having considerable experience in working with universities. Despite the semblance of organisational proximity through having engaged in similar collaborations previously, in this case it did not emerge. The following quote outlines their situation:

> we have a long history of working with universities. I've got close contacts … we've got a very strong, you know, academic background here and we're very, very keen on the relationship between, you know, academy and industry. However, in this case, the West of Scotland University were really quite disgraceful and could not deliver what we required. (Blue Finance)

The collaboration failed for Pink-Soft due to their failings in terms of the organisation and engagement of the internal project team. As a result, they considered that they failed to properly embed the Associate into the team, leading to this individual leaving the project seven months early to take up another job. This is illustrated in the following quote:

> I wouldn't regard the KTP as an unqualified success. I don't think the knowledge was embedded as widely within [the company] as it should have been. I don't think we got as much done as we could have done. I would ascribe that to our failure to manage it as closely as we needed to. I think our associate needed more support than we gave him. And we should have worked harder on a) distributing the knowledge around [the company] but b) really pushing that side of the project harder to work out what it was that we should have been doing, what the functionality was that we should have been embedding and how it was going to work and getting everybody working on the same thing. (Pink-Soft)

The lack of engagement by the KTP Associate is blamed by Marine-Consultants for the failure of their project. In this case, after nine months, and despite the fact the firm had invested in getting him certified and qualified to work at sea (which was crucial for the project), the Associate left after deciding that it was not the right job for him. Subsequently, the project was curtailed.

The reasons behind the failure of a project are not always clear. For example, for Motor-Tech the lack of success was not attributed to either party but instead was due to the project's lack of financial viability. While the real-isation that their project was not going to be a financial success was apparent part way through the project, the firm took a broader view of it recognising that it managed to fulfil secondary aims such as recruiting a graduate programmer. For Brown Media, while a functioning output was developed, the project was not regarded as a success by the firm because the KTP Associate left the business towards the end of the project. This exposes just how much of the project's knowledge and capabilities were embedded within this person and not the firm. They were understandably disappointed and resentful when the Associate left, as illustrated in the following quote:

> So as we came to the end of the project … we picked up two big international clients and a large wholesaler client which we started to tailor the sites to, and [the Associate] left and left us high and dry. I mean, literally high and dry. We obviously invested in [the Associate] two years of time, so you can imagine, we didn't realise 'til the day it ended that that was it and we were told he had gone. So, for us, it was massively disappointing. And so that meant, you know, the work couldn't progress because the person had gone. (Brown Media)

A similar scenario was experienced by Patient-Tech, whose Associate also left the business at the end of the project leaving a small amount of work to be undertaken on the project before it was ready to sell. However, this parting of ways appears to have been more amicable as the Associate was involved in recruiting the consultants required to finish the work. Therefore, the success or failure of the project was perceived in terms of the development of an output and whether it functioned as intended, and the subsequent sales it generated. Broadening the focus of the relative success of the project from concentrating on the output towards a series of outcomes enables a broader assessment of the relative success of the projects through providing a more holistic understanding of what the project delivered.

One way of assessing success is to consider whether SMEs intend to collaborate again with their academic partner, which is summarised in Table 9.2. Here a strong relationship between the development of a successful output is observed and the existence of an ongoing relationship between the partners. Of the 14 firms who regarded their project to be a success in delivering the required outputs, ten had maintained an ongoing relationship with the university partner. Therefore, where SMEs regard their project to have been successful, they will maintain the relationship with their university partner.

Table 9.2 also indicates that an enduring relationship between the two is unlikely to develop if the project was not regarded as successfully meeting its objectives. Of the eight firms reporting this, seven stated that they had not maintained the relationship, with only a single firm reporting an enduring relationship. For these firms, the prospect of engaging in a future project with the same university partner was sometimes dismissed as a non-starter.

Table 9.2   *Perceived success of project and ongoing relationships*

Perceived Success of Output	Ongoing relationship with Partner University	
	Yes	No
Successful	• Arc-Tech	• Data-Tech
	• Blue-Design	• Edu-Tech
	• Indigo- Consultants	• Magnolia-Support
	• Magenta-Design	• Patient-Tech
	• Mine-Tech	
	• Pink-Soft	
	• Purple Media	
	• Red-Soft	
	• White-Electronics	
	• Yellow-Soft	
Unsuccessful	• Green-Soft	• Black-Electronics
		• Blue Finance
		• Brown Media
		• Cyan-Soft
		• Gen-Tech
		• Marine Consultants
		• Motor-Tech

In the cases where a successful project was delivered, the absence of an enduring relationship between the firm and their university partner did not mean that the firm had severed ties with the university. Instead, these cases meant that SMEs did not maintain an active contact with their partner, with the link between the two becoming dormant in character, allowing the connection to be reactivated should a suitable project arise. This is illustrated by the following quote from Magnolia-Support who regarded their project as successful but did not report an active ongoing relationship:

> there are touch points, but no, but that's us, not them, or the KTP. We'd do another one. We would absolutely do another one and we'd probably think of them first, so I don't … It created conditions for an enduring relationship, but there has to be a project you want to do. (Magnolia-Support)

Table 9.3   *Perceived success of project and further university collaboration*

Perceived Success of Output	Openness to Further University Collaboration	
	Yes	No
Successful	• Arc-Tech	
	• Blue-Design	
	• Data-Tech	
	• Edu-Tech	
	• Indigo-Consultants	
	• Magenta-Design	
	• Magnolia-Support	
	• Mine-Tech	
	• Patient-Tech	
	• Pink-Soft	
	• Purple Media	
	• Red-Soft	
	• White-Electronics	
	• Yellow-Soft	
Unsuccessful	• Brown Media	• Black-Electronics
	• Cyan-Soft	• Blue Finance
	• Green-Soft	• Gen-Tech
	• Marine Consultants	• Motor-Tech

The absence of an ongoing relationship does not preclude a revival and renewal of the collaborative partnership in the future among those firms whose projects had been successful in meeting their objectives. Nevertheless, meeting the project's objectives does not always guarantee an enduring link between a firm and its university partner, but it appears to be a significant influence on the endurance of the relationship between the two parties.

Table 9.3 suggests that the future engagement of SMEs with the wider university sector is less closely linked to their perceived success of the project. In terms of future collaborations with universities more generally, 18 of the firms were happy to pursue more collaborations, with only four reporting that they would not subsequently engage in these collaborations again. Those SMEs that were reluctant to pursue further collaborations with a university were those whose projects had not succeeded in developing a tangible output. Therefore, the failure of one project is not always a sign that a firm will not re-engage with *another* university partner, but generally ended the relationship with the partner university. Consequently, it appears that engaging in U–I collaboration does, overall, encourage the participating firms to re-engage in similar partnerships.

As with SMEs' original assessments of credibility in the partner selection process, the success of the relationship tends to be judged at the individual rather than the organisational level, that is, respondents stated that they are happy to maintain the relationship primarily with the individual academic rather than their university. Therefore, enduring relationships are focused on the individuals involved. The strength of these relationships was further highlighted by the fact that when individuals subsequently moved to another university the SMEs maintained their partnership with them and not the university. This was also true even in cases where the academic moved abroad as the following quote from Mine-Tech highlights:

> … well, [the academic partner has] moved now actually. He's no longer in Southampton, he's gone out over to Canada. But, yeah, we continue to work with him. In fact, he's writing the … he's leading on the paper and we're contributing to that at the moment. (Mine-Tech)

Conversely, where the relationship had broken down with an individual academic, there was still a respect for the link with the university itself, as illustrated by this quote from Patient-Tech:

> I presume it wasn't the university that caused the problem; I presume it was that particular academic or that particular department. So no, yeah, I don't brand the whole organisation as a mess; it was just him or that department that was a mess. So yes, I would [collaborate again]. (Patient-Tech)

Engaging with universities through these formal collaboration mechanisms also encourages SMEs to connect and interact with their university partners through other means. In fact, several of the firms had subsequently engaged in taught courses, seminars, and workshops hosted by their university partners. Therefore, these initial projects had opened the eyes of the firms to the broader range of 'third mission' activities offered by the universities and thereby induced an extension of the link to include the utilisation of other services offered by the university. This highlights another potential success mechanism through which U–I collaboration can be judged.

Several other success factors emerged from the analysis. Firstly, for some SMEs university collaboration is regarded as not just a method for leveraging knowledge and expertise into the business but also a method of recruiting

Table 9.4   *Fate of the KTP Associates*

Firm	Fate of the Associate
Arc-Tech	Left after the completion of the project
Black-Electronics	Left the firm at the end of the project
Blue-Design	No Associate recruited
Blue Finance	Employed in the business following the collapse of the project
Brown Media	Left the firm prior to the project's conclusion
Cyan-Soft	Employed in the business following the completion of the project
Data-Tech	Employed in the business following the completion of the project
Edu-Tech	Left the firm at the end of the project
Gen-Tech	Left the firm prior to the project's conclusion
Green-Soft	Employed in the business following the collapse of the project
Indigo-Consultants	Left the firm prior to the project's conclusion
Magenta-Design	Employed in the business following the completion of the project
Magnolia-Support	Employed in the business following the completion of the project
Marine Consultants	Left the firm prior to the project's conclusion
Mine-Tech	Employed in the business following the completion of the project
Motor-Tech	Employed in the business following the completion of the project
Patient-Tech	Left the firm at the end of the project
Pink-Soft	Left the firm prior to the project's conclusion
Purple Media	Employed in the business following the completion of the project
Red-Soft	Left after the completion of the project
White-Electronics	Left after the completion of the project
Yellow-Soft	Left after the completion of the project

skilled workers. Typically, for SMEs located in more peripheral and rural locations of the UK, such as Shropshire or Cornwall, difficulties in recruiting skilled workers were a major motivation to engage in a collaborative project with a university.

The fate of the KTP Associates also provides evidence of the relative success of the projects. In many cases, the KTP Associates ended up being employed permanently by the SME, with nine of the firms reporting that the Associate remained with the firm after the completion or collapse of the project (see Table 9.4 for a summary of the fate of the Associates). In addition, three of the firms reported that they would have liked to have kept their Associate employed within the firm but that the individual chose to leave for another opportunity. As the Associate is the conduit for the knowledge created in the course of the project there is a strong rationale for SMEs to retain them as these individuals represent an investment in a tangible resource for the firm.

For some SMEs, the development of academic outputs from their projects is regarded as a sign of success. For Mine-Tech, part of the ongoing relationship between the firm and the academic partner was the development of academic papers; this was due to the fact that they perceived the outputs of the project to be scientifically useful as well as commercially viable and were very keen to share their findings with others working in the field. Arc-Tech had a similar viewpoint, as they wished to contribute to the field overall by highlighting how their processes could be used to not only benefit other users of the technology but society in general. Therefore, they were keen to see the development of the technology attributed to their firm in multiple ways, as illustrated in the following quote:

> [We] want to see it published through the context of our practice. But it'll also be then published in a meaningful way in an academic context, which would inform the development of better ways of achieving better environmental standards for schools and for classrooms. It's enormous really ... It's quite a challenge to ensure that you get good air quality and good environmental quality and combine that with low energy in our buildings. That's kind of a huge challenge to achieve those things. We've got a long way to go but hope that this study in its different ways would feed into that kind of process. (Arc-Tech)

Kudos by association can be regarded as another successful outcome of the project, whereby the project's findings are published to an academic audience and the firms then use these outputs as evidence of their innovativeness as well as desire and ability to generate new knowledge. This demonstrates that the SMEs possess the capabilities to develop a commercially viable idea through their project, while also being able to share the underlying science/knowledge for the good of society.

The findings from Chapter 8 also suggest that SMEs are able to use the knowledge created during the project prior to its conclusion. Through examining the SMEs' perceptions of success, it is clear that those regarding their project as producing a successful output at the end are those that have been utilising the knowledge during the project. Therefore, for SMEs it appears that the early exploitation of knowledge from the project is a signal that it is likely to succeed in achieving its objectives.

Finally, through assessing SMEs' experience of working with universities at the outset of the project and the perceived success at the project's conclusion, several findings are noted. In order to assess this, SMEs are grouped according to whether they had no experience of working with universities prior to the project, an intermediate level of experience in working with universities (typically, informal links or contacts that did not involve collaborations), or extensive experience of working with universities (those that had previously been involved in formal collaborations). Table 9.5 presents these groupings, showing that SMEs with more extensive experience of working with universities at the outset of their project are more likely to perceive that their projects were successful as six of the eight SMEs with extensive experience reported this outcome. Conversely, the opposite is observed for those with no experience, with only four of the nine SMEs reporting a successful outcome.

Table 9.5   *Perceptions of project success and level of prior engagement with universities*

	Project Perceived as Successful?	
Experience	Yes	No
None	• Data-Tech	• Black-Electronics
	• Magnolia-Support	• Brown Media
	• Pink-Soft	• Gen-Tech
	• Purple Media	• Green-Soft
		• Motor-Tech
Intermediate	• Blue-Design	• Cyan-Soft
	• Indigo-Consultants	
	• Patient-Tech	
	• Red-Soft	
Extensive	• Arc-Tech	• Blue Finance
	• Edu-Tech	• Marine Consultants
	• Magenta-Design	
	• Mine-Tech	
	• White-Electronics	
	• Yellow-Soft	

The second relationship examined is that between prior experience of university engagement and the creation of an enduring relationship with the university partner following the completion of the project. The analysis shows that this follows a similar pattern as before, with Table 9.6 indicating that SMEs lacking any experience of working with a university are less likely to carry on working with their partner than those with extensive prior experience.

Table 9.6   Enduring relationship and level of prior engagement with universities

	Enduring Relationship with Partner?	
Experience	Yes	No
None	• Green-Soft	• Black-Electronics
	• Pink-Soft	• Brown Media
	• Purple Media	• Data-Tech
		• Gen-Tech
		• Magnolia-Support
		• Motor-Tech
Intermediate	• Blue-Design	• Cyan-Soft
	• Indigo-Consultants	• Patient-Tech
	• Red-Soft	
Extensive	• Arc-Tech	• Blue Finance
	• Magenta-Design	• Edu-Tech
	• Mine-Tech	• Marine Consultants
	• White-Electronics	
	• Yellow-Soft	

Finally, we examine the relationship between prior experience of working with a university and the SMEs' openness to working with any other university in the future. Table 9.7 indicates that less of a relationship exists between SMEs' prior experience of working with universities and their openness to working with other universities in the future. The table shows that SMEs with no experience of working with a university were split roughly evenly, with six willing to collaborate again compared with three who were not. For SMEs with intermediate and extensive levels of experience, there was a general willingness to subsequently engage in this type of collaboration regardless of the perceived success.

Table 9.7   Openness to further univeristy collaboration and level of prior engagement with universities

	Open to Working with other Universities Again?	
Experience	Yes	No
None	• Brown Media	• Black-Electronics
	• Data-Tech	• Gen-Tech
	• Green-Soft	• Motor-Tech
	• Magnolia-Support	
	• Pink-Soft	
	• Purple Media	
Intermediate	• Blue-Design	
	• Cyan-Soft	
	• Indigo-Consultants	
	• Patient-Tech	
	• Red-Soft	
Extensive	• Arc-Tech	• Blue Finance
	• Edu-Tech	
	• Magenta-Design	
	• Marine Consultants	
	• Mine-Tech	
	• White-Electronics	
	• Yellow-Soft	

9.3   DISCUSSION AND CONCLUSIONS

The findings presented in this chapter focus on the completion of collaborative projects and the factors used by SMEs to judge their success. According to Cohen, Nelson, and Walsh (2002), many firms view the university's role as contributing to the completion of a project, which suggests that success is focused on the degree to which the project is completed. This mirrors the arguments of Das and Teng (2001), who argue that the success of alliance is the degree to which objectives are met.

As Chapter 6 outlined, in collaborating with a university the primary aim for SMEs is to be able to bring to fruition an idea that has been developed in order to extend the firms' competitiveness through the development of a new product or process. Given this, the primary assessment of the success of the project by SMEs revolves around the development of a tangible output and its associated benefits to the business. Conversely, failure tends to be understood in terms of disappointment with the collaborative process and lack of knowledge transfer in creating a tangible output. In general, the findings echo previous work in this field which emphasises the importance of these quantitative metrics for understanding the impact of the collaboration and the effect it has on the firm (Bishop, D'Este, and Neely 2011; Fontana, Geuna and Matt 2006).

The findings also suggest that the contribution of universities to their business partners can be broader than simply completing the objectives of the collaboration. Therefore, the success of U–I collaboration can be assessed more accurately if it is interpreted in terms of the overall satisfaction an SME gains from such a relationship (Plewa and Quester 2006). From an SME perspective, the success of university collaboration is better understood in terms of Perkmann, Neely and Walsh's (2011) categorisation of 'outputs' and 'impacts'. These impacts, or outcomes, can be interpreted not only in terms of the tangible success of the project but also provide an assessment of the development of the relationship between SMEs and their university partner.

Outcomes such as the development of an enduring relationship between the parties signal that SMEs are likely to be sufficiently close to their university partner both relationally and cognitively to continue their collaboration. As Bjerregaard (2010) suggests, institutional convergence between the parties is likely to have occurred. This is an important result as it highlights the existence of organisational learning from the collaboration (Dada and Fogg 2016). Therefore, a narrow focus on outputs can overlook important outcomes of SME–university collaboration, that is, the reduction of relational and cognitive distances between the actors involved.

Successful university collaboration can also be interpreted as the creation of additional knowledge, expertise, and human capital within SMEs through permanent post-project employment opportunities for the KTP Associates. The Associate is typically a pivotal part of the project team, not only acting as a bridge between the university and the firm but also working at the fulcrum of the project as a permanent member of the team. Therefore, the loss of the Associate has serious consequences for the success of a collaboration. However, this risk may be inherent in the design of the KTP programme, that is, their structure necessitates that the Associates are employed on a two-year fixed-term contract. It is perhaps inevitable that towards the end of a project, in the absence of an offer, or at least a discussion, of a contract extension or ongoing employment within the firm, they are likely to be taking steps to secure employment elsewhere.

Therefore, the assessment of U–I collaboration is more usefully understood in terms of overall satisfaction. This provides a broader understanding of how SMEs may have learned and developed as a result of their collaboration, rather than simply concentrating on what was produced. The result being that less tangible benefits can be considered when assessing 'success' of university collaboration, the impacts of which may provide significant benefits to the firm. For example, establishing an ongoing relationship with the academic partner can provide SMEs with a powerful future tool for furthering their ability to innovate. Furthermore, additional human capital and knowledge resources gained through the employment of Associates will only enhance SMEs' competitiveness.

For universities, assessments of the success of their technology transfer activities usually focus on headline metrics such as income from a range of business interactions from collaborative research to the provision of equipment and facilities (Rossi 2010; Rossi and Rosli 2015). Indeed, this approach essentially adopts the 'out the door' criterion, whereby 'success' is viewed as the facilitation of a collaborative link and evaluated in terms of the funding or revenue it generates (Bozeman, Rimes, and Youtie 2015). This means that any other activities and impacts are not captured in these assessments. However, the findings presented in this chapter suggest that this is an oversimplification of the various impacts of their collaborative activities. Indeed, for SMEs, a successful grant application for the project does not feature in their evaluation of success. For universities, a focus on 'softer' factors, such as building medium-to-long-term relationships with SMEs, may produce a more holistic idea of their success in terms of industry collaborations. Indeed, the current moves towards developing a 'Knowledge Exchange Framework' (KEF)[1] for UK universities should take this into account if it is to capture the true impact of universities on the business community.

In summary, these findings indicate that the success of SME–university collaborations is more contextual than objective in nature, covering a range of results and consequences from the collaboration. These findings back up calls within the literature for the evaluations of success of U–I collaborations to take a holistic perspective that examines their success or failure according to a broad range of factors including: working practices and processes; how the actors communicate; whether project objectives are met; and the environment in which the collaboration occurs (Rybnicek and Königsgruber 2019).

This last point echoes calls for the evaluation of university–industry collaboration to involve the continuous monitoring of alliances as they progress in order to assist with adjusting and improving their performance. Continuous monitoring of their collaborative projects may assist SMEs in maintaining the interest of the whole project team and indicate the likely success in terms of producing an output that fulfils the objectives of the project.

NOTE

1. Further details of the Knowledge Exchange Framework are available at https:// re.ukri.org/knowledge-exchange/knowledge-exchange-framework/ (accessed 21 July 2020).

10. Conclusions and implications

This chapter summarises the findings from the empirical analysis presented in the book. The premise of this book is to provide a thorough examination of the process of SME–university collaboration from the perspective of the SMEs involved. The basis for undertaking the study was the fact that SMEs are widely regarded as being less likely to collaborate with universities than larger firms. While this assertion may be true, it does not mean that SMEs do not engage with universities at all. Indeed, the literature reviewed in Chapter 4 highlights that where SMEs do engage with universities, they are less likely to engage in formal collaborations, instead engaging in less formal ways. Furthermore, the dynamics of their interactions may differ from larger firms, being less likely to patent the outcomes and more focused on organisational learning than the creation of a commercial output.

Dispelling the myth of disengagement is an important point, as it is unsatisfactory to merely dismiss SMEs as potential partners for universities but instead to understand how they go about unlocking these ivory towers. Given the fact that 99% of firms are SMEs in the economy of the UK as well as many other nations, placing too much emphasis on large firms means that understanding U–I collaboration reflects only the experiences of a small proportion of firms. Through providing an examination of collaboration between SMEs and universities, this book not only raises the profile of these collaborations, but also provides answers to questions around their formation and function.

Via an analysis of in-depth interviews with SMEs, the material within this book presents a comprehensive account of the factors underlying their university collaborations. The findings highlight the origins of these ideas, the reasons why the firm collaborated with a university partner, the selection of that partner, how the project was delivered, and what factors could be taken to indicate the nature of a successful project. In doing so, the analysis avoids picking out individual characters, instead endeavouring to present an overview of the process as experienced by SMEs without promoting a heroic individual or a set of traits to maximise effectiveness. Therefore, the nuances of the projects are revealed, along with the specific cases of certain behaviours while still presenting a general overview of the process. Clearly, this means the analysis may not offer a generalised account of these events and it must be noted that focusing on a different set of firms may highlight a different set of factors. Yet, there is enough similarity in the individual stories for the findings to be taken as a reasonably typical account of university collaboration from an SME perspective.

The absence of a formal market for university knowledge and the associated mechanisms through which collaboration may be coordinated, that is, a price system, means that the development of such collaborations is akin to systems based on mutual exchange and embeddedness. Therefore, the book adopts a realist position, which supports the use of what Polanyi (2001) termed 'substantivism', whereby economic exchange is understood through reciprocity and redistribution rather than price. Indeed, the conceptualisation of SME–university collaboration as a socio-technical process, whereby relational and cognitive similarities between the partners underpin their formation and function, reinforces this view (Al-Tabbaa and Ankrah 2019; Ankrah and Al-Tabbaa 2015). This description suggests that for these collaborations to occur, both sets of actors must be able to discover, connect, *and* understand one another.

Collaborations are based around networks and networking and driven by proximities, or the closeness, of the actors in terms of physical distances, methods of working, organisational culture, and technical language. Added to this, broadening the analysis of SME–university collaboration beyond the 'out the door' criterion, examining every stage of the process instead of seeing the formation of a link as the end point, allows the roles of these socio-technical characteristics to be assessed at each stage.

To draw this analysis to a close, this final chapter is organised as follows. The overall conclusions are outlined and discussed in turn. This is followed by a discussion of the policy implications of these findings to highlight what policymakers, academics, and knowledge exchange practitioners can learn from this and activities that can be implemented to further promote SME–university collaboration. Finally, limitations and directions for future research are examined.

10.1 CONCLUSIONS

UK universities are increasingly recognised by policymakers as a conduit for knowledge creation. The first two decades of the twenty-first century have seen multiple reviews of the higher education sector, each coming to the same broad conclusion that universities and the knowledge they create represent a key economic resource. Prior to this, driven by the requirements of two world wars, the twentieth century saw the increasing involvement of academics in the invention of military technologies such as radar. The second half of the twentieth century also saw an increasing focus on the use of university knowledge for non-military activity, particularly from the mid-1960s onwards, as greater emphasis was placed on utilising knowledge and technology to pursue economic growth. In the early 1970s 'The Docksey Report' revealed substantial links between universities and industry (Russell, 1971). However, the two decades that followed presented a rather piecemeal and confused approach to science policy, which meant that it was not until the late 1990s that utilising university knowledge became an explicit aspect of innovation policy.

In light of this significant and enduring policy push towards stronger involvement of universities in the innovation system, Chapter 5 illustrates that UK universities appear to have taken this mission seriously as levels of engagement with industry (in terms of the income generated by these contracts) have increased substantially. As a result, industry engagement was worth over £4 billion in 2018–19. Importantly, the fact that university engagement remains lower than for other actors such as customers, suppliers, and rival firms for SMEs, suggests sufficient scope to grow this engagement.

The finding that SMEs develop their project ideas alone and achieve this prior to engaging an external partner is significant as this means there was no university involvement in the development of the ideas that underpinned these projects. Consequently, the genesis of the collaboration is when SMEs begin to search for a university partner while in possession of a fully formed project idea. Indeed, this search resulted not from the wish to collaborate with a university but from the fact that SMEs simultaneously possess sufficient knowledge and capabilities to develop an idea but lack the knowledge and capability required to tackle the project alone. Accordingly, the nature of these fully formed project ideas means that the university partner was required to possess complementary knowledge that matched the firms' requirements.

In practice, these explorations led SMEs to the doors of the ivory towers in a bid to pursue their project ideas with a partner that possesses complementary knowledge that matches their own requirements. The key message here is that the motive of these SMEs was to innovate rather than to engage in university collaboration. This distinction suggests that for SMEs, university collaboration results from innovation, and these motivations reveal the offensive nature of this activity, SMEs are seeking to develop new products to expand and improve the business rather than merely survive.

In general, there is a mixture of embedded and emergent links, whereby the collaborations result from existing networks or the actions of those involved. In short, these collaborative links developed organically and are not engineered by a third party bringing the partners together.

Examining the motivations for seeking a university partner provided the first evidence of the importance of proximities in this process. SMEs' familiarity with universities and their respect for them as sources of high-quality knowledge revealed a degree of organisational and technological proximity. The familiarity was the result of prior collaborations with other universities as well as less formal interactions such as providing placement opportunities or guest lectures, both of which allowed firms to develop an understanding of working practices and cultures within universities. Likewise, these proximities are complemented by the social proximity of the actors, with shared networks often being an important means for accessing a university partner. However, it must be noted that for all but one of these collaborations, the project represented the first time the SME had collaborated with their university partner.

In general, the results reinforce the idea that 'nothing is in the air' (Fitjar and Rodríguez-Pose 2017), as the receipt of university knowledge requires cognitive and relational similarities to access. There is no evidence that SMEs merely absorb knowledge created within universities through unintended spillovers. Interaction between the parties is the key. Therefore, unlocking the ivory tower is possible where SMEs can access a university partner through possessing sufficient networking capabilities to search for and find a partner as well as the cognitive abilities to understand them.

The importance of both networking activities and proximities between partners is evident at every stage of the collaboration process. For example, networks play a crucial role in both the development of relationships and assessment of their credibility. This allows the SMEs to find a new contact, whether through an existing tie or the development of new ties. Therefore, both strong and weak ties are important.

Furthermore, this social proximity was more in evidence at the beginning of the project for search and selection activities. Yet, during the operation of the project it was technological and organisational proximity between the partners that was important, assisting SMEs in both understanding and absorbing the knowledge generated. Therefore, different proximities may play different roles at different stages of the project.

Despite its prominent position in the U–I collaboration literature, spatial proximity was largely absent as an important factor in the motivation for seeking a university partner. Instead, it is connectivity rather than a localised focus that drives SMEs to collaborate in this manner. However, the analysis highlights a more implicit role for spatial proximity that underlies rather than drives the process. Since the average distance between the partners was 76 km, which is approximately an hour's drive, the collaborators were reasonably close to one another. In addition, as several of SMEs were located less than 5 km from their university partner, the results reinforce the idea that these are predominantly localised collaborations. Indeed, the spatial profile of these collaborations appears to result from the local networking focus of the SMEs, which means that this activity took place within the locale of the SMEs. This may not be a deliberate strategy to find local partners but a result of how the networking opportunities present themselves. As the SMEs' networks were mainly centred on their location, so were their collaborative partners, highlighting an implicit role for spatial proximity in the process.

The analysis further reveals that collaborations did occur without the presence of spatial proximity, with some partnerships occurring over hundreds of kilometres. Given this, the co-location of the actors was not necessarily sufficient to promote the development of a link, instead the existence of a network connection was the important criterion (Boschma and ter Wal 2007). Therefore, it is non-spatial proximities, in terms of the closeness of the partners socially, organisationally, and technologically, that are prominent in the findings.

The book also sheds light on the operations of these collaborative projects. Two key findings emerged from this analysis. Firstly, running the project consumes resources within SMEs, and embedding the project team, particularly the Knowledge Transfer Partnership (KTP) Associate, into SMEs is important for the transfer of knowledge. In general, undertaking collaborative projects with universities involves the consumption of resources within the firm and university collaboration may involve a trade-off between the pursuit of 'everyday' activities with the project's objectives. The second finding regards the KTP Associate as a boundary spanner meaning that the project team requires embedding within the firm to ensure that the knowledge can be used within the whole organisation. Similarly, the importance of the Associates to the functioning of the project means that they are required to minimise cognitive and relational distances with both the firm and the university. Indeed, where this did not occur the projects tended to run into barriers either through lack of knowledge transfer or the failure to embed the knowledge in the firm.

The analysis highlights how the project team typically requires a period to embed itself. However, once this had been achieved, usable knowledge was generated during the projects, negating the need to wait for the conclusion of the project to exploit this knowledge. Significantly, SMEs that are able to begin to utilise the knowledge prior to the completion of the project are more likely to perceive the project as being successful.

Importantly, the results highlight the fact that the focus of these projects is based on individual agency and reputations not organisations. For example, credibility is evaluated according to both the source and message conferred by individual academics. Throughout the analysis, it is the role of individual academics that is highlighted rather than the university as an organisation. This provides an important insight into the formation and function of these links in that the organisational relationships are predicated on individuals involved.

The book illuminates factors that may influence the perceived success of these collaborative projects. Understandably the principal concern for SMEs is that their project fulfils its objectives and provides them with a new product to sell or process with which to create new products and services. Yet, the outcomes can also be considered as successful if they facilitate the development of an enduring relationship between the firm and the university, generating permanent employment opportunities for the KTP Associates, the creation of academic outputs, and the associated kudos from working with a university.

Furthermore, the evidence suggests that the successful creation of outputs means that SMEs are more likely to develop an enduring relationship with the university. Conversely, the lack of a successful output ends the relationship between the SME and its university partner. Despite this, the perceived failure of a project does not necessarily mean that SMEs are discouraged from pursuing another collaboration with a different university partner.

There is also evidence that the starting levels of organisational proximity may influence the success of the project outputs, as those SMEs that have higher levels of interaction with universities prior to their collaboration typically reported the creation of a successful output from the project. On the other hand, SMEs with less experience of working with universities are more likely to report an unsuccessful output. Therefore, there appears to be a link between the experience of working with universities and the ultimate success of the project in terms of achieving its objectives. This finding hints at the fact that there may be a need to learn how to work with universities in order to successfully collaborate.

Accordingly, the findings presented within the book make several key contributions to understanding U–I collaboration from a theoretical perspective. To summarise, the analysis suggests that:

- Relational and cognitive factors are important for both the formation and function of collaborative links between SMEs and universities.
- Spatial proximity plays an implicit role in the collaboration process between SMEs and universities.
- The closeness of the actors in terms of social, technological, and organisational proximity may evolve through the collaboration process.
- A broad range of outputs and outcomes underpins the success of the project.
- Successful projects are more likely to result in enduring relationships between SMEs and universities.
- Collaborative projects between SMEs and universities are path dependent in nature, with prior experience of working with universities likely to result in more successful projects.

The closeness of the actors is important at every stage of the projects and the findings clearly contribute to evidence that outlines the socio-technical nature of the process of SME–university collaboration. This socio-technical description captures the importance of the existing networks for identifying a university, plus the prior experiences of engagement and the associated organisational and technological proximity between the parties that this promotes.

The importance of relational and cò27gnitive factors to the formation and function of SME–university links provides an insight into why this type of engagement is rarer than collaboration between other actors. It may be that an absence of cognitive and relational factors is a limiting factor for most SMEs, as the closeness between the majority of firms and universities is just not present. Therefore, the higher levels of interaction with other actors is the result of greater similarities to these actors. As a result, the key to encouraging greater interaction between SMEs and universities may lie in encouraging network connections between the two parties to promote understanding.

The analysis reveals degrees of proximity in terms of the organisational, technological, or social familiarity and understanding of the actors. These may evolve during the lifetime of the project and are, therefore, dynamic in nature. In terms of the two-worlds paradox, which suggests that there may be fundamental barriers to the effective collaboration of firms and universities, it appears that these barriers may diminish through the course of projects. Based on these findings, revisiting the proximity matrix captures the cognitive and relational basis for SME–university collaboration (See Table 10.1). The matrix provides a useful framework for assessing how the distance between the partners either physically, through network membership, their knowledge base, and working practices may influence the formation and function of these collaborations. Based on the analysis presented here, the matrix does not assume primacy for any single proximity but maps the extent to which each exists within a given dyad in order to assess the drivers of the collaborative link. Importantly, the analysis presented in the preceding chapters has demonstrated that these factors are also dynamic and may ebb and flow as the actors learn to work together, join new networks, accumulate new knowledge and expertise, or change location.

Finally, the results contribute to enhancing the understanding of SME–university collaboration through charting the broad set of success factors that may underpin U–I collaboration. Specifically, the findings contribute to debates within the literature that have broadened the set of factors used to judge success (Albats, Fiegenbaum, and Cunningham 2018; Perkmann, Neely, and Walsh 2011). Furthermore, the results reveal that these collaborations were to a certain extent path dependent, with the success of the outputs being related to the starting levels of SMEs' experience of prior working with universities.

Table 10.1   *The Proximity matrix revisited*

	Spatial (physical distance)	Social (network participation)	Organisational (working methods and culture)	Technological (knowledge bases)
Total Proximity	Located on same science park/ industrial estate	Members of identical networks	Identical working culture and practices	Utilise identical scientific language and knowledge base
Comprehensive Proximity	Located within same city/town	Significant overlap of actors within networks	Significant overlap of working culture, practice, and procedures	Significant overlaps in scientific language used and knowledge base
Intermediate Proximity	Located within the same region	Some overlap of actors within networks	Some similarity of working culture, practice, and procedures	Some similarity in scientific language used and knowledge base
Limited Proximity	Located within adjacent regions	Few common actors within networks	Little similarity in working culture, practice, and procedures	Little similarity in scientific language and knowledge base
No Proximity	Located in non-adjacent regions	No common actors within networks	No common working culture, practice, and procedures	No common scientific language or knowledge base

10.2   IMPLICATIONS FOR SMES, PRACTITIONERS, AND POLICYMAKERS

The findings from the analysis presented in this book have set out several new insights into the formation and function of SME–university collaborative projects. This section considers the findings in terms of their implications for SMEs, academics, knowledge exchange practitioners, and policymakers.

For SMEs, the promise of university collaboration is the development of new products and processes with which to enhance the competitive position of the business. The first implication is the need for SMEs to develop their ideas prior to pursuing university collaboration. Based on this, it appears that university collaboration follows innovation rather than vice versa. The implication here is that only SMEs seeking to innovate may collaborate with universities. Yet, this need not discourage those SMEs that are nascent innovators and lack fully developed ideas. Indeed, while universities must not be regarded as a panacea for delivering successful innovation, they can still offer multiple levels of assistance to SMEs from the provision of equipment or facilities, informal advice, or signposting to relevant sources of assistance to promote innovation. In short, for SMEs, engagement with a university can assist with the development of ideas from any starting point.

SMEs must also expect the collaboration to consume resources. The process is based around the co-creation of knowledge based on working together. Therefore, SMEs should further appreciate that the collaboration process is also about learning to work with the university partner. Learning to work with the partner is also closely related to the evolution of commonalities between the SME and university. While proximities, or the closeness of the actors, clearly played an important role in the formation and function of these SME–university links, the fact that these may also develop and evolve during the project means that low levels or even an absence do not preclude the formation and function of these projects. Therefore, SMEs should not necessarily be discouraged if they consider there are few similarities with their partner at the outset as this can develop during the collaboration.

SMEs must further appreciate that success may be more contextual than objective in nature as perceptions can cover a range of results and conse-quences from the collaboration. The creation of jobs, the development of aca-demic outputs and the kudos of collaboration may all be regarded as measures of success for SMEs in the course of U–I collaboration. Firms may wish to consider a broader range of factors for success – particularly those with less experience of university collaboration, for whom the process may involve more learning. Here, SMEs are encouraged to look beyond the project outputs when considering the impacts on the business.

From the perspective of academics and knowledge exchange practitioners, there are clear implications in terms of how they may connect to SMEs. Two of the insights from this research may be useful to this group, the first concerns the focus on the individual rather than the institution, and the second around the importance of networks and networking. The focus on the individual is important because universities tend to market themselves as an organisation and are increasingly judged in these terms. For example, rankings metrics tend to focus on the overall university performance in terms of teaching, research, and, in the future, knowledge transfer. However, this broad-brush approach may miss key strengths in specific areas among academics, and importantly may not be useful to the SME community who typically do not refer to any of these metrics. Instead, they judge the partner in terms of the individual academic and it is these individuals and their message that is important to the firms.

Highlighting the expertise of individual academics to the business com-munity and encouraging these individuals to develop their networks, and of course providing the time and incentives to do so, would appear to be a fruitful policy progression. In doing so, the academic community can pursue a course of action that enables connections with the SME community to be established. Care should also be taken by academics to make their backgrounds understandable by the business community. For example, ensuring that websites are configured so that Google searches may pick up simple queries as well as highlighting their knowledge and expertise in accessible terms. This will then have the effect of reducing cognitive distances between the actors.

Furthermore, if cognitive and relational similarity between the actors is important, differences between SMEs and universities can be eradicated. It has been long argued that universities are distinct from firms in their activities and motivations (Lavie and Drori 2012) and consequently conceptualised as ivory towers that are somewhat removed from society. However, this is possibly the fundamental advantage of universities in that this difference places them in a unique position to work alongside SMEs to promote and support open innovation. While the differing focus and priorities may result in dissimilarities between the actors, it would be foolish to advocate the promotion of homogeneity between the two. Instead, it is important that universities and the business communities are related, so that overlapping concerns and objectives exist, but are still distinct, so that they are free to pursue their relative strengths.

In terms of the promotion of proximities, encouraging the active participation of academics in firm-based networks may increase the social proximity of actors where it may not exist or be limited in nature. The effective dissemination of university knowledge in an accessible manner, in terms of both the language used and the openness of access, may also enable higher levels of technological proximity. However, the division of activities with universities focusing on the creation of knowledge and firms concentrating on its commercialisation means the activities of the two actors will run in parallel rather than merge. Indeed, as the differences between these actors allow SMEs and universities to learn from one another it is not desirable to eradicate it completely.

Given these arguments, it would be valuable to urge greater levels of interaction between SMEs and universities to gain experience as to how each other works, their culture, and their knowledge and expertise. However, this need not be achieved through formal collaboration alone, and therefore we encourage knowledge exchange practitioners to promote the interaction of academics and SMEs through less formal activities such as placements, assistance with equipment, and guest lectures on their activities to cultivate interaction and relationships.

In general, a broader set of initiatives may be required to support the interaction of academics with SMEs. A lack of a market means that this type of open innovation may be subject to information access failures. Indeed, proposed measures to tackle this have been suggested in terms of providing information about potential partners (Hewitt-Dundas and Roper 2017). Based on the findings presented in this book, this should be targeted at the individual level to provide information on who possesses the knowledge and expertise required.

10.3   LIMITATIONS AND DIRECTIONS FOR FUTURE RESEARCH

Through an in-depth examination of university collaboration from the point of view of SMEs, this book has provided a thorough and comprehensive account of their experiences. However, it is acknowledged that this does not necessarily paint the whole picture as the voices of the university partners are absent from our findings. Given this, it would be pertinent to encourage further work in this area to provide a mixed account of these partnerships, giving voice to the academic partners. The most likely route to achieve this is through focusing on fewer projects with a larger number of participants.

As noted earlier, the book does not claim to provide a generalisable account nonetheless an overview of the typical experiences of SMEs when collaborating with universities. As such, the characters involved in the storytelling remain somewhat in the background, emerging through the reported quotes to illustrate specific events that were pertinent to the findings. The growth in narrative research in the business and management discipline has begun to provide much deeper accounts of phenomena under investigation. For example, work in the entrepreneurship field has yielded interesting insights into new venture creation, while innovation biographies have also led to more comprehensive understandings of the process.

Finally, future research should seek to further test the empirical and theoretical findings presented in this book, particularly at a larger scale so that generalisations can be analysed. Furthermore, it may be fruitful for scholars to further investigate proximities between SMEs and universities in order to assess whether an optimal level may exist, particularly in terms of non-spatial proximities focused on social, organisational, and technological similarities. The existing literature on U–I collaboration has identified that the relationship between both firm size and spatial proximity and the probability of a collaborative link developing is non-linear in nature (D'Este, Guy, and Iammarino 2013; Fukugawa 2013; Johnston and Huggins 2016), suggesting that an optimal level for both exists. Therefore, further investigation of the relationship between social, organisational, and technological proximities and the formation of collaborative links can shed further light on the success factors for SME–university collaboration.

References

Abelson, Philip H. 1966. 'The Tea Leaves or the Record?' *Science* 151(3712):781.

Abreu, M. and V. Grinevich. 2013. 'The Nature of Academic Entrepreneurship in the UK: Widening the Focus on Entrepreneurial Activities.' *Research Policy* 42(2):408–22.

Abreu, M., V. Grinevich, A. Hughes, M. Kitson, and P. Ternouth. 2008. *Universities, Business and Knowledge Exchange.* London: The Council for Industry and Higher Education.

Acs, Z. and D.B. Auderetsch. 1990. *Innovation and Small Firms.* Cambridge, MA: MIT Press.

Acs, Z., L. Anselin, and A. Varga. 2002. 'Patents and Innovation Counts as Measures of Regional Production of New Knowledge.' *Research Policy* 21(7):1069–85.

Agar, J. 2019. 'Science Policy since the 1960s.' Pp. 21–30 in *Lessons from the History of UK Science Policy*, edited by British Academy. Available at https://www.thebritishacademy.ac.uk/documents/243/Lessons-History-UK-science-policy.pdf (accessed 15 June 2020).

Agrawal, Ajay K. 2001. 'University-to-Industry Knowledge Transfer: Literature Review and Unanswered Questions.' *International Journal of Management Reviews* 3(4):285–302.

Agrawal, Ajay and Rebecca Henderson. 2002. 'Putting Patents in Context: Exploring Knowledge Transfer from MIT.' *Management Science* 48(1):44–60.

Aguilera, A., V. Lethiais, and A. Rallet. 2012. 'Spatial and Non-Spatial Proximities in Inter-Firm Relations: An Empirical Analysis.' *Industry and Innovation* 19(3):187–202.

Ahuja, G. 2000. 'The Duality of Collaboration: Inducements and Opportunities in the Formation of Interfirm Linkages.' *Strategic Management Journal* 21(3):317–43.

Al-Ashaab, Ahmed, Myrna Flores, Athanasia Doultsinou, and Andrea Magyar. 2011. 'A Balanced Scorecard for Measuring the Impact of Industry–University Collaboration.' *Production Planning & Control* 22(5–6):554–70.

Al-Tabbaa, Omar and Samuel Ankrah. 2016. 'Social Capital to Facilitate "Engineered" University–Industry Collaboration for Technology Transfer: A Dynamic Perspective.' *Technological Forecasting and Social Change* 104:1–15.

Al-Tabbaa, Omar and Samuel Ankrah. 2019. '"Engineered" University-Industry Collaboration: A Social Capital Perspective.' *European Management Review* 16(3):543–65.

Alam, Ian. 2006. 'Removing the Fuzziness from the Fuzzy Front-End of Service Innovations through Customer Interactions.' *Industrial Marketing Management* 35(4):468–80.

Albats, Ekaterina, Irina Fiegenbaum, and James A. Cunningham. 2018. 'A Micro Level Study of University Industry Collaborative Lifecycle Key Performance Indicators.' *The Journal of Technology Transfer* 43(2):389–431.

Almeida, P., G. Dokko, and L. Rosenkopf. 2003. 'Startup Size and the Mechanisms of External Learning: Increasing Opportunity and Decreasing Ability?' *Research Policy* 32(2):301–15.

Andrade, Rita, Gabriela Fernandes, and Anabela Tereso. 2016. 'Benefits Management in University-Industry R&D Collaborative Projects: A Review on Benefits and Success Factors.' *Procedia Computer Science*. 100:921–7.

Ankrah, Samuel and Omar Al-Tabbaa. 2015. 'Universities–Industry Collaboration: A Systematic Review.' *Scandinavian Journal of Management* 31(3):387–408.

Arranz, Nieves and J. Carlos Fdez de Arroyabe. 2008. 'The Choice of Partners in R&D Cooperation: An Empirical Analysis of Spanish Firms.' *Technovation* 28(1–2):88–100.

Arrow, K. 1962. 'Economic Welfare and the Allocation of Resources for Invention.' Pp. 609–26 in *The Rate and Direction of Inventive Activity*, edited by R. Nelson. Princton, NJ: Princeton University Press.

Asheim, B. and M. Gertler. 2005. 'The Geography of Innovation: Regional Innovation Systems.' Pp. 291–317 in *The Oxford Handbook of Innovation*, edited by J. Fagerberg, D. Mowery, and R. Nelson. Oxford: Oxford University Press.

Autant-Bernard, C., P. Billand, D. Frachisse, and N. Massard. 2007. 'Social Distance versus Spatial Distance in R&D Cooperation: Empirical Evidence from European Collaboration Choices in Micro and Nanotechnologies.' *Papers in Regional Science* 86(3):495–519.

Azagra-Caro, Joaquín M., David Barberá-Tomás, Mónica Edwards-Schachter, and Elena M. Tur. 2017. 'Dynamic Interactions between University–Industry Knowledge Transfer Channels: A Case Study of the Most Highly Cited Academic Patent.' *Research Policy* 46(2):463–74.

Baba, Yasunori, Naohiro Shichijo, and Silvia Rita Sedita. 2009. 'How Do Collaborations with Universities Affect Firms' Innovative Performance? The Role of "Pasteur Scientists" in the Advanced Materials Field.' *Research Policy* 38(5):756–64.

Balconi, M. and A. Laboranti. 2006. 'University-Industry Interactions in Applied Research: The Case of Microelectronics.' *Research Policy* 35(10):1616–30.

Balland, Pierre-Alexandre, Ron Boschma, and Koen Frenken. 2015. 'Proximity and Innovation: From Statics to Dynamics.' *Regional Studies* 49(6):907–20.

Bansal, Pratima, Stephanie Bertels, Tom Ewart, Peter MacConnachie, and James O'Brien. 2012. 'Bridging the Research–Practice Gap.' *Academy of Management Perspectives*. 26: 73–92.

Barnes, Tina, Ian Pashby, and Anne Gibbons. 2002. 'Effective University–Industry Interaction: A Multi-Case Evaluation of Collaborative R&D Projects.' *European Management Journal* 20(3):272–85.

Barney, J. 1991. 'Firm Resources and Sustained Competitive Advantage.' *Journal of Management* 17(1):99–120.

Bartunek, J.M. and S.L. Rynes. 2014. 'Academics and Practitioners Are Alike and Unlike: The Paradoxes of Academic–Practitioner Relationships.' *Journal of Management* 40(5):1181–201.

Bathelt, H. 2005. 'Cluster Relations in the Media Industry: Exploring the "Distanced Neighbour" Paradox in Leipzig.' *Regional Studies* 39(1):105–27.

Bathelt, Harald and Patrick Cohendet. 2014. 'The Creation of Knowledge: Local Building, Global Accessing and Economic Development – toward an Agenda.' *Journal of Economic Geography* 14(5):869–82.

Bathelt, H., A. Malmberg, and P. Maskell. 2004. 'Clusters and Knowledge: Local Buzz, Global Pipelines and the Process of Knowledge Creation.' *Progress in Human Geography* 28(1):31–56.

Bauer, M. 1996. *The Narrative Interview: Comments on a Technique for Qualitative Data Collection*. Papers in Social Research Methods. London School of Economics and Political Science, Methodology Institute.

Beckman, C.M., P.R. Haunschild, and D.J. Phillips. 2004. 'Friends or Strangers? Firm-Specific Uncertainty, Market Uncertainty, and Network Partner Selection.' *Organisation Science* 15(3):259–75.

Beech, N., R. MacIntosh, and D. MacLean. 2010. 'Dialogues between Academics and Practitioners: The Role of Generative Dialogic Encounters.' *Organization Studies* 31(9–10):1341–67.

Belderbos, René, Martin Carree, Bert Diederen, Boris Lokshin, and Reinhilde Veugelers. 2004. 'Heterogeneity in R&D Cooperation Strategies.' *International Journal of Industrial Organization* 22(8–9):1237–63.

Belderbos, René, Martin Carree, and Boris Lokshin. 2004. 'Cooperative R&D and Firm Performance.' *Research Policy* 33(10):1477–92.

di Benedetto, A. 2010. 'Comment on "Is Open Innovation a Field of Study or a Communication Barrier to Theory Development?"' *Technovation* 30:557.

Bhaskar, R. 2008. *A Realist Theory of Science*. Abingdon: Routledge.

Bigliardi, Barbara and Francesco Galati. 2016. 'Which Factors Hinder the Adoption of Open Innovation in SMEs?' *Technology Analysis & Strategic Management* 28(8):869–85.

Bishop, Kate, Pablo D'Este, and Andy Neely. 2011. 'Gaining from Interactions with Universities: Multiple Methods for Nurturing Absorptive Capacity.' *Research Policy* 40(1):30–40.

Bjerregaard, Toke. 2009. 'Universities-Industry Collaboration Strategies: A Micro-Level Perspective.' *European Journal of Innovation Management* 12(2):161–76.

Bjerregaard, Toke. 2010. 'Industry and Academia in Convergence: Micro-Institutional Dimensions of R&D Collaboration.' *Technovation* 30(2):100–8.

Bodas Freitas, Isabel Maria, Aldo Geuna, and Federica Rossi. 2013. 'Finding the Right Partners: Institutional and Personal Modes of Governance of University-Industry Interactions.' *Research Policy* 42(1):50–62.

Boje, D.M. 2001. *Narrative Methods for Organisational and Communication Research*. London: Sage.

Bonaccorsi, Andrea and Andrea Piccaluga. 1994. 'A Theoretical Framework for the Evaluation of University-Industry Relationships.' *R&D Management* 24(3):229–47.

Boschma, R.A. 2005. 'Proximity and Innovation: A Critical Assessment.' *Regional Studies* 39(1):61–74.

Boschma, R.A. and Anne L.J. ter Wal. 2007. 'Knowledge Networks and Innovative Performance in an Industrial District: The Case of a Footwear District in the South of Italy.' *Industry and Innovation* 14(2):177–99.

Bozeman, Barry, Heather Rimes, and Jan Youtie. 2015. 'The Evolving State-of-the-Art in Technology Transfer Research: Revisiting the Contingent Effectiveness Model.' *Research Policy* 44(1):34–49.

Broekel, T. and R. Boschma. 2012. 'Knowledge Networks in the Dutch Aviation Industry: The Proximity Paradox.' *Journal of Economic Geography* 12(2):409–33.

Broström, Anders. 2010. 'Working with Distant Researchers – Distance and Content in University–Industry Interaction.' *Research Policy* 39(10):1311–20.

Brouthers, Keith D., Lance Eliot Brouthers, and Timothy J. Wilkinson. 1995. 'Strategic Alliances: Choose Your Partners.' *Long Range Planning* 28(3):18–25.

Bruneel, Johan, Pablo D'Este, and Ammon Salter. 2010. 'Investigating the Factors That Diminish the Barriers to University–Industry Collaboration.' *Research Policy* 39(7):858–68.

Bud, R. and P. Gummett. 2002. *Cold War, Hot Science: Applied Research in Britain's Defence Laboratories, 1945–1990.* London: Science Museum.

Budyldina, Natalia. 2018. 'Entrepreneurial Universities and Regional Contribution.' *International Entrepreneurship and Management Journal* 14(2):265–77.

Caldera, A. and O. Debande. 2010. 'Performance of Spanish Universities in Technology Transfer: An Empirical Analysis.' *Research Policy* 39(9):1160–73.

Caloffi, Annalisa, Federica Rossi, and Margherita Russo. 2015. 'What Makes SMEs More Likely to Collaborate? Analysing the Role of Regional Innovation Policy.' *European Planning Studies* 23(7):1245–64.

Capaldo, Antonio and Antonio Messeni Petruzzelli. 2014. 'Partner Geographic and Organizational Proximity and the Innovative Performance of Knowledge-Creating Alliances.' *European Management Review* 11(1):63–84.

Capone, Francesco and Luciana Lazzeretti. 2018. 'The Different Roles of Proximity in Multiple Informal Network Relationships: Evidence from the Cluster of High Technology Applied to Cultural Goods in Tuscany.' *Industry and Innovation* 25(9):897–917.

Capone, Francesco and Vincenzo Zampi. 2019. 'Proximity and Centrality in Inter-Organisational Collaborations for Innovation: A Study on an Aerospace Cluster in Italy.' *Management Decision* 58(2):239–54.

CBI. 2015. *Best of Both Worlds: Guide to Business–University Collaboration.* London: Middlesex University London.

Centobelli, Piera, Roberto Cerchione, Emilio Esposito, and Shashi Aggrawal. 2019. 'Exploration and Exploitation in the Development of More Entrepreneurial Universities: A Twisting Learning Path Model of Ambidexterity.' *Technological Forecasting and Social Change* 141:172–94.

Charles, D. 2006. 'Universities as Key Knowledge Infrastructures in Regional Innovation Systems.' *Innovation* 19(1):117–30.

Charles, D. 2016. 'The Rural University Campus and Support for Rural Innovation.' *Science and Public Policy* 43(6):763–73.

Charles, D. and P. Benneworth. 2002. *Evaluating the Regional Contribution of an HEI.* Bristol: HEFCE.

Chatterton, P. and J.B. Goddard. 2000. 'The Response of Higher Education Institutions to Regional Needs.' *European Journal of Education* 35(4):475–96.

Chen, Ming Jer. 1996. 'Competitor Analysis and Interfirm Rivalry: Toward a Theoretical Integration.' *Academy of Management Review* 21(1):100–34.

Chesbrough, H.W. 2003. *Open Innovation: The New Imperative for Creating and Profiting from Technology.* Cambridge, MA: Harvard Business School Press.

Chesbrough, Henry. 2007. 'Business Model Innovation: It's Not Just about Technology Anymore.' *Strategy & Leadership* 35(6):12–17.

Chesbrough, Henry. 2017. 'The Future of Open Innovation.' *Research-Technology Management* 60(1):35–8.

Christensen, C.M. 1997. *The Innovator's Dilemma: When New Technolgies Cause Great Firms to Fail.* Boston, MA: Harvard Business School Press.

Clandinin, D.J. and F.M. Connelly. 2000. *Narrative Inquiry: Experience and Story in Narrative Research.* San Francisco, CA: Jossey-Bass.

Clark, B. 1998. *Creating Entrepreneurial Universities: Organisational Pathways of Transformation*. Oxford: Elsevier.

Cohen, W.M. and Daniel A. Levinthal. 1990. 'Absorptive Capacity: A New Perspective on Learning and Innovation.' *Administrative Science Quarterly* 35(1):128–52.

Cohen, Wesley M., Richard R. Nelson, and John P. Walsh. 2002. 'Links and Impacts: The Influence of Public Research on Industrial R&D.' *Management Science* 48(1):1–23.

Coleman, James S. 1988. 'Social Capital in the Creation of Human Capital.' *American Journal of Sociology* 94:S95–S120.

Colombo, M., E. Piva, and Cristina Rossi-Lamastra. 2014. 'Open Innovation and Within-Industry Diversification in Small and Medium Enterprises: The Case of Open Source Software Firms.' *Research Policy* 43(5):891–902.

Contractor, F. and P. Lorange. 2002. 'The Growth of Alliances in the Knowledge-Based Economy.' *International Business Review* 11(4):205–485.

Cooke, P. and K. Morgan. 1998. *The Associational Economy*. Oxford: Oxford University Press.

Cowan, R. and N. Jonard. 2003. 'The Dynamics of Collective Invention.' *Journal of Economic Behavior & Organization* 52(4):513–32.

Cowan, R., P. David, and D. Foray. 2000. 'The Explicit Economics of Knowledge Codification and Tacitness.' *Industrial and Corporate Change* 9(2):211–53.

Crescenzi, Riccardo, Andrea Filippetti, and Simona Iammarino. 2017. 'Academic Inventors: Collaboration and Proximity with Industry.' *The Journal of Technology Transfer* 42(4):730–62.

Cunningham, James A. and Paul O'Reilly. 2018. 'Macro, Meso and Micro Perspectives of Technology Transfer.' *The Journal of Technology Transfer* 43(3):545–57.

Czarniawska, B. 1998. *A Narrative Approach to Organisation Studies*. London: Sage.

D'Este, P. and S. Iammarino. 2010. 'The Spatial Profile of University-Business Research Partnerships.' *Papers in Regional Science* 89(2):335–50.

D'Este, P. and P. Patel. 2007. 'University–Industry Linkages in the UK: What Are the Factors Underlying the Variety of Interactions with Industry?' *Research Policy* 36(9):1295–313.

D'Este, Pablo and Markus Perkmann. 2010. 'Why Do Academics Engage with Industry? The Entrepreneurial University and Individual Motivations.' *The Journal of Technology Transfer* 36(3):316–39.

D'Este, Pablo, Frederick Guy, and Simona Iammarino. 2013. 'Shaping the Formation of University–Industry Research Collaborations: What Type of Proximity Does Really Matter?' *Journal of Economic Geography* 13(4):537–58.

Dacin, M. Tina, Christine Oliver, and Jean-Paul Roy. 2007. 'The Legitimacy of Strategic Alliances: An Institutional Perspective.' *Strategic Management Journal* 28(2):169–87.

Dada, Olufunmilola (Lola) and Helen Fogg. 2016. 'Organizational Learning, Entrepreneurial Orientation, and the Role of University Engagement in SMEs.' *International Small Business Journal: Researching Entrepreneurship* 34(1):86–104.

Dahlander, L. and D. Gann. 2010. 'How Open Is Innovation?' *Research Policy* 39(6):699–709.

Das, T.K. and B.S. Teng. 2001. 'Trust, Control, and Risk in Strategic Alliances: An Integrated Framework.' *Organization Studies* 22(2):251–83.

Dasgupta, Partha and Paul A. David. 1994. 'Toward a New Economics of Science.' *Research Policy* 23(5):487–521.

Davenport, S. 2005. 'Exploring the Role of Proximity in SME Knowledge-Acquisition.' *Research Policy* 34(5):683–701.

David, Paul A. 1998. 'Common Agency Contracting and the Emergence of "Open Science" Institutions.' *American Economic Review* 88(2):15–21.

Debackere, Koenraad and Reinhilde Veugelers. 2005. 'The Role of Academic Technology Transfer Organizations in Improving Industry Science Links.' *Research Policy* 34(3):321–42.

Delfmann, Heike and Sierdjan Koster. 2012. 'Knowledge Transfer between SMEs and Higher Education Institutions.' *Industry and Higher Education* 26(1):31–42.

Devarakonda, Shivaram V. and Jeffrey J. Reuer. 2018. 'Knowledge Sharing and Safeguarding in R&D Collaborations: The Role of Steering Committees in Biotechnology Alliances.' *Strategic Management Journal* 39(7):1912–34.

Devigili, M., T. Pucci, and L. Zanni. 2019. 'Looking for the Red Thread: A Systematic Literature Review on Proximity and Innovation.' Paper Presented at DRUID19 Copenhagen Business School, Copenhagen, Denmark, 19–21 June.

DiMaggio, P.J. 1988. 'Interest and Agency in Institutional Theory.' Pp. 3–22 in *Institutional Patterns and Organizations*, edited by L. Zucker. Cambridge, MA: Ballinger.

Discua Cruz, Allan, Eleanor Hamilton, and Sarah L. Jack. 2020. 'Understanding Entrepreneurial Opportunities through Metaphors: A Narrative Approach to Theorizing Family Entrepreneurship.' *Entrepreneurship & Regional Development*: 1–22. https://doi.org/10.1080/08985626.2020.1727089.

Dittrich, Koen and Geert Duysters. 2007. 'Networking as a Means to Strategy Change: The Case of Open Innovation in Mobile Telephony.' *Journal of Product Innovation Management* 24(6):510–21.

Dornbusch, Friedrich and Peter Neuhäusler. 2015. 'Composition of Inventor Teams and Technological Progress – the Role of Collaboration between Academia and Industry.' *Research Policy* 44(7):1360–75.

Dosi, G. 1990. 'The Nature of the Innovative Process.' Pp. 221–38 in *Technical Change and Economic Theory*, edited by G. Dosi, C. Freeman, and R. Nelson. London: Frances Pinter.

Doyle, Joanne. 2018. 'Reconceptualising Research Impact: Reflections on the Real-World Impact of Research in an Australian Context.' *Higher Education Research & Development* 37(7):1366–79.

Drejer, I., F.S. Kristensen, and K. Laursen. 1999. 'Studies of Clusters as a Basis for Industrial and Technology Policy in the Danish Economy.' Pp. 293–313 in *Boosting Innovation: The Cluster Approach*, edited by OECD. Paris: OECD.

DTI. 1998. *Our Competitive Future: Building the Knowledge Driven Economy – Analytical Report*. London: HMSO.

Dyer, J.H. 1996. 'Specialized Supplier Networks as a Source of Competitive Advantage: Evidence from the Auto Industry.' *Strategic Management Journal* 17(4):271–91.

Dyer, Jeffrey H. and Harbir Singh. 1998. 'The Relational View: Cooperative Strategy and Sources of Interorganizational Competitive Advantage.' *The Academy of Management Review* 23(4):660.

Dyer, Jeffrey H., Harbir Singh, and William S. Hesterly. 2018. 'The Relational View Revisited: A Dynamic Perspective on Value Creation and Value Capture.' *Strategic Management Journal* 39(12):3140–62.

Easton, G. 2010. 'Critical Realism in Case Study Research.' *Industrial Marketing Management* 39(1):118–28.

Ebersberger, B., C. Bloch, S. Herstad, and E. Van De Velde. 2012. 'Open Innovation Practices and Their Effect on Innovation Performance.' *International Journal of Innovation and Technology Management* 9(6):1–12.

Edgerton, D. 2019. 'What Has British Science Policy Really Been?' Pp. 31–9 in *Lessons from the History of UK Science Policy*, edited by British Academy. Available at https://www.thebritishacademy.ac.uk/documents/243/Lessons-History -UK-science-policy.pdf (accessed 15 June 2020).

Edler, Jakob and Jan Fagerberg. 2017. 'Innovation Policy: What, Why, and How.' *Oxford Review of Economic Policy* 33(1):2–23.

Eisenhardt, Kathleen M. and Claudia Bird Schoonhoven. 1996. 'Resource-Based View of Strategic Alliance Formation: Strategic and Social Effects in Entrepreneurial Firms.' *Organization Science* 7(2):136–50.

Enkel, Ellen, Oliver Gassmann, and Henry Chesbrough. 2009. 'Open R&D and Open Innovation: Exploring the Phenomenon.' *R&D Management* 39(4):311–16.

Eom, Boo-Young and Keun Lee. 2010. 'Determinants of Industry–Academy Linkages and Their Impact on Firm Performance: The Case of Korea as a Latecomer in Knowledge Industrialization.' *Research Policy* 39(5):625–39.

Ericson, M. 2010. *A Narrative Approach to Business Growth*. Cheltenham, UK and Northampton, MA, USA: Edward Elgar.

Etzkowitz, H. 2003a. 'Innovation in Innovation: The Triple Helix of University-Industry-Government Relations.' *Social Science Information* 42(3):293–337.

Etzkowitz, H. 2003b. 'Research Groups as "Quasi-Firms": The Invention of the Entrepreneurial University.' *Research Policy* 32(1):109–21.

Etzkowitz, Henry and Loet Leydesdorff. 2000. 'The Dynamics of Innovation: From National Systems and "Mode 2" to a Triple Helix of University–Industry–Government Relations.' *Research Policy* 29(2):109–23.

Etzkowitz, H. and C. Zhou. 2006. 'Triple Helix Twins: Innovation and Sustainability.' *Science and Public Policy* 33(1):77–83.

European Communities. 1986. 'Single European Act.' Official Journal of the European Communities No. L 169/1.

Faems, Dries, Bart Van Looy, and Koenraad Debackere. 2005. 'Interorganizational Collaboration and Innovation: Toward a Portfolio Approach.' *Journal of Product Innovation Management* 22(3):238–50.

Feldman, M.P. 1999. 'The New Economics of Innovation, Spillovers and Agglomeration: A Review of Empirical Studies.' *Economics of Innovation and New Technology* 8(1–2):5–25.

Fini, Riccardo, Einar Rasmussen, Donald Siegel, and Johan Wiklund. 2018. 'Rethinking the Commercialization of Public Science: From Entrepreneurial Outcomes to Societal Impacts.' *Academy of Management Perspectives* 32(1):4–20.

Fitjar, Rune Dahl and Andrés Rodríguez-Pose. 2017. 'Nothing Is in the Air.' *Growth and Change* 48(1):22–39.

Fitjar, Rune Dahl and Martin Gjelsvik. 2018. 'Why Do Firms Collaborate with Local Universities?' *Regional Studies* 52(11):1525–36.

Flanagan, Kieron and Elvira Uyarra. 2016. 'Four Dangers in Innovation Policy Studies – and How to Avoid Them.' *Industry and Innovation* 23(2):177–88.

Fletcher, D. 2007. '"Toy Story": The Narrative World of Entrepreneurship and the Creation of Interpretive Communities.' *Journal of Business Venturing* 22(5):649–72.

Fontana, Roberto, Aldo Geuna, and Mireille Matt. 2006. 'Factors Affecting University–Industry R&D Projects: The Importance of Searching, Screening and Signalling.' *Research Policy* 35(2):309–23.

Freel, Mark. 2000. 'External Linkages and Product Innovation in Small Manufacturing Firms.' *Entrepreneurship & Regional Development* 12(3):245–66.

Freel, Mark and Richard Harrison. 2006. 'Innovation and Cooperation in the Small Firm Sector: Evidence from "Northern Britain".' *Regional Studies* 40(4):289–305.

Freeman, C. 1992. 'Formal Scientific and Technical Institutions in the National System of Innovation.' Pp. 173–92 in *National Systems of Innovation: Towards a Theory of Innovation and Interactive Learning*, edited by B. Lundvall. London: Pinter.

Fu, Xiaolan. 2012. 'How Does Openness Affect the Importance of Incentives for Innovation?' *Research Policy* 41(3):512–23.

Fukugawa, Nobuya. 2013. 'University Spillovers into Small Technology-Based Firms: Channel, Mechanism, and Geography.' *The Journal of Technology Transfer* 38(4):415–31.

Garcia-Perez-de-Lema, Domingo, Antonia Madrid-Guijarro, and Dominique Philippe Martin. 2017. 'Influence of University–Firm Governance on SMEs Innovation and Performance Levels.' *Technological Forecasting and Social Change* 123:250–61.

Garman, Andrew N. 2011. 'Shooting for the Moon: How Academicians Could Make Management Research Even Less Irrelevant.' *Journal of Business and Psychology* 26(2):129–33.

Gartner, W. 2010. 'A New Path to the Waterfall: A Narrative on a Use of Entrepreneurial Narrative.' *International Small Business Journal* 28(1):6–19.

Gassmann, Oliver. 2006. 'Opening up the Innovation Process: Towards an Agenda.' *R&D Management* 36(3):223–8.

George, Gerard, Shaker A. Zahra, and D. Robley Wood Jr. 2002. 'The Effects of Business–University Alliances on Innovative Output and Financial Performance: A Study of Publicly Traded Biotechnology Companies.' *Journal of Business Venturing* 17(6):577–609.

Gertler, M. 1995. '"Being There"': Proximity, Organization, and Culture in the Development and Adoption of Advanced Manufacturing Technologies.' *Economic Geography* 71(1):1–26.

Gertler, M. 2003. 'Tacit Knowledge and the Economic Geography of Context, or the Undefinable Tacitness of Being (There).' *Journal of Economic Geography* 3(1):75–99.

Gertner, Drew, Joanne Roberts, and David Charles. 2011. 'University-Industry Collaboration: A CoPs Approach to KTPs.' *Journal of Knowledge Management* 15(4):625–47.

Geuna, Aldo and Alessandro Muscio. 2009. 'The Governance of University Knowledge Transfer: A Critical Review of the Literature.' *Minerva* 47(1):93–114.

Gibbons, M., C. Limoges, H. Nowotny, S. Schartzman, P. Scott, and M. Trow. 1994. *The New Production of Knowledge*. London: Sage.

Gimeno, Javier, Robert E. Hoskisson, Brent D. Bea, and William P. Wan. 2005. 'Explaining the Clustering of International Expansion Moves: A Critical Test in the U.S. Telecommunications Industry.' *Academy of Management Journal* 48(2):297–319.

Giuliani, Elisa and Valeria Arza. 2009. 'What Drives the Formation of "Valuable" University–Industry Linkages?' *Research Policy* 38(6):906–21.

Goddard, J. 1999. 'Universities and Regional Development: An Overview.' Pp. 36–47 in *Universities and the Creation of Wealth*, edited by G. Gray. Milton Keynes: Open University Press.

Goddard, J. and P. Chatterton. 1999. 'Regional Development Agencies and the Knowledge Economy: Harnessing the Potential of Universities.' *Environment and Planning C: Government and Policy* 17(6):685–99.

Goddard, J. and P. Vallance. 2013. *The University and the City*. Abingdon: Routledge.

Goddard, J., M. Coombes, L. Kempton, and P. Vallance. 2014. 'Universities as Anchor Institutions in Cities in a Turbulent Funding Environment: Vulnerable Institutions and Vulnerable Places in England.' *Cambridge Journal of Regions, Economy and Society* 7(2):307–25.

Goddard, J., E. Hazelkorn, and P. Vallance. 2016. *The Civic University: The Policy and Leadership Challenges*. Cheltenham, UK and Northampton, MA, USA: Edward Elgar.

Goel, Rajeev K., Devrim Göktepe-Hultén, and Christoph Grimpe. 2017. 'Who Instigates University–Industry Collaborations? University Scientists versus Firm Employees.' *Small Business Economics* 48(3):503–24.

Goerzen, Anthony. 2007. 'Alliance Networks and Firm Performance: The Impact of Repeated Partnerships.' *Strategic Management Journal* 28(5):487–509.

Granovetter, M. 1973. 'The Strength of Weak Ties.' *American Journal of Sociology* 78(6):1360–80.

Granovetter, M. 1985. 'Economic Action and Social Structure: The Problem of Embeddedness.' *American Journal of Sociology* 91(3):481–510.

Grant, R. 1996. 'Towards a Knowledge-based Theory of the Firm.' *Strategic Management Journal* 17(Winter special issue):109–22.

Greco, M., M. Grimaldi, and L. Cricelli. 2016. 'An Analysis of the Open Innovation Effect on Firm Performance.' *European Management Journal* 34(5):501–16.

Di Gregorio, D. and S. Shane. 2003. 'Why Do Some Universities Generate More Start-Ups Than Others?' *Research Policy* 32(2):209–27.

Gretsch, Oliver, Edmund Christian Salzmann, and Alexander Kock. 2019. 'University-Industry Collaboration and Front-End Success: The Moderating Effects of Innovativeness and Parallel Cross-Firm Collaboration.' *R&D Management* 49(5):835–49.

Grimpe, Christoph and Heide Fier. 2010. 'Informal University Technology Transfer: A Comparison between the United States and Germany.' *The Journal of Technology Transfer* 35(6):637–50.

Grimpe, Christoph and Katrin Hussinger. 2013. 'Formal and Informal Knowledge and Technology Transfer from Academia to Industry: Complementarity Effects and Innovation Performance.' *Industry and Innovation* 20(8):683–700.

Gruber, Marc, Dietmar Harhoff, and Karin Hoisl. 2013. 'Knowledge Recombination across Technological Boundaries: Scientists vs. Engineers.' *Management Science* 59(4):837–51.

Guerrero, Maribel and David Urbano. 2012. 'The Development of an Entrepreneurial University.' *The Journal of Technology Transfer* 37(1):43–74.

Guerrero, Maribel, James A. Cunningham, and David Urbano. 2015. 'Economic Impact of Entrepreneurial Universities' Activities: An Exploratory Study of the United Kingdom.' *Research Policy* 44(3):748–64.

Gulati, Ranjay. 1995. 'Does Familiarity Breed Trust? The Implications of Repeated Ties for Contractual Choice in Alliances.' *The Academy of Management Journal* 38(1):85–112.

Gulati, R. 1999. 'Network Location and Learning: The Influence of Network Resources and Firm Capabilities on Alliance Formation.' *Strategic Management Journal* 20(5):397–420.

Gulati, R. 2007. *Managing Network Resources: Alliances, Affiliations and Other Relational Assets*. Oxford: Oxford University Press.

Gulati, Ranjay, Dovev Lavie, and Harbir Singh. 2009. 'The Nature of Partnering Experience and the Gains from Alliances.' *Strategic Management Journal* 30(11):1213–33.

Gupta, A. and D. Wilemon. 1988. 'The Credibility-Cooperation Connection at the R&D-Marketing Interface.' *Journal of Product Innovation Management* 5(1):20–31.

Hadjimanolis, Athanasios. 2000. 'A Resource-Based View of Innovativeness in Small Firms.' *Technology Analysis & Strategic Management* 12(2):263–81.

Hagerdoorn, J., A. Link, and N. Vonortas. 2000. 'Research Partnerships.' *Research Policy* 29(4–5):567–86.

Hansen, Teis. 2015. 'Substitution or Overlap? The Relations between Geographical and Non-Spatial Proximity Dimensions in Collaborative Innovation Projects.' *Regional Studies* 49(10):1672–84.

Hassink, Robert and Michelle Wood. 1998. 'Geographic "Clustering" in the German Opto Electronics Industry: Its Impact on Rand Collaboration and Innovation.' *Entrepreneurship & Regional Development* 10(4):277–96.

Healy, Adrian and Kevin Morgan. 2012. 'Spaces of Innovation: Learning, Proximity and the Ecological Turn.' *Regional Studies* 46(8):1041–53.

Heath, H.F. and A.L. Heatherington. 1946. *Industrial Research and Development in the United Kingdom*. London: Faber and Faber.

Henderson, R. and I. Cockburn. 1996. 'Scale, Scope and Spillovers: The Determinants of Research Productivity in Drug Discovery.' *Rand Journal of Economics* 27(1):32–59.

Hendry, J. 1989. *Innovating for Failure*. Cambridge, MA: MIT Press.

Henry, N. and S. Pinch. 2001. 'Neo-Marshallian Nodes, Institutional Thickness, and Britain's "Motor Sport Valley": Thick or Thin?' *Environment and Planning A* 33(7):1169–83.

Hermannsson, Kristinn, Katerina Lisenkova, Patrizio Lecca, Peter G. McGregor, and J. Kim Swales. 2017. 'The External Benefits of Higher Education.' *Regional Studies* 51(7):1077–88.

Herrmann, Andrea Monika, Janne Louise Taks, and Ellen Moors. 2012. 'Beyond Regional Clusters: On the Importance of Geographical Proximity for R&D Collaborations in a Global Economy – the Case of the Flemish Biotech Sector.' *Industry and Innovation* 19(6):499–516.

Hewitt-Dundas, Nola. 2011. 'The Role of Proximity in University-Business Cooperation for Innovation.' *The Journal of Technology Transfer* 38(2):93–115.

Hewitt-Dundas, Nola. 2012. 'Research Intensity and Knowledge Transfer Activity in UK Universities.' *Research Policy* 41(2):262–75.

Hewitt-Dundas, Nola and Stephen Roper. 2017. 'Exploring Market Failures in Open Innovation.' *International Small Business Journal* 36(1):23–40.

Hewitt-Dundas, Nola, Areti Gkypali, and Stephen Roper. 2019. 'Does Learning from Prior Collaboration Help Firms to Overcome the "Two-Worlds" Paradox in University-Business Collaboration?' *Research Policy* 48(5):1310–22.

HM Government. 2017. *Industrial Strategy. Building a Britain Fit for the Future*. London: Department for Business, Energy & Industrial Strategy.

Hoang, Ha and Frank T. Rothaermel. 2005. 'The Effect of General and Partner-Specific Alliance Experience on Joint R&D Project Performance.' *Academy of Management Journal* 48(2):332–45.

Huggins, R. 2010. 'Forms of Network Resource: Knowledge Access and the Role of Inter-Firm Networks.' *International Journal of Management Reviews* 12(3):335–52.

Huggins, R. and A. Johnston. 2009a. 'Knowledge Networks in an Uncompetitive Region: SME Growth and Innovation.' *Growth and Change* 40(2):227–59.

Huggins, R. and A. Johnston. 2009b. 'The Economic and Innovation Contribution of Universities: A Regional Perspective.' *Environment and Planning C: Government and Policy* 27(6):1088–106.

Huggins, R and A. Johnston. 2010. 'Knowledge Flow across Inter-Firm Networks: The Influence of Network Resource, Spatial Proximity and Firm Size.' *Entrepreneurship & Regional Development* 22(5):457–84.

Huggins, R. and F. Kitagawa. 2012. 'Regional Policy and University Knowledge Transfer: Perspectives from Devolved Regions in the UK.' *Regional Studies* 46(6):817–32.

Huggins, R. and P.Thompson. 2017. 'Entrepreneurial Networks and Open Innovation: The Role of Strategic and Embedded Ties.' *Industry and Innovation* 24(4):403–35.

Huggins, R., A. Johnston, and R. Steffenson. 2008. 'Universities, Knowledge Networks and Regional Policy.' *Cambridge Journal of Regions, Economy and Society* 2(1):321–40.

Huggins, R., A. Johnston, and C. Stride. 2012. 'Knowledge Networks and Universities: Locational and Organisational Aspects of Knowledge Transfer Interactions.' *Entrepreneurship & Regional Development* 24(7–8):475–502.

Huggins, R., A. Johnston, and P. Thompson. 2012. 'Network Capital, Social Capital and Knowledge Flow: How the Nature of Inter-Organizational Networks Impacts on Innovation.' *Industry and Innovation* 19(3):203–32.

Huggins, R., D. Prokop, R. Steffenson, A. Johnston, and N. Clifton. 2014. 'The Engagement of Entrepreneurial Firms with Universities: Network Formation, Innovation and Resilience.' *Journal of General Management* 40(1):23–51.

Huggins, R., H. Izushi, and D. Prokop. 2016. 'Networks, Space and Organizational Performance: A Study of the Determinants of Industrial Research Income Generation by Universities.' *Regional Studies* 50(12):2055–68.

Huggins, R., D. Prokop, and P. Thompson. 2020. 'Universities and Open Innovation: The Determinants of Network Centrality.' *The Journal of Technology Transfer* 45(3):718–57.

Hughes, Alan and Michael Kitson. 2012. 'Pathways to Impact and the Strategic Role of Universities: New Evidence on the Breadth and Depth of University Knowledge Exchange in the UK and the Factors Constraining Its Development.' *Cambridge Journal of Economics* 36(3):723–50.

Huizingh, E. 2011. 'Open Innovation: State of the Art and Future Perspectives.' *Technovation* 31(1):2–9.

Hung, Kuang-Peng and Christine Chou. 2013. 'The Impact of Open Innovation on Firm Performance: The Moderating Effects of Internal R&D and Environmental Turbulence.' *Technovation* 33(10–11):368–80.

Inauen, Matthias and Andrea Schenker-Wicki. 2011. 'The Impact of Outside-in Open Innovation on Innovation Performance' (edited by S. Carlsson), *European Journal of Innovation Management* 14(4):496–520.

Jaffe, A.B. 1989. 'Real Effects of Academic Research.' *American Economic Review* 79(5):957–70.

Jain, S. and G. George. 2007. 'Technology Transfer Offices as Institutional Entrepreneurs: The Case of Wisconsin Alumni Research Foundation and Human Embryonic Stem Cells.' *Industrial and Corporate Change* 16(4):483–98.

Jessop, Bob. 2017. 'Varieties of Academic Capitalism and Entrepreneurial Universities.' *Higher Education* 73(6):853–70.

Jessop, Bob. 2018. 'On Academic Capitalism.' *Critical Policy Studies* 12(1):104–9.

Johansson, A.W. 2004. 'Narrating the Entrepreneur.' *International Small Business Journal* 22(3):273–93.

John, G. and J. Martin. 1984. 'Effects of Organisational Structure of Marketing Planning on Credibility and Utilization of Plan Output.' *Journal of Marketing* 21(2):170–83.

Johnston, A. 2019. 'The Roles of Universities in Knowledge-Based Urban Development: A Critical Review.' *International Journal of Knowledge-Based Development* 10(3):213–31.

Johnston, A. 2020a. 'Open Innovation and the Formation of University–Industry Links in the Food Manufacturing and Technology Sector: Evidence from the UK.' *European Journal of Innovation Management.* doi:https://doi.org/10.1108/ejim-06 -2019-0163.

Johnston, A. 2020b. 'University-Industry Collaboration: Are SMEs Different?' Available at https://www.enterpriseresearch.ac.uk/wp-content/uploads/2020/06/ No41-University-Industry-Collaboration-Are-SMEs-Different-Johnston-FINAL-1 .pdf: ERC State of the Art Review No. 41 (accessed 14 July 2020).

Johnston, A. and R. Huggins. 2016. 'Drivers of University-Industry Links: The Case of Knowledge Intensive Business Service Firms in Rural Locations.' *Regional Studies* 58(8):1330–45.

Johnston, A. and R. Huggins. 2017. 'University-Industry Links and the Determinants of Their Spatial Scope: A Study of the Knowledge Intensive Business Services Sector.' *Papers in Regional Science* 96(2):247–60.

Johnston, A. and R. Huggins. 2018. 'Partner Selection and University–Industry Linkages: Assessing Small Firms' Initial Perceptions of the Credibility of Their Partners.' *Technovation* 78:15–26.

Johnston, A. and D. Prokop. 2019. 'University Engagement and Productivity in Innovative SMEs: An Empirical Assessment.' ERC Working Paper No. 78. Available at https://www.enterpriseresearch.ac.uk/ (accessed 25 June 2020).

Johnston, A and P. Wells. 2020 'Assessing the role of universities in a place-based Industrial Strategy: Evidence from the UK' *Local Economy* 35(4):384–402.

Johnston, R. and P. Lawrence. 1988. 'Beyond Vertical Integration – the Rise of the Value-Adding Partnership.' *Harvard Business Review.* Available at https://hbr .org/1988/07/beyond-vertical-integration-the-rise-of-the-value-adding-partnership (accessed 4 May 2020).

Kale, Prashant and Harbir Singh. 2007. 'Building Firm Capabilities through Learning: The Role of the Alliance Learning Process in Alliance Capability and Firm-Level Alliance Success.' *Strategic Management Journal* 28(10):981–1000.

Kale, Prashant, Harbir Singh, and Howard Perlmutter. 2000. 'Learning and Protection of Proprietary Assets in Strategic Alliances: Building Relational Capital.' *Strategic Management Journal* 21(3):217–37

Kapetaniou, Chrystalla and Soo Hee Lee. 2019. 'Geographical Proximity and Open Innovation of SMEs in Cyprus.' *Small Business Economics* 52(1):261–76.

Kenney, Martin and Donald Patton. 2009. 'Reconsidering the Bayh-Dole Act and the Current University Invention Ownership Model.' *Research Policy* 38(9):1407–22.

Khanna, Tarun, Ranjay Gulati, and Nitin Nohria. 1998. 'The Dynamics of Learning Alliances: Competition, Cooperation, and Relative Scope.' *Strategic Management Journal* 19(3):193–210.

Kim, Dong-Young, Vinod Kumar, and Uma Kumar. 2010. 'Performance Assessment Framework for Supply Chain Partnership.' *Supply Chain Management: An International Journal* 15(3):187–95.

Kirby, David A., Maribel Guerrero, and David Urbano. 2011. 'Making Universities More Entrepreneurial: Development of a Model.' *Canadian Journal of Administrative Sciences/Revue Canadienne Des Sciences de l'Administration* 28(3):302–16.

Kitagawa, Fumi, Mabel Sánchez-Barrioluengo, and Elvira Uyarra. 2016. 'Third Mission as Institutional Strategies: Between Isomorphic Forces and Heterogeneous Pathways.' *Science and Public Policy* 43(6):scw015.

Knoben, J. and L. Oerlemans. 2006. 'Proximity and Inter-Organizational Collaboration: A Literature Review.' *International Journal of Management Reviews* 8(2):71–89.

Koschatzky, K. 2001. 'Networks in Innovation Research and Innovation Policy – an Introduction.' Pp. 3–23 in *Innovation Networks: Concepts and Challenges in the European Perspective*, edited by K. Koschatzky, M. Kulicke, and A. Zenker. Heidelberg: Physica Verlag.

Lagendijk, A. and D. Charles. 1999. 'Clustering as a New Growth Strategy for Regional Economies? A Discussion of New Forms of Regional Industrial Policy in the United Kingdom.' Pp. 127–53 in *Boosting Innovation: The Cluster Approach*, edited by OECD. Paris: OECD.

Lam, Alice. 2011. 'What Motivates Academic Scientists to Engage in Research Commercialization: "Gold", "Ribbon" or "Puzzle"?' *Research Policy* 40(10):1354–68.

Lambert, R. 2003. *Lambert Review of Business University Collaboration*. Norwich: HMSO.

Larty, J. and E. Hamilton. 2011. 'Structural Approaches to Narrative Analysis in Entrepreneurship Research: Exemplars from Two Researchers.' *International Small Business Journal* 29(3):220–37.

Laursen, K. and A. Salter. 2004. 'Searching High and Low: What Types of Firms Use Universities as a Sources of Innovation?' *Research Policy* 33(8):1201–15.

Laursen, K. and A. Salter. 2006. 'Open for Innovation: The Role of Openness in Explaining Innovation Performance among UK Manufacturing Firms.' *Strategic Management Journal* 27(1):131–50.

Laursen, K., T. Reichstein, and A. Salter. 2011. 'Exploring the Effect of Geographical Proximity and University Quality on University-Industry Collaboration in the United Kingdom.' *Regional Studies* 45(4):507–23.

Lauvås, Thomas and Marianne Steinmo. 2019. 'The Role of Proximity Dimensions and Mutual Commitment in Shaping the Performance of University-Industry Research Centres.' *Innovation: Organisation and Management*: 1–27. doi: https://doi.org/10.1080/14479338.2019.1662725

Lavie, Dovev and Israel Drori. 2012. 'Collaborating for Knowledge Creation and Application: The Case of Nanotechnology Research Programs.' *Organization Science* 23(3):704–24.

Lawson, C., B. Moore, D. Keeble, H. Lawton Smith, and F. Wilkinson. 1998. 'Inter-Firm Links between Regionally Clustered High-Technology SMEs; A Comparison of Cambridge and Oxford Innovation Networks.' Pp. 181–96 in *New Technology-Based Firms in the 1990s Volume Four*, edited by W. During and R. Oakey. London: Paul Chapman Publishing.

Lechner, Christian and Michael Dowling. 2003. 'Firm Networks: External Relationships as Sources for the Growth and Competitiveness of Entrepreneurial Firms.' *Entrepreneurship & Regional Development* 15(1):1–26.

Lee, Sungjoo, Gwangman Park, Byungun Yoon, and Jinwoo Park. 2010. 'Open Innovation in SMEs – an Intermediated Network Model.' *Research Policy* 39(2):290–300.

Letaifa, Soumaya Ben and Karine Goglio-Primard. 2016. 'How Does Institutional Context Shape Entrepreneurship Conceptualizations?' *Journal of Business Research* 69(11):5128–34.

Lhuillery, Stéphane and Etienne Pfister. 2009. 'R&D Cooperation and Failures in Innovation Projects: Empirical Evidence from French CIS Data.' *Research Policy* 38(1):45–57.

Lichtenthaler, U. 2005. 'External Commercialization of Knowledge: Review and Research Agenda.' *International Journal of Management Reviews* 7(4):231–55.

Lichtenthaler, U. 2008. 'Open Innovation in Practice: An Analysis of Strategic Approaches to Technology Transactions.' *IEEE Transactions on Engineering Management* 55(1):148–57.

Link, Albert N., Donald S. Siegel, and Barry Bozeman. 2017. 'An Empirical Analysis of the Propensity of Academics to Engage in Formal University Technology Transfer.' Pp. 97–111 in *Universities and the Entrepreneurial Ecosystem*, edited by D.B. Audretsch and A.N. Link. Cheltenham, UK and Northampton, MA, USA: Edward Elgar.

Lioukas, Constantinos S. and Jeffrey J. Reuer. 2015. 'Isolating Trust Outcomes from Exchange Relationships: Social Exchange and Learning Benefits of Prior Ties in Alliances.' *Academy of Management Journal* 58(6):1826–47.

Lissoni, Francesco, Jacques Mairesse, Fabio Montobbioy, and Michele Pezzoni. 2011. 'Scientific Productivity and Academic Promotion: A Study on French and Italian Physicists.' *Industrial and Corporate Change* 20(1):253–94.

Liu, Hung Yao, Annapoornima M. Subramanian, and Chang Chieh Hang. 2020. 'Marrying the Best of Both Worlds: An Integrated Framework for Matching Technology Transfer Sources and Recipients.' *IEEE Transactions on Engineering Management* 67(1):70–80.

Lokshin, Boris, John Hagedoorn, and Wilko Letterie. 2011. 'The Bumpy Road of Technology Partnerships: Understanding Causes and Consequences of Partnership Mal-Functioning.' *Research Policy* 40(2):297–308.

Lööf, Hans and Anders Broström. 2006. 'Does Knowledge Diffusion between University and Industry Increase Innovativeness?' *The Journal of Technology Transfer* 33(1):73–90.

Lorenzoni, Gianni and Andrea Lipparini. 1999. 'The Leveraging of Interfirm Relationships as a Distinctive Organizational Capability: A Longitudinal Study.' *Strategic Management Journal* 20(4):317–38.

Lundvall, B. 1992. *National Systems of Innovation: Towards a Theory of Innovation and Interactive Learning*. London: Pinter.

Madrid-Guijarro, Antonia, Domingo Garcia, Howard Van Auken, and H. Van Auken. 2009. 'Barriers to Innovation among Spanish Manufacturing SMEs.' *Journal of Small Business Management* 47(4):465–88.

Maietta, O. 2015. 'Determinants of University–Firm R&D Collaboration and Its Impact on Innovation: A Perspective from a Low-Tech Industry.' *Research Policy* 44(7):1341–59.

Mäkimattila, Martti, Timo Junell, and Tero Rantala. 2015. 'Developing Collaboration Structures for University-Industry Interaction and Innovations.' *European Journal of Innovation Management* 18(4):451–70.

Mansfield, E. 1995. 'Academic Research Underlying Industrial Innovations: Sources, Characteristics, and Financing.' *The Review of Economics and Statistics* 77(1):55–65.

Mansfield, E. 1998. 'Academic Research and Industrial Innovation: An Update of Empirical Findings.' *Research Policy* 26(8):773–6.

Marques, Pedro, Kevin Morgan, Adrian Healy, and Paul Vallance. 2019. 'Spaces of Novelty: Can Universities Play a Catalytic Role in Less Developed Regions?' *Science and Public Policy* 46(5):763–71.

Marrocu, Emanuela, Raffaele Paci, and Stefano Usai. 2013. 'Proximity, Networking and Knowledge Production in Europe: What Lessons for Innovation Policy?' *Technological Forecasting and Social Change* 80(8):1484–98.

Marshall, A. 1970. *Industry and Trade*, fourth edn. New York: Augustus M. Kelley.

Martin, F. 1998. 'The Economic Impact of Canadian University R&D.' *Research Policy* 27(7):677–87.

Marullo, Cristina, Alberto Di Minin, Chiara De Marco, and Andrea Piccaluga. 2020. 'Is Open Innovation Always the Best for SMEs? An Exploratory Analysis at the Project Level.' *Creativity and Innovation Management.*

Maskell, Peter, Harald Bathelt, and Anders Malmberg. 2006. 'Building Global Knowledge Pipelines: The Role of Temporary Clusters.' *European Planning Studies* 14(8):997–1013.

Mattes, Jannika. 2012. 'Dimensions of Proximity and Knowledge Bases: Innovation between Spatial and Non-Spatial Factors.' *Regional Studies* 46(8):1085–99.

Mazzucato, Mariana. 2016. 'From Market Fixing to Market-Creating: A New Framework for Innovation Policy.' *Industry and Innovation* 23(2):140–56.

McGahan, A. 2007. 'Academic Research That Matters to Managers: On Zebras, Dogs, Lemmings, Hammers, and Turnips.' *Academy of Management Journal* 50(4):748–53.

Meagher, K. and M. Rogers. 2004. 'Network Density and R&D Spillovers.' *Journal of Economic Behavior & Organization* 53(2):237–60.

Menon, A. and P.R. Varadarajan. 1992. 'A Model of Marketing Knowledge Use within Firms.' *Journal of Marketing* 56(4):53–71.

Metcalfe, J. Stanley. 2010. 'University and Business Relations: Connecting the Knowledge Economy.' *Minerva* 48(1):5–33.

Mindruta, Denisa. 2013. 'Value Creation in University–Firm Research Collaborations: A Matching Approach.' *Strategic Management Journal* 34(6):644–65.

Mindruta, Denisa, Mahka Moeen, and Rajshree Agarwal. 2016. 'A Two-Sided Matching Approach for Partner Selection and Assessing Complementarities in Partners' Attributes in Inter-Firm Alliances.' *Strategic Management Journal* 37(1):206–31.

Miotti, Luis and Frédérique Sachwald. 2003. 'Co-operative R&D: Why and with Whom?' *Research Policy* 32(8):1481–99.

Mishler, E.G. 1986. *Research Interviewing: Context and Narrative.* Cambridge, MA: Harvard University Press.

Mohnen, P. and C. Hoareau. 2003. 'What Type of Enterprise Forges Close Links with Universities and Government Labs? Evidence from CIS 2.' *Managerial and Decision Economics* 24(1):133–46.

Mokyr, J. 2002. *The Gifts of Athena: Historical Origins of the Knowledge Economy.* Princeton, NJ: Princeton University Press.

Monjon, Stéphanie and Patrick Waelbroeck. 2003. 'Assessing Spillovers from Universities to Firms: Evidence from French Firm-Level Data.' *International Journal of Industrial Organization* 21(9):1255–70.

Montoya-Weiss, Mitzi M. and Tony M. O'Driscoll. 2000. 'From Experience: Applying Performance Support Technology in the Fuzzy Front End.' *Journal of Product Innovation Management* 17(2):143–61.

Moodysson, J. and O. Jonsson. 2007. 'Knowledge Collaboration and Proximity: The Spatial Organization of Biotech Innovation Projects.' *European Urban and Regional Studies* 14(2):115–31.

Morgan, Kevin. 2004. 'The Exaggerated Death of Geography: Learning, Proximity and Territorial Innovation Systems.' *Journal of Economic Geography* 4(1):3–21.

Mothe, Caroline and Bertrand V. Quelin. 2001. 'Resource Creation and Partnership in R&D Consortia.' *The Journal of High Technology Management Research* 12(1):113–38.

Motohashi, K. 2005. 'University–Industry Collaborations in Japan: The Role of New Technology-Based Firms in Transforming the National Innovation System.' *Research Policy* 34(5):583–94.

Motoyama, Yasuyuki. 2014. 'Long-Term Collaboration between University and Industry: A Case Study of Nanotechnology Development in Japan.' *Technology in Society* 36(1):39–51.

Mowery, D. and B. Sampat. 2004. 'The Bayh-Dole Act of 1980 and University–Industry Technology Transfer: A Model for Other OECD Governments?' *The Journal of Technology Transfer* 30(1):140–56.

Mowery, D.C., J.E. Oxley, and B.S. Silverman. 1998. 'Technological Overlap and Interfirm Cooperation: Implications for the Resource-Based View of the Firm.' *Research Policy* 27(5):507–23.

Murray, Fiona. 2002. 'Innovation as Co-evolution of Scientific and Technological Networks: Exploring Tissue Engineering.' *Research Policy* 31(8–9):1389–403.

Muscio, Alessandro. 2013. 'University-Industry Linkages: What Are the Determinants of Distance in Collaborations?' *Papers in Regional Science* 92(4):715–39.

Narula, Rajneesh. 2004. 'R&D Collaboration by SMEs: New Opportunities and Limitations in the Face of Globalisation.' *Technovation* 24(2):153–61.

Nelson, R. 2001. 'Observations on the Post-Bayh-Dole Rise of Patenting at American Universities.' *The Journal of Technology Transfer* 26(1–2):13–19.

Nelson, Richard R. 2004. 'The Market Economy, and the Scientific Commons.' *Research Policy* 33(3):455–71.

Nelson, R. and N. Rosenberg. 1993. 'Technical Innovation and National Systems.' Pp. 3–28 in *National Innovation Systems: A Comparative Analysis*, edited by R. Nelson. Oxford: Oxford University Press.

Nieto, M. and L. Santamaria. 2010. 'Technological Collaboration: Bridging the Innovation Gap between Small and Large Firms.' *Journal of Small Business Management* 48(1):44–69.

Nonaka, I., R. Toyama, and A. Nagata. 2000. 'A Firm as a Knowledge-Creating Entity: A New Perspective on the Theory of the Firm.' *Industrial and Corporate Change* 9(1):1–20.

OECD. 2019. *Main Science and Technology Indicators*. doi:https://doi.org/10.1787/6a56fcfa-en.

Oerlemans, L. and M. Meeus. 2005. 'Do Organizational and Spatial Proximity Impact on Firm Performance.' *Regional Studies* 39(1):89–104.

Office for National Statistics (ONS). 2020. 'Gross Domestic Expenditure on Research and Development'. Available at https://www.ons.gov.uk/economy/government publicsectorandtaxes/researchanddevelopmentexpenditure accessed 16/06/2020 (accessed 25 November 2020).

Okamuro, Hiroyuki. 2007. 'Determinants of Successful R&D Cooperation in Japanese Small Businesses: The Impact of Organizational and Contractual Characteristics.' *Research Policy* 36(10):1529–44.

Owen-Smith, Jason and Walter W. Powell. 2001. 'To Patent or Not: Faculty Decisions and Institutional Success at Technology Transfer.' *The Journal of Technology Transfer* 26(1/2):99–114.

Oxley, J.E. 1997. 'Appropriability Hazards and Governance in Strategic Alliances: A Transaction Cost Approach.' *Journal of Law, Economics, and Organization* 13(2):387–409.

Parida, Vinit, Mats Westerberg, and Johan Frishammar. 2012. 'Inbound Open Innovation Activities in High-Tech SMEs: The Impact on Innovation Performance.' *Journal of Small Business Management* 50(2):283–309.

Park, Seung Ho and Kim Dongcheol. 1997. 'Market Valuation of Joint Ventures: Joint Venture Characteristics and Wealth Gains.' *Journal of Business Venturing* 12(2):83–108.

Park, Seung Ho and Gerardo R. Ungson. 2001. 'Interfirm Rivalry and Managerial Complexity: A Conceptual Framework of Alliance Failure.' *Organization Science* 12(1):37–53.

Parkhe, Arvind. 1993. 'Strategic Alliance Structuring: A Game Theoretic and Transaction Cost Examination of Interfirm Cooperation.' *Academy of Management Journal* 36(4):794–829.

Penrose, E. 1959. *The Theory of the Growth of the Firm.* New York: John Wiley & Sons.

Perkmann, Markus and Kathryn Walsh. 2007. 'University–Industry Relationships and Open Innovation: Towards a Research Agenda.' *International Journal of Management Reviews* 9(4):259–80.

Perkmann, Markus, Zella King, and Stephen Pavelin. 2011. 'Engaging Excellence? Effects of Faculty Quality on University Engagement with Industry.' *Research Policy* 40(4):539–52.

Perkmann, Markus, Andy Neely, and Kathryn Walsh. 2011. 'How Should Firms Evaluate Success in University–Industry Alliances? A Performance Measurement System.' *R&D Management* 41(2):202–16.

Perkmann, Markus, Valentina Tartari, Maureen McKelvey et al. 2013. 'Academic Engagement and Commercialisation: A Review of the Literature on University–Industry Relations.' *Research Policy* 42(2):423–42.

Petruzzelli, Antonio Messeni. 2011. 'The Impact of Technological Relatedness, Prior Ties, and Geographical Distance on University–Industry Collaborations: A Joint-Patent Analysis.' *Technovation* 31(7):309–19.

Petruzzelli, Antonio Messeni and Daniele Rotolo. 2015. 'Institutional Diversity, Internal Search Behaviour, and Joint-Innovations.' *Management Decision* 53(9):2088–106.

Philpott, K., L. Dooley, C. O'Reilly, and G. Lupton. 2011. 'The Entrepreneurial University: Examining the Underlying Academic Tensions.' *Technovation* 31(4):161–70.

Pickernell, David, Nick Clifton, and Julienne Senyard. 2009. 'Universities, SMEs and Innovation Frameworks: Think Global, Act Local?' *Industry and Higher Education* 23(2):79–89.

Pinch, S., N. Henry, M. Jenkins, and S. Tallman. 2003. 'From "Industrial Districts" to "Knowledge Clusters": A Model of Knowledge Dissemination and Competitive Advantage in Industrial Agglomerations.' *Journal of Economic Geography* 3(4):373–88.

Piore, M. and C. Sabel. 1984. *The Second Industrial Divide*. New York: Basic Books.

Plewa, Carolin and Pascale Quester. 2006. 'Satisfaction with University-Industry Relationships: The Impact of Commitment, Trust and Championship.' *International Journal of Technology Transfer and Commercialisation* 5(1/2):79.

Plewa, Carolin, Nisha Korff, Thomas Baaken, and Greg Macpherson. 2013. 'University-Industry Linkage Evolution: An Empirical Investigation of Relational Success Factors.' *R&D Management* 43(4):365–80.

Plewa, Carolin, Nisha Korff, Claire Johnson, Gregory Macpherson, Thomas Baaken, and Giselle Camille Rampersad. 2013. 'The Evolution of University–Industry Linkages – a Framework.' *Journal of Engineering and Technology Management* 30(1):21–44.

Plewa, Carolin, Giselle Rampersad, and Joanne Ho. 2019. 'The Dynamics of Managing Evolving University-Industry Linkages.' Pp. 127–48 in *Developing Engaged and Entrepreneurial Universities*, edited by Thorsten Kliewe, Tobias Kesting, Carolin Plewa, Thomas Baaken. Singapore: Springer.

Polanyi, K. 2001. *The Great Transformation*, second edn. Boston, MA: Beacon.

Ponds, R., F. van Oort, and K. Frenken. 2007. 'The Geographical and Institutional Proximity of Research Collaboration.' *Papers in Regional Science* 86(3):423–43.

Porter, M. 1990. *The Competitive Advantage of Nations*. Worcester: Billing and Sons.

Porter, M. 2003. 'The Economic Performance of Regions.' *Regional Studies* 37(6&7):549–78.

Porter, M.E. and C.H.M. Ketels. 2003. *UK Competitiveness: Moving to the Next Stage*. London: Department of Trade and Industry.

Powell, W.W., K. Koput, and L. Smith-Doerr. 1996. 'Interorganizational Collaboration and the Locus of Innovation: Networks of Learning in Biotechnology.' *Administrative Science Quarterly* 41(1):116–45.

Pugh, Rhiannon, Eleanor Hamilton, Sarah Jack, and Amy Gibbons. 2016. 'A Step into the Unknown: Universities and the Governance of Regional Economic Development.' *European Planning Studies* 24(7):1357–73.

Pyatt, E. 1983. *The National Physical Laboratory – a History*. Bristol: Adam Hilger.

Rajalo, Sigrid and Maaja Vadi. 2017. 'University-Industry Innovation Collaboration: Reconceptualization.' *Technovation* 62–63:42–54.

Randhawa, Krithika, Ralf Wilden, and Jan Hohberger. 2016. 'A Bibliometric Review of Open Innovation: Setting a Research Agenda.' *Journal of Product Innovation Management* 33(6):750–72.

Ranga, Marina and Henry Etzkowitz. 2013. 'Triple Helix Systems: An Analytical Framework for Innovation Policy and Practice in the Knowledge Society.' *Industry and Higher Education* 27(3):237–62.

Rasche, A. and M. Behnam. 2009. 'As If It Were Relevant: A Systems Theoretical Perspective on the Relation between Science and Practice.' *Journal of Management Inquiry* 18(3):243–55.

Rasmussen, Einar, Øystein Moen, and Magnus Gulbrandsen. 2006. 'Initiatives to Promote Commercialization of University Knowledge.' *Technovation* 26(4):518–33.

Reuer, Jeffrey J. and Shivaram V. Devarakonda. 2016. 'Mechanisms of Hybrid Governance: Administrative Committees in Non-Equity Alliances.' *Academy of Management Journal* 59(2):510–33.

Rinallo, D., H. Bathelt, and F. Golfetto. 2017. 'Economic Geography and Industrial Marketing Views on Trade Shows: Collective Marketing and Knowledge Circulation.' *Industrial Marketing Management* 61(1):93–103.

Ring, Peter Smith, Yves L. Doz, and Paul M. Olk. 2005. 'Managing Formation Processes in R&D Consortia.' *California Management Review* 47(4):137–56.

Roper, Stephen and Nola Hewitt-Dundas. 2015. 'Knowledge Stocks, Knowledge Flows and Innovation: Evidence from Matched Patents and Innovation Panel Data.' *Research Policy* 44(7):1327–40.

Rosli, Ainurul, Muthu de Silva, Federica Rossi, and Nick Yip. 2018. 'The Long-Term Impact of Engaged Scholarship: How Do SMEs Capitalise on Their Engagement with Academics to Explore New Opportunities?' *International Small Business Journal: Researching Entrepreneurship* 36(4):400–28.

Rossi, Federica. 2010. 'The Governance of University-Industry Knowledge Transfer.' *European Journal of Innovation Management* 13(2):155–71.

Rossi, Federica and Ainurul Rosli. 2015. 'Indicators of University–Industry Knowledge Transfer Performance and Their Implications for Universities: Evidence from the United Kingdom.' *Studies in Higher Education* 40(10):1970–91.

Rouvinen, Petri. 2002. 'Characteristics of Product and Process Innovators: Some Evidence from the Finnish Innovation Survey.' *Applied Economics Letters* 9(9):575–80.

Roy, Rustum. 1972. 'University-Industry Interaction Patterns.' *Science* 178(4064): 955–60.

Russell, John. 1971. 'The Docksey Report: Industry, Science and the Universities.' *R&D Management* 1(2):107–8.

Rutten, Roel. 2017. 'Beyond Proximities: The Socio-Spatial Dynamics of Knowledge Creation.' *Progress in Human Geography* 41(2):159–77.

Rybnicek, Robert and Roland Königsgruber. 2019. 'What Makes Industry–University Collaboration Succeed? A Systematic Review of the Literature.' *Journal of Business Economics* 89(2):221–50.

Saebi, T. and N. Foss. 2015. 'Business Models for Open Innovation: Matching Heterogeneous Open Innovation Strategies with Business Model Dimensions.' *European Management Journal* 33(3):201–13.

Salomaa, Maria. 2019. 'Third Mission and Regional Context: Assessing Universities' Entrepreneurial Architecture in Rural Regions.' *Regional Studies, Regional Science* 6(1):233–49.

Sánchez-Barrioluengo, M. and P. Benneworth. 2019. 'Is the Entrepreneurial University Also Regionally Engaged? Analysing the Influence of University's Structural Configuration on Third Mission Performance.' *Technological Forecasting and Social Change* 141:206–18.

Santoro, Michael D. 2000. 'Success Breeds Success: The Linkage between Relationship Intensity and Tangible Outcomes in Industry–University Collaborative Ventures.' *The Journal of High Technology Management Research* 11(2):255–73.

Sarason, Yolanda, Tom Dean, and Jesse F. Dillard. 2006. 'Entrepreneurship as the Nexus of Individual and Opportunity: A Structuration View.' *Journal of Business Venturing* 21(3):286–305.

Sarasvathy, S. 2001. 'Causation and Effectuation: Toward a Theoretical Shift from Economic Inevitability to Entrepreneurial Contingency.' *Academy of Management Review* 26(3):375–90.

Saxenian, A. 1994. *Regional Advantage: Culture and Competition in Silicon Valley and Route 128*. Cambridge, MA: Harvard University Press.

Scandura, Alessandra. 2016. 'University–Industry Collaboration and Firms' R&D Effort.' *Research Policy* 45(9):1907–22.

Schofield, T. 2013. 'Critical Success Factors for Knowledge Transfer Collaborations between University and Industry.' *Journal of Research Administration* 44(2):38–56.

Schumpeter, J.A. 2014. *Capitalism, Socialism and Democracy*, second edn. Floyd, VA: Impact Books (originally published 1942).

Sengupta, A. and A. Ray. 2017. 'University Research and Knowledge Transfer: A Dynamic View of Ambidexterity in British Universities.' *Research Policy* 46(5):881–97.

Shane, S. 2004. *Academic Entrepreneurship: University Spinoffs and Wealth Creation.* Cheltenham, UK and Northampton, MA, USA: Edward Elgar.

Shane, S. and S. Venkataraman. 2000. 'The Promise of Entrepreneurship as a Field of Research.' *Academy of Management Review* 25(1):217–26.

Sharifi, Hossein, Weisheng Liu, and Hossam S. Ismail. 2014. 'Higher Education System and the "Open" Knowledge Transfer: A View from Perception of Senior Managers at University Knowledge Transfer Offices.' *Studies in Higher Education* 39(10):1860–84.

Shepherd, Neil Gareth and John Maynard Rudd. 2014. 'The Influence of Context on the Strategic Decision-Making Process: A Review of the Literature.' *International Journal of Management Reviews* 16(3):340–64.

Sieg, Jan Henrik, Martin W. Wallin, and Georg Von Krogh. 2010. 'Managerial Challenges in Open Innovation: A Study of Innovation Intermediation in the Chemical Industry.' *R&D Management* 40(3):281–91.

Siegel, Donald S., David A. Waldman, Leanne E. Atwater, and Albert N. Link. 2003. 'Commercial Knowledge Transfers from Universities to Firms: Improving the Effectiveness of University–Industry Collaboration.' *The Journal of High Technology Management Research* 14(1):111–33.

Siegel, D.S., R. Veugelers, and M. Wright. 2007. 'Technology Transfer Offices and Commercialization of University Intellectual Property: Performance and Policy Implications.' *Oxford Review of Economic Policy* 23(4):640–60.

Siegel, Donald, Mike Wright, Wendy Chapple, and Andy Lockett. 2008. 'Assessing the Relative Performance of University Technology Transfer in the US and UK: A Stochastic Distance Function Approach.' *Economics of Innovation and New Technology* 17(7–8):717–29.

Simard, C. and J. West. 2006. 'Knowledge Networks and the Geographic Locus of Innovation.' Pp. 220–40 in *Open Innovation: Researching a New Paradigm*, edited by H. Chesbrough, W. Vanhaverbeke, and J. West. Oxford: Oxford University Press.

Sisodiya, Sanjay R., Jean L. Johnson, and Yany Grégoire. 2013. 'Inbound Open Innovation for Enhanced Performance: Enablers and Opportunities.' *Industrial Marketing Management* 42(5):836–49.

Situm, M. 2019. 'Corporate Performance and Diversification from a Resource-Based View: A Comparison between Small and Medium-Sized Austrian Firms.' *Journal of Small Business Strategy* 29(3):78–96.

Sivadas, Eugene and F. Robert Dwyer. 2000. 'An Examination of Organizational Factors Influencing New Product Success in Internal and Alliance-Based Processes.' *Journal of Marketing* 64(1):31–49.

Slaughter, S. and L. Leslie. 1997. *Academic Capitalism: Politics, Policies, and the Entrepreneurial University.* Baltimore, MD: Johns Hopkins University Press.

Smith, Helen Lawton and Sharmistha Bagchi-Sen. 2010. 'Triple Helix and Regional Development: A Perspective from Oxfordshire in the UK.' *Technology Analysis & Strategic Management* 22(7):805–18.

Snow, C.P. 1959. *The Two Cultures and the Scientific Revolution.* London: Cambridge University Press.

Soetanto, Danny and Sarah Jack. 2016. 'The Impact of University-Based Incubation Support on the Innovation Strategy of Academic Spin-Offs.' *Technovation* 50–51:25–40.

Soh, Pek-Hooi and Annapoornima M. Subramanian. 2014. 'When Do Firms Benefit from University–Industry R&D Collaborations? The Implications of Firm R&D Focus on Scientific Research and Technological Recombination.' *Journal of Business Venturing* 29(6):807–21.

Spithoven, André, Wim Vanhaverbeke, and Nadine Roijakkers. 2013. 'Open Innovation Practices in SMEs and Large Enterprises.' *Small Business Economics* 41(3):537–62.

Steinmo, Marianne. 2015. 'Collaboration for Innovation: A Case Study on How Social Capital Mitigates Collaborative Challenges in University–Industry Research Alliances.' *Industry and Innovation* 22(7):597–624.

Steinmo, Marianne and Einar Rasmussen. 2018. 'The Interplay of Cognitive and Relational Social Capital Dimensions in University-Industry Collaboration: Overcoming the Experience Barrier.' *Research Policy* 47(10):1964–74.

Steyaert, C. 2007. 'Of Course That Is Not the Whole (Toy) Story: Entrepreneurship and the Cat's Cradle.' *Journal of Business Venturing* 22(5):733–51.

Storper, M. and A. Venables. 2004. 'Buzz: Face-to-Face Contact and the Urban Economy.' *Journal of Economic Geography* 4(4):351–70.

Striukova, Ludmila and Thierry Rayna. 2015. 'University-Industry Knowledge Exchange.' *European Journal of Innovation Management* 18(4):471–92.

Suckling, Charles. 1980. 'The Role of Universities in National R &D Strategy.' *R&D Management* 10(s1):173–6.

Teece, D. 1998. 'Capturing Value from Knowledge Assets: The New Economy, Markets for Know-How, and Intangible Assets.' *California Management Review* 40(3):55–79.

Ternouth, Philip, Cathy Garner, Laurie Wood, and Peter Forbes. 2012. *Key Attributes for Successful Knowledge Transfer Partnerships.* London: CIHE.

Terziovski, Milé. 2010. 'Innovation Practice and Its Performance Implications in Small and Medium Enterprises (SMEs) in the Manufacturing Sector: A Resource-Based View.' *Strategic Management Journal* 31(8):892–902.

Tether, B.S., Qian Cher Li, and A. Mina. 2012. 'Knowledge-Bases, Places, Spatial Configurations and the Performance of Knowledge-Intensive Professional Service Firms.' *Journal of Economic Geography* 12(5):969–1001.

Thorp, H. and B. Goldstein. 2010. *Engines of Innovation: The Entrepreneurial University in the Twenty-First Century.* Chapel Hill, NC: University of North Carolina Press.

Thorpe, R., R. Holt, A. Macpherson, and L. Pittaway. 2005. 'Using Knowledge within Small and Medium-Sized Firms: A Systematic Review of the Evidence.' *International Journal of Management Reviews* 7(4):257–81.

Thune, Taran and Magnus Gulbrandsen. 2014. 'Dynamics of Collaboration in University–Industry Partnerships: Do Initial Conditions Explain Development Patterns?' *The Journal of Technology Transfer* 39(6):977–93.

Thursby, J.G. and M.C. Thursby. 2002. 'Who Is Selling the Ivory Tower? Sources of Growth in University Licensing.' *Management Science* 48(1):90–104.

Thursby, J.G. and M.C. Thursby. 2004. 'Are Faculty Critical? Their Role in University–Industry Licensing.' *Contemporary Economic Policy* 22(2):162–78.

Torre, Andre and Jean-Pierre Gilly. 2000. 'On the Analytical Dimension of Proximity Dynamics.' *Regional Studies* 34(2):169–80.

Torre, Andre and Alain Rallet. 2005. 'Proximity and Localization.' *Regional Studies* 39(1):47–59.

Uyarra, E. 2010. 'Conceptualizing the Regional Roles of Universities, Implications and Contradictions.' *European Planning Studies* 18(8):1227–46.

Vahter, Priit, James H. Love, and Stephen Roper. 2014. 'Openness and Innovation Performance: Are Small Firms Different?' *Industry and Innovation* 21(7–8):553–73.

Valdés-Llaneza, Ana and Esteban García-Canal. 2015. 'The Devil You Know? A Review of the Literature on the Impact of Prior Ties on Strategic Alliances.' *Management Research* 13(3):334–58.

Valero, Anna and John Van Reenen. 2019. 'The Economic Impact of Universities: Evidence from across the Globe.' *Economics of Education Review* 68:53–67.

Van de Vrande, V., J.P.J. de Jong, W. Vanhaverbeke, and M. de Rochemont. 2009. 'Open Innovation in SMEs: Trends, Motives and Management Challenges.' *Technovation* 29(6–7):423–37.

Van Wijk, Raymond and Anna Nadolska. 2020. 'Making More of Alliance Portfolios: The Role of Alliance Portfolio Coordination.' *European Management Journal* 38(3):388–99.

Vanino, Enrico, Stephen Roper, and Bettina Becker. 2019. 'Knowledge to Money: Assessing the Business Performance Effects of Publicly-Funded R&D Grants.' *Research Policy* 48(7):1714–37.

Vossen, R. 1999. 'Relative Strengths and Weaknesses of Small Firms in Innovation.' *International Small Business Journal* 16(3):88–94.

Walsh, J.P., M.L. Tushman, J.R. Kimberly, B. Starbuck, and S. Ashford. 2007. 'On the Relationship between Research and Practice: Debate and Reflections.' *Journal of Management Inquiry* 16(2):128–54.

Walter, Jorge, Christoph Lechner, and Franz W. Kellermanns. 2007. 'Knowledge Transfer between and within Alliance Partners: Private versus Collective Benefits of Social Capital.' *Journal of Business Research* 60(7):698–710.

Wasserman, I.C. and K.E. Kram. 2009. 'Enacting the Scholar–Practitioner Role: An Exploration of Narratives.' *The Journal of Applied Behavioral Science* 45(1):12–38.

Wernerfelt, B. 1984. 'A Resource-Based View of the Firm.' *Strategic Management Journal* 5(1):171–80.

Williamson, O. 1993. 'Calculativeness, Trust and Economic Organisation.' *Journal of Law and Economics* 36(1 Part 2):453–86.

Wilson, T. 2012. *A Review of Business–University Collaboration*. London: Department for Business Innovation and Skills.

Wirsich, Alexander, Alexander Kock, Christoph Strumann, and Carsten Schultz. 2016. 'Effects of University–Industry Collaboration on Technological Newness of Firms.' *Journal of Product Innovation Management* 33(6):708–25.

de Wit-de Vries, Esther, Wilfred A. Dolfsma, Henny J. van der Windt, and M.P. Gerkema. 2019. 'Knowledge Transfer in University–Industry Research Partnerships: A Review.' *The Journal of Technology Transfer* 44(4):1235–55.

Wood, G.A. and J.B. Parr. 2005. 'Transaction Costs, Agglomeration Economies, and Industrial Location.' *Growth and Change* 36(1):1–15.

Woolcott, Geoff, Robyn Keast, and David Pickernell. 2020. 'Deep Impact: Re-Conceptualising University Research Impact Using Human Cultural Accumulation Theory.' *Studies in Higher Education* 45(6):1197—216.

World Bank. 2017. 'World Bank Education Overview: Higher Education.' Available at http://documents.worldbank.org/curated/en/610121541079963484/World-Bank -Education-Overview-Higher-Education: World Bank Bank Group (accessed 23 July 2020).

Wright, Mike and Andy Lockett. 2003. 'The Structure and Management of Alliances: Syndication in the Venture Capital Industry.' *Journal of Management Studies* 40(8):2073–102.

Wright, Mike, Bart Clarysse, Andy Lockett, and Mirjam Knockaert. 2008. 'Mid-Range Universities' Linkages with Industry: Knowledge Types and the Role of Intermediaries.' *Research Policy* 37(8):1205–23.

Yasuda, Hiroshi. 2005. 'Formation of Strategic Alliances in High-Technology Industries: Comparative Study of the Resource-Based Theory and the Transaction-Cost Theory.' *Technovation* 25(7):763–70.

Yegros-Yegros, Alfredo, Joaquín M. Azagra-Caro, Mayte López-Ferrer, Robert J.W. Tijssen. 2016. 'Do University–Industry Co-publication Outputs Correspond with University Funding from Firms?' *Research Evaluation* 25(2):136–50.

Yigitcanlar, T. 2014. 'Position Paper: Benchmarking the Performance of Global and Emerging Knowledge Cities.' *Expert Systems with Applications* 41(12):5549–59.

Zeller, Christian. 2009. 'North Atlantic Innovative Relations of Swiss Pharmaceuticals and the Proximities with Regional Biotech Arenas.' *Economic Geography* 80(1):83–111.

Zollo, Maurizio, Jeffrey J. Reuer, and Harbir Singh. 2002. 'Interorganizational Routines and Performance in Strategic Alliances.' *Organization Science* 13(6):701–13.

De Zubielqui, Graciela Corral, Janice Jones, and Laurence Lester. 2016. 'Knowledge Inflows from Market- and Science-Based Actors, Absorptive Capacity, Innovation and Performance – a Study of SMES.' *International Journal of Innovation Management* 20(6):1–31.

Index